An Anthropological Inquiry into Confucianism

An Anthropological Inquiry into Confucianism

Ritual, Emotion, and Rational Principle

Guo Wu

LEXINGTON BOOKS
Lanham • Boulder • New York • London

Published by Lexington Books

An imprint of The Rowman & Littlefield Publishing Group, Inc.
4501 Forbes Boulevard, Suite 200, Lanham, Maryland 20706
www.rowman.com
86-90 Paul Street, London EC2A 4NE

British Library Cataloguing in Publication Information Available

Library of Congress Cataloging-in-Publication Data
ISBN: 978-1-7936-5431-1 (cloth)
ISBN: 978-1-7936-5432-8 (electronic)

To my father Wu Yuanxin (1935–2012), my mother Feng Xuezhen, my wife Ranhee Pyo, and my son Tianyi Wu

Contents

Introduction: Confucianism through Anthropological Lenses

My memory of my father's funeral in October 2012 is still vivid: unending Buddhist music with sutras being chanted; wearing traditional white cloth headband and hanging a piece of hemp on my coat, I was instructed by a Daoist ritual master to perform a series of actions, from walking while holding a stick to telling the master my and my wife's names. As a sorrowful "filial son" in the Confucian funerary sense, I knelt down to thank all the guests who offered condolences, every time, one by one, touching my forehead to the ground. Incenses were burned and candles lit, and the funeral home that night was saturated with their mixed smell, with which I had been familiar since childhood.

In the Confucian sense, I would have failed to fulfill the obligation of a filial son had I not flown back to China from the United States to attend the funeral. Yet I made it. The evening that I arrived at the site was already the fourth—the traditional three-day period to keep vigil had been extended for me because I also had to fulfill my public duty as a teacher who had to cancel classes. I still felt some degree of guilt for my lateness. However, the most important thing was that despite the Daoist rituals and Buddhist music, which for me ornamented the funeral, I was evaluated and then endorsed by the grief-stricken families, relatives, and old friends of my father as a "filial son," in a quintessential Confucian way. Hence, Confucianism was something that I experienced as a core value and an uncodified rule. The relatives, who did not self-consciously think they adhered to the principles of "Confucianism," would subconsciously allude to this value of filial piety to judge me while all my actions and reactions at the site for them were a spectacle.

All this led me to consider some key issues of central importance: What does Confucianism mean in textual, ritualistic, and metaphysical senses? How is it experienced in real life? If my presence suffices to prove my (self-)image of a "filial son," did the Daoist death ritual buttressed it, did it help express my grief, or did it build and enhance the ties between me and the soul of my father? According to popular Buddhist belief, in the first several days after the death, the soul is still wandering, searching for a better reincarnation, so we children must also attend to that. On an academic level, I became interested in the entangled relationship between Confucian values and rituals and that between the rituals and true human emotions. I have often been asked by my American students and colleagues, "Is Confucianism a philosophy or a religion?" Certain books trace the origin and evolution of the debate but still do not provide a straightforward answer.[1] I agree with Vincent Goossaert that we should first acknowledge that "[i]t is very well known that in Chinese, as in many other languages, there is no precise equivalent for the modern western concept 'religion.'"[2]

A *LI-QING-LI* TRIAD

I see Confucianism as a mixed belief and value system that has both philosophical and certain vestiges of pre-textual rites from early human society. In this book, I will analyze its historical origin and evolution based upon textual analysis and focus on three key terms, *Li-qing-li*, and my hypothesis of a Confucian conceptual triad. Confucianism is relational, practical, ritualist, emotional, and metaphysical, and it is experienced by ordinary people, often without self-consciousness and self-identity even it fits the four qualifying criteria: "a priesthood, a liturgy, a canon (defining orthodoxy) and educational centres."[3] As Robert Cummings Neville points out, metaphysics, which should not be overlooked in modern philosophical inquiries, seeks "what is ultimately real," and what is "fundamental."[4] And it had a place in the Confucian reflection on the world, lying in Song Neo-Confucian thinkers' proposition of "Heavenly principle," or "*tianli.*" Yet Song dynasty's (Heavenly) rational principle, *li*, as a core Chinese concept, was not elaborated on in the abstract, detached from secular emotions, desires, and practical rites. To perferm this analysis effectively, I shall turn to anthropology and sometimes psychology rather than engaging in the endless exegesis of the received texts and reading of later interpretations of the classics.

The assertion that "Western philosophy has largely neglected the topic of emotions" such as "anger, fear, sadness, joy, and compassion"[5] might have gone too far, and Ludwig Wittgenstein talks at length about human emotions.[6] Yet it might be true that in the Western tradition "[t]here is a long history of viewing women and non-Caucasian Euro-Americans as irrational and unable to control emotions, and thus more susceptible to hysteria, depression . . . and violence."[7] While emotions are seen in the American intellectual traditional as irrational, immature, and private, rather than social, situational, and relational, "passion" is sometimes seen as sacred.[8] This neglect of the centrality of both emotions, *qing*, and the Confucian order of ritual, *Li*, is based on an ethno-centric "narrow definition of philosophy," and it contributes to the "Western prejudices against Chinese culture" and has hampered the cross-cultural dialogue between Western philosophy and "non-Western moral and philosophical traditions," which was hardly treated as "truly legitimate voices deserving serious consideration."[9] In communication theory studies, scholars also borrow the notion of modern Confucian philosopher Tu Weiming's critique of the "Enlightenment mentality" for its overemphasis on the rational individual and neglect of non-Western conceptions of self and discourses of feeling, body, and morality to question the Cartesian dichotomy of "cognition" and "feeling" and the lack of the concern with "human fellow-feeling" in American communication discipline.[10] Overall, it is undeniable that "Anglo-American and most European philosophers have simply ignored the rich philosophical traditions of Africa, Asia, Latin and Native America, and the rest of the world."[11] Thus, excavating conceptual categories internal to the Confucian tradition helps shift the vantage point from the West to China.

This study approaches Confucian ritualism first as a historical phenomenon rooted in the pre-textual sacrificial rites of early China, which later progressed into Confucian rites, propriety, and social etiquette.[12] Eastern Han Dynasty philologist Xu Shen (58–148) defines *Li* as "That's how people serve gods and acquire their blessing" by capturing its spiritual character.[13] For Xunzi (300–230 BCE), a rationalist Confucian thinker, *Li* had become "a comprehensive idea, involving ceremonies, rituals, the rules of social conduct, the norms of political behavior, and the private standards by which one governs his own emotions and actions."[14] The ritualistic-ceremonial *Li*, whose first letter I capitalize, as core concept of Confucianism has yet to receive deeper analysis from an anthropological perspective, and merely studying "how" Confucius and other Confucian philosophers (here philosophers are defined as people who engage in systematic critical thinking about some transcendental issues) discussed *Li* is inadequate. We need to bring the ritual methods into the studies of (comparative) philosophy. In daily life, the Chinese practice of exchanging gifts is another way of performing social etiquette and ritual propriety through materials. The Chinese word for "gift" is simply *Liwu*, or "ritual object," literally, and as in ancient societies, accepting something from another person means "to accept some part of his spiritual essence."[15] To be sure, *Li* was extended to encompass not only ceremonies but conventions.[16]

Chinese, as well as East Asian, traditions are rarely confined to pure intellectual activities, but "often involve ritualized or repetitive exercises that do not appeal directly to the intellect."[17] The "body-mind cultivation practices," as Leah Kalmanson calls them, involve the stimulation of *qing*, or emotions, and their correct regulations through music and rites. By the time of

Confucius (551–479 BCE) and Mencius (372–289 BCE), for instance, the Eastern Zhou Dynasty (770–221 BCE), moral emotions had become a core issue of the Confucian intellectual contemplation.[18] Since the nonintellectual, emotional element is intrinsic to Confucian teachings, often embodied by the expectation from a "filial son or daughter," its appropriate expression and its relationship with rituals must be studied as a dual structure in Confucianism. These behaviors would finally contribute to the construction of a Confucian ideal human world: benevolent, hierarchical, and reciprocal. As a partial moral philosophy, Confucianism contains many utterances of brief aphorisms such as "People may not be shameless" and "The benevolent love everyone" by Mencius. This type of proposition itself fits the modern definition of "emotivism" since "they are *nothing but* (italicization original) expressions of preference, expressions of attitude and feeling, in so far as they are moral and evaluative in character," according to Alasdair MacIntyre.[19] From an anthropological point of view, it is valid to ask if it is the emotions that bring about the rites, or the other way around, though emotions usually accompany rites.[20]

Another structure inherent in the Confucian tradition is the relationship between rationality and emotion, which is fraught with tensions and integrations. The English term "rationality" is somewhat equivalent to the Chinese word *li*, for which I use the lowercase "l" to mark its difference with the capitalized ritualist *Li*. The word *li* has a complex history of changing connotation and it can mean "pattern," "principle," "order," "truth," "reason," and "coherence" in different times and different circumstances. The English rendition "coherence" perhaps catches its fundamental character of entailing certain stable value.[21] Philologist Xu Shen defined *li* as a technique of carving jade.[22] Gaining a prominent position only in the tenth century, *li* is neither a set of external etiquette, nor human emotions, let along craftmanship, but invoked an abstract, transcendental being by Song Confucians. "It is at once the fundamental principle of the universe and the highest good for man," as Wing-Tsi Chan posits.[23] I also translate the lowercase *li* in this study as "rational principle," and a key phrase that symbolizes the distinctiveness of Neo-Confucianism since the Northern Song dynasty (960–1127) is "Heavenly rational principle." The concept *li* in the Song was about "the existence of the laws of nature," and the unified, cohesive, and pervasive *li* was both normative and prescriptive.[24] In the Song philosophical discourse, the rational *li* is often paired with *qi*, which is often translated as matter, energy, substance, etc., and sometimes it is paired with *yu*, desires. The relationship between rational principle and desires was replete with tensions, if they were not irreconcilable.

As we will see in later chapters, *li* was gradually enmeshed in the conflicts with individual emotions and desire, and the tension between transcendental *li* and practical ritual propriety, *Li,* was pinpointed by eighteenth-century

Confucian scholars. Today, Chinese still often use expressions like *"fa hu qing, zhi hu liyi"*—(one's action ought to) "start from following emotions, yet stop at observing ritual propriety and righteousness," and *"he qing he li"*—(the handling of one thing ought to) "be congruent with both situation-emotion and modern secular rationality" to describe social norms. The Chinese scholar of religious studies Zhuo Xinping, however, cautions that the Chinese concept of *li* "as a universal law of nature or supernatural principle has nothing to do with a 'personal God.'"[25]

To be sure, these three categories, particularly *Li* and *qing*, have multifarious connotations to fit in different times and contexts in the Chinese lexicon of philosophy, literature, and daily practice. *Li* began with sacrificial ceremonies and was extended to rites, etiquettes, manners, propriety, and social norms pertinent to one's roles, relations, and proper behavior in society.[26] In political practices, *Li* as social convention often overlaps with or supplants law in traditional Chinese society. Its semantic field can hardly "be grasped by any single Western notion."[27] In this book, I will use contextualized English renditions and "*Li*" interchangeably.

The etymology and usage of the keywords, as well as their changing meaning, all need to be scrutinized, and the "anthropological primacy of language" and "oral and written communication" will receive ample attention in this study.[28] Michael Puett posits that *qing* has a broad semantic range, including such meanings as basic tendencies, inclinations, dispositions (including emotional dispositions), and fundamental qualities.[29] It may simply mean a concrete situation in both classical and modern Chinese, but it will mislead people to understand *qing* simply as " the Aristotelian 'essence,'" as A.C. Graham suggests.[30] "Essence" for Aristotle is an objective substance, but *qing* for Zhuangzi involved "judging between right and wrong," as well as inward "likes and dislikes," as A.C. Graham also suggests.[31] Thus this subjective and judgmental *qing* is much less an essence than just instinctive human sentiments, or sometimes "gut feelings."

The term *Qing* can also be understood as both subjective and objective "situation-emotion" in the Chinese context. Recent studies of classical Chinese literature focused on the spatial structures and projection of emotions in Chinese theatricality and referred to Chinese expressions that demonstrate the integration of (subjective) emotion with the (objective) landscape, such as *qingjing jiaorong*, "emotion-landscape mingling," and another word used in aesthetics: *qingjing*, "emotion-realm."[32] The external situation and the inner emotion are so related that sometimes when the term *qing* is used, the tacit understanding of it includes a balanced consideration of both the situation and human emotions. For instance, when an official is going to investigate *"minqing,"* a composite word with *qing* as its root, it implies both "people's feelings" and "people's (objective) living conditions." Chinese rarely distinguish these two usages in either spoken or written languages while seeing the investigation of *minqing* as a fact-gathering action with sympathy, and such an investigation is in fact a situational interaction. Another common word in modern Chinese is *shiqing*, usually translated as "something" that happens or something that A wants to tell B, but the word is also a composite ending with *qing*. Regarding the philosophers, in later chapters we will see them becoming "conceptual personae" who, through a variety of "vital anecdotes," epitomized humans' relationship with foodstuff (Confucius), animals (Mencius), clothes (Zhu Xi), and plants (Wang Yangming).[33]

From the perspective of paleography and the Chinese language's emotional lexicon, the composite character *qing* contains a "heart-mind" radical and was interpreted by Eastern Han philologist Xu Shen as related to "desire" and "heart-mind."[34] In the *Book of Rites*, there was a statement: "What are the feelings of men [*renqing*]? They are joy, anger, sadness, fear, love, disliking, and liking."[35] The association of "subjective" feeling with desire, embodied by the Chinese composite word *qingyu*, can be found in Immanuel Kant's writing when he asserts "First, pleasure and displeasure, susceptibility to which is called *feeling*, is always connected with desire or aversion. (Italicization original)"[36] It is a character, just like *Li* and *li*, that is qualified for structural analysis, for their parts and radicals all convey a specific meaning.[37]

Scholars have found that "emotion is a complex, culture-specific concept, a term from ordinary English borrowed by psychology and roughly meaning 'feelings based on thoughts,'" while "*feel*"(italicization original) is more basic than emotion and cannot be explained by it, and whereas a definition of emotion requires a feeling component."[38] Another similar theory suggests that feelings are specific bodily sensations, and it is "first and foremost about the body."[39] Yet emotions are "motives by which people's higher-level behavior is explained."[40] Hence, we need to pay attention to a variety of *qing*: Some are thought-oriented ideas, some are more sensory feelings, like hunger and coldness, and some should be more appropriately understood and translated as "mood."[41] *Qing* might be the best rendition of "passions" as used in Western philosophical tradition if passions imply only strong and positive emotions. When interpreting Spinoza, Bertrand Russell points out that "Emotions are called 'passions' when they spring from inadequate ideas."[42] *Qing* is also associated with moral sentiments. Anthropologist Ruth Benedict uses the Japanese word *on* (*en* in Chinese and in Chinese there is a compound word *enqing*) to capture the Japanese/East Asian feeling of the parental sacrifice for children and children's feeling of indebtedness to parents through remembering and returning the owed *en*. On-*en* is love, but as Ruth Benedict points out, "we (Americans) think of love as something freely given unfettered by obligation."[43] Hence, this non-Western sentiment of love fettered by obligation and indebtedness should be studied as a distinct cultural pattern. From a comparative perspective, Confucianism underwent a "religion to philosophy"[44] transition, but its philosophizing process and metaphysical dimension were also inhibited by its irrevocable concern with inner emotions and their expressions, as well as the meaning of external rites in fostering the cohesion of a community.

MY APPROACHES TO STUDYING
THE THREE CONCEPTS

My approach to investigating the triad is to track the rise and interplay of the three key conceptual categories as a history of ideas yet at both the textual-theoretical level and the practical level, paying attention to the life-world pertinent to anthropological analysis. Anthropologist Michael Puett believes that study of Confucian rituals in history "opens up some interesting possibilities for anthropological theory in general, and more particularly some interesting issues for ways to bring together anthropological theory with philosophy."[45] He sees Confucianism as a cultural system that is taken out of "lived experience," and he is particularly interested in the Confucian dealing with not only ritual and lived experience, but "negative feelings."[46] I will first unravel the cultural origin of the Confucian belief system by tracing it back to the pre-textual years in Chinese history and the Shang dynasty (c.1600–1046 BCE) based on archaeological evidence and oracle bone inscriptions.

It is arguable that Confucianism stems and moves away from the tribal cult of this period, transcending it, yet keeping many of its worldviews and rites.[47] A product of a complex agricultural society, early Confucianism is not too different from some agrarian tribal cultures in Africa. Even the well-known Confucian deep concern with kinship relations between father and son, husband and wife, brother and brother, and friend and friend was typical to a tribal society under the study of Marshall Sahlins.[48] There are three elements in common: agriculture, which symbolizes a more complex society compared with fishing and hunting societies, and its natural interest in animals; the disparity between the views of the religious thinker and the mass of people; and the worship of ancestors, which was a later development.[49]

Confucian values and concepts, as mentioned above, are humanistic, practical, ethical, and pertinent to regulating self and society through the control of the emotions, performing rites and observation of social protocols, as well as the consideration of rational principles, and this study is informed by anthropological studies of rituals and emotions and their connections. As contemporary anthropologists George E. Marcus and Michael M. J. Fischer point out, anthropologists looked to ritual as the appropriate means to understand human sentiment and experience. Marcus and Fischer recognized that there was a thread from Émile Durkheim to Victor Turner that analyzed ritual as a means to convert the obligatory norms of society into the desires of the individual, of creating socialized sentiments, of transforming statuses, effecting cures, acting out mythic charters for social action, and reintegrating agonistic social groups.[50] Here, the notion of the ritual is a means of expression and transformation to facilitate dynamic actions and becoming is congruent with the Confucian understanding of the function of the rituals, *Li*. What we need to overhaul now is how exactly *Li* performed these roles, how it helped people understand emotion, and how it reintegrated social groups.

Sociologists and anthropologists have been turning to philosophy for valid interpretative frameworks to distance themselves from immediate field experiences. Max Weber noticed that *Li*, or "propriety," and also "ceremonies" or "forms of etiquette" were practiced by the educated Chinese to control "all his activities, physical gestures, movements, as well with politeness and with grace in accordance with status mores. . . ."[51] A. R. Radcliffe-Brown affirmed that "[a]t any rate the most complete elaboration of the idea [of the union of opposites] is to be found in the Yin-Yang philosophy of ancient China," and he believed that "this Yin-Yang philosophy of ancient China . . . can be used to define the social structure of the moieties in Australian tribes."[52] Radcliffe-Brown admitted his exposition of rites as having "a specific social function" of expressing . . . of a sense of dependence on a power outside ourselves," and "producing and maintaining an orderly human society," but he immediately referred to Confucian philosopher Xunzi and the *Book of Rites* (*Liji*, or *Li Chi* in the old spelling), claiming that his theory was "by no means new" compared with ancient Chinese thoughts.[53] Some anthropologists are inspired by the philosopher Gilles Deleuze's concern with "life's immanence and horizontal transcendence," as well as his interest in the idea of "becoming."[54] Some argue that philosophy should learn from anthropology and make the core empirical of "living" "more central to its own concerns with epistemology, ontology, and ethical principles."[55] A recent trend is to engage ethical issues intrinsic to speech and action with anthropological studies and to examine "ordinary ethical sensibilities" by drawing from "the insights of philosophers."[56]

Fostering the ethical–emotional bonds was a pertinent intrinsic value in Chinese lineages, and its reinforcement was the goal of Confucian ritualism at the societal level. This was a historical process and the result of the self-conscious promotion and conceptualization of the Confucian thinkers since the Song dynasty.[57] Chinese anthropologist Li Anzhai argues that the origin of *Li*, which for him means both "mores" and "institution," was nothing but *renqing*, which for him means natural human condition and tendency before artificial improvement.[58] Based on her fieldwork in urban

China, anthropologist Mayfair Mei-hui Yang too captures this key Chinese cultural trait of emphasizing "human feelings," *renqing,* in both contemporary social connections, *guanxi,* and its ideological origin in the Confucian classic the *Book of Rites, Liji,* in which human sentiments were considered to be the source of reciprocal ritual propriety, *Li.*[59] In rural southeast China, anthropologist Wang Mingming has also observed the significance of *renqing* and its maintenance is essential in the villages through rotational sacrifices, banqueting, exchange of gifts, and mutual aid. I argue that the philosophical accentuation of the concept *qing* from Confucius's time to the Song dynasty buttressed the folk tradition of cultivating and maintaining *renqing* in practice, which I translate as "reciprocal empathy and favor."[60]

For this current study of Confucianism centering on the dynamics of the triad of *Li, qing,* and *li,* Émile Durkheim has provided felicitous, pertinent definitions and descriptions. He defines (religious) rituals as "ways of acting that are generated only within assembled groups and are meant to stimulate and sustain or recreate certain mental states in these groups."[61] Durkheim also argues that a "religion" cannot be a collection of fragmentary beliefs, but must develop its conception of the universe. This cosmological or even mysterious dimension in Confucianism was embodied by the *Book of Changes* (*Yijing,* or *I-Ching* in old spelling) and later given prominence by Southern Song Confucians such as Zhu Xi. Durkheim's discussion of emotions and "religious feelings," including the "deference" that may lead one to "keep a distance from a high-ranking person," is salient to this study's consideration of Confucius and Xunzi's elaboration of human emotions toward ghosts and deities and to families, and very similar expressions.[62] When Confucius was quoted as saying he had not "dreamed of" the sagely Duke of Zhou for a while, he showed a quasi-religious feeling; as Carl Jung says, "I hold that our dream really speaks of religion and that it means to do so."[63] In another place, Durkheim compares a moral law to a rite for both "prescribe ways of acting" although toward different objects, yet a rite always has "sacred character."[64] For our detailed discussion in the following chapters on the funeral, the death ritual, and the ancestor cult, Durkheim also provides an invaluable way of understanding. He points out that in human history, "the first rites are funeral rites," and "the first sacrifices food offerings meant to satisfy the needs of the departed, and the first altars were graves."[65] However, the ancestor cult, one core practice and belief in Confucianism, was only prevalent in advanced early societies such as China, Egypt, and Greek and Latin cities, but it is absent in Australian tribes. From here I will examine when and in what context Chinese culture continued the ancestor cult while ancient Greeks departed from it.[66]

To further tackle the human-non-human relationship in the lifeworld, I find the "ontological turn" of anthropology which emphasizes the role of objects, artifact, and animals as devices of "memory" and "thinking about history" pertinent.[67] James Frazer's study of the beliefs and institutions of humankind can relate to my inquiry into some features of early Confucianism. First, Frazer notes that the Indians in California had their custom of using "living persons" to represent the "souls" of the deceased at "annual ceremonies of mourning for the dead."[68] As we will discuss later, this resembles an important content of the Chinese sacrificial rite and a recurring topic of Confucius's elaboration, the use of *shī*, impersonator of the deceased father. One noteworthy contribution by Frazer to the modern understanding of early human history is his concern with the "agricultural significance" of ancient rituals. Frazer paid attention to the corn-spirit, and each kind of crop—wheat, barley, oats, flax, beans, lentils, etc., as well as fig tree used as sacrificial offerings in various ancient cultures. He also wrote about the use of animal meat and blood in ritual performance. Frazer's interest in the distinction between man and other animals and in men's killing of animals is relatable to early Confucian texts which contain many discussions on the difference between man and beasts, allusions to the slaughtering of divine animals, and how the sages treated animals such as horses and oxen.[69] In his reflective assessment, Bronislaw Malinowski aptly captured Frazer's "insight in linking up ritual with the practical production of food."[70] This interest was taken further by Roy Rappaport, who delved into the study of "the interaction of humans with local materials, foodstuffs, and animals."[71]

While anthropology is now heading toward more transactional "relational ethnography,"[72] the current research employs a relational perspective at three levels: (1) The dynamic relationships among *Li*, *qing*, and *li* in intellectual discourses and practice; (2) The relationships between humans and non-humans, and those among humans as perceived by Confucians; (3) The relationship between cultural elites and commoners in transmitting, instructing and practicing *Li*, *qing*, and *li*. In terms of a changed perception of the relationship between humans and non-humans, which is deeply embedded in the Confucian worldview, anthropologists Marshall Sahlins' study of production and Tim Ingold's focus on the relationships between humans and non-human animals and mutual perceptions while "dwelling" in the same ecological landscape were inspirational.[73] A relational analytical perspective also helps shift from a concept of substance to a concept of relationship, seeing emotions not as "entities" in individuals but inherent in "*situational* (italicization original) ways of acting in conversational encounters."[74]

The following chapters examine the historical evolution of Confucian ritualism in conjunction with emotion and rational principle. Their interplay occurred in very concrete, historicized situations as a nexus of practices, textualization, codification, institutionalization, and abstraction over an extended time span, and kinship was a crucial institution to sustain the

Confucian creeds as well as an object of Confucian contemplations on human relations. Claude Lévi-Strauss is pertinent here in that he emphasized the meaning of kinship studies as "the anthropologist's special and privileged share in the science of communication."[75] The two keywords here, "kinship" and "communication" will both emerge in my analysis of Confucian rituals and emotions as social processes of communication inside and outside of kinship. Ritual is, as Cliff Geertz asserts, "not just a pattern of meaning; it is also a form of social interactions."[76] Yet this interaction embedded in ritual is often an emotional one, and ritual is a site for the display of a great variety of feelings, while the human body, as modern anthropologists argue, is a source of symbols.[77]

THE SCOPE AND STRUCTURE OF THE BOOK

In the first chapter, I trace the pre-Confucian roots of Chinese state sacrificial rites and how these rites, as well as non-ritual human emotions, were textualized. Based on an anthropological perspective, I will examine the participants and spectators of the rituals and the objects, e.g., food, and animals used in the rituals and referred to in the received texts. From a comparative perspective, I agree with A.C. Graham that "even in the Axial Age Chinese rational demonstration had a much smaller place in Chinese than in Greek thought,"[78] but my explanation is that Chinese thought was more fraught with properly performing sacrificial rites at the elite level and the free expression of human emotions at the grassroots level than Greek thought. The collection and canonization of folksong and sacrificial eulogies and legitimization of non-philosophical expression of human emotions in the *Classic of Odes* distinguishes Confucianism, although the authorship of Confucian classics remains a moot question.

In the second chapter, I rethink some key texts of Confucian and Daoist classics, paying particular attention to how Confucius himself treated ritual practice and human emotions, and how he and his disciples grappled with the legitimacy, meaning, and possible failure of rituals. I trace how the texts on Chu State bamboo slips disclose the rising interest in the origin of *qing* and its relation to *xing*, nature. I also examine how Mencius hypothesized four scenarios involving human-animal relations, to test people's possible choices between moral sentiment and sacrificial procedure/ritual propriety. I provide an alternative interpretation to the classic *Zhuangzi* and argue that the Daoist philosopher Zhuangzi was more rational than free of worries. I also argue that the Confucian philosopher Xunzi can be considered a proto-anthropologist who studied ritual and emotional issues in an analytical and detached way, and for Xunzi, *li* assumed its earliest meaning as "pattern."

In the third chapter, I focus on Song Confucian philosophers, for example, the Cheng brothers and Zhu Xi's promotion of the metaphysical rational-principle, *li*, to enhance Confucianism's ontological foundation, yet they also tried to balance the cosmological principle with the proper expression of human emotions and practice of rituals at the grassroots level. The Tang-Song intellectual transition gave prominence to the concept *li*, and it was reinvented to be the supreme cosmological rational principle as the culmination of Neo-Confucian metaphysics. The rational *li* was idealistically combined with a moderate consideration of human emotions whose ontological origin was associated with the human heart-mind, while *li* was defined as synonymous with *xing*, intrinsic human disposition. In the lifeworld, *li* was concretized as detailed procedures of "family rituals" designed by Zhu Xi to guide common people. Hence, Zhu Xi accomplished the full integration of the cosmological/ethical principle, internal human emotions, and external ceremonial actions through his writing and personal practice, e.g., his compiling of *Family Rituals* and his wearing of the pre-Qin Confucian robe *shenyi* as an artifact.

In chapter 4, I investigate how Confucian ritualism and sentimentalism took root in the Ming and Qing dynasties and how the imperial courts, critical Confucian intellectuals, and the communal level society contributed to the interplay of *Li*, *qing*, and *li*. Both Ming and Qing rulers attempted to reinforce ritualism and the unity of groups at the village level, and early Qing emperors appealed to intra-family emotions by compiling handbooks. In the Confucian discourse, human emotions and desires, or in one composite word *qingyu*, loomed large and led to a cult of sensibility. Ming Confucian philosophers emphasized individual autonomy and entertained the legitimacy of human emotions and desires embedded in quotidian life. Qing philosophers challenged the entrenched supremacy of cosmological rationality and rediscovered the value of ritual, which could be more secular, flexible and adaptive to suit and reflect the emotion-situation. This chapter also details how Zhu Xi's guidebook *Family Rituals* penetrated to the village level based on the research of historical anthropology on Ming-Qing rural China.

In the conclusion and concluding remarks, I extend the discussion to a quick glimpse into contemporary Chinese intellectual and popular cultural landscapes partially based on my fieldwork. There has been a "revival" of Confucianism in mainland China in the early twentieth-first century, and Xunzi, who equally emphasized "ritual" and "emotion" yet had been overshadowed by Mencius and marginalized by the Song dynasty neo-Confucian tradition has received increasing attention. On the popular level, ritual forms such as the rite of "ancient-style" initiation, wedding, and matriculation are being reinvented; gift-exchange and funerary wailing, clothing, and kowtow persist as the expression of emotions. While the Song dynasty notion of metaphysical "Heavenly principle" has diminished, "law" has supplanted it and continues to interact with the more malleable emotion and ritual.

The *Li-qing-li* triad is an assemblage of three interrelated conceptual categories and a contingent relational construction of a latent Chinese mode of philosophical reflection. I place this triad in a conceptual-historical framework that embodies how China's indigenous categories encompass pure philosophical thinking and the lifeworld. The internal tensions of these three elements do not follow the Western pattern of the dichotomy between rationality and non-rationality, nor does the book's narrative attempt to demonstrate how Confucianism was teleologically "rationalized" in history. Instead, I suggest that Confucianism is characterized by an emphasis on the balance of human emotions, ritual practices, and rationality, although the right proportion is often contested both polemically and in real-life. Epistemologically, this triad may help ameliorate the radical dualisms of mind/soul, body/mind, emotion/rationality, etc.

In this book, I examine the Confucian attempt to balance ritual, emotion, rationality, its shifting focuses over time, and its responses and adaptations to the changing times and folk customs, its internal debates, as well as the contemporary revival of ritualism and rethinking of the relationship between rational principle and law. In fact, the ideal sage-ruler in the Chinese imagination is a person who is emotional, empathic, and rational, and is respectful to ritual propriety. At the same time, *Li* was expected to restrain and discipline political rulers.[79] But I believe ordinary people today can learn from this balancing without aspiring to become a sage. I hope my historicized narrative and interpretation of Confucianism informed by the perspectives of anthropology can provide a new angle of vision to revisit the thought-world of ancient China and its cultural legacy in the post-pandemic world and to facilitate a more effective cross-cultural understanding.

NOTES

1. For instance, Anna Sun's *Confucianism as a World Religion: Contested Histories and Contemporary Realities* (Princeton, NJ: Princeton University Press, 2013) shows "how" *Confucianism* became a world religion by tracking the development of the scholarly discourses and controversies on this issue. But I suspect the scholars think Confucianism "is" a religion because they entertain a more religion-oriented understanding of it based on the later institutionalization of Confucianism and canonization of Confucian classics after Confucius's death.

2. Vincent Goossaert, "The Concepts of Religion in China and the West," *Diogenes* 52, no.1 (2005):14.

3. Ibid.

4. Robert Cummings Neville, *Ritual and Deference: Extending Chinese Philosophy in a Comparative Context* (Albany: State University of New York Press, 2008), 2–3, 90.

5. Robert Feleppa, "Zen, Emotions, and Social Engagement," *Philosophy East and West* 59, no. 3 (2009): 264.

6. See Ludwig Wittgenstein, *Major Works: Selected Philosophical Writings* (New York: Harper Collins Publishers, 2009).

7. James Davis and Dimitrina Spencer eds., *Emotions in the Field: The Psychology and Anthropology of Fieldwork Experience* (Stanford, CA: Stanford University Press, 2010), 30.

8. Catherine A. Lutz, *Unnatural Emotions: Everyday Sentiments on a Micronesian Atoll and Their Challenge to Western Theory* (Chicago: University of Chicago Press, 1988), 40–41.

9. Huaiyu Wang, "From the Principle of Rational Autonomy of the Virtuosity of Empathetic of Embodiment: Reclaiming the Modern Significance of Confucian Civilization," *Philosophy East and West* 67, no. 4 (2007): 1222, 1223, 1237.

10. Ronald D. Gordon, "Beyond the Failure of Western Communication Theory," *Journal of Multicultural Discourses* 2, no. 2 (2007): 89, 93–94.

11. Robert C. Solomon, "'What Is Philosophy?' The Status of World Philosophy in the Profession," *Philosophy East and West* 51, no. 1 (2001): 100.

12. "Ritual" and "ceremonial" are not totally identical, while *Li* in Chinese encompasses both meanings. Ritual is an action mainly to establish continuity with "invisible entities," while ceremonial is only about inter-human relations. See Sébastien Billioud and Joël Thoraval, *The Sage and the People: The Confucian Revival in China* (Oxford, UK: Oxford University Press, 2014), 250–51.

13. Xu, *Shuo wen jie zi*, 1. However, I argue that what Xu Shen did was interpretation, not explanation, because *lü* (treading) and *Li* (sacrificial ceremonies) were two unrelated words in Shang oracle bone inscriptions, and perhaps only in the Zhou dynasty were the words become connected.

14. Frederic W. Mote, *Intellectual Foundations of China* (New York: Alfred A. Knopf, 1971), 64.

15. Marcel Mauss, *The Gift: The Form and Reason for Exchange in Archaic Societies* (New York: W. W. Norton, 1990), 12.

16. Neville, *Ritual and Deference,* 29.

17. Leah Kalmanson, "The Ritual Methods of Comparative Philosophy," *Philosophy East and West* 67, no. 2 (April 2017): 400.

18. Ryan Nichols, "A Genealogy of Early Confucian Moral Psychology," *Philosophy East and West* 61, no. 4 (October 2011): 609–29.

19. Alasdair Macintyre, *After Virtue: A Study in Moral Philosophy*, 3rd ed. (Notre Dame, IN: University of Notre Dame Press, 2007), 11–12.

20. E.E., Evans-Pritchard, *Theories of Primitive Religion* (Oxford, UK: Oxford University Press, 1965), 45.

21. Brook Ziprin, *Ironies of Oneness and Difference: Coherence in Early Chinese Thought; Prolegomena to the Study of Li* (Albany: State University of New York Press, 2012), 9–12.

22. Xu Shen, *Shuo wen jie zi* [*Explication of Words and Characters*] (Beijing: Zhonghua shuju, 2013), 6. In this entry, Xu Shen defines *li* the same as other characters related to jade-carving, *zhiyu*.

23. Wing-Tsi Chan, *Chu Hsi: New Studies* (Honolulu: University of Hawaii Press, 1989), 199.

24. Jeeloo Liu, *Neo-Confucianism: Metaphysics, Mind, and Morality* (Hoboken, NJ: Wiley-Blackwell, 2018), 85, 87–88.

25. Xinping Zhuo, "Western and Chinese Philosophical and Religious Thought in the Twentieth Century," *Studies in Chinese Religions* 1, no. 1 (2015): 93.

26. Many scholars have discussed the connotations of *Li*. For one example, see A.C. Graham, *Disputers of the Tao: Philosophical Argument in Ancient China* (La Salle, Il: Open Court, 1989), 11.

27. Geir SigurÐsson, *Confucian Propriety and Ritual Learning: A Philosophical Interpretation* (Albany: State University of New York Press, 2015), 12.

28. For an emphasis on the anthropological dimension of conceptual history, see Reinhart Koselleck, *The Practice of Conceptual History: Timing History, Spacing Concepts*, trans. Todd Samuel Presner et al. (Stanford, CA: Stanford University Press, 2002), 27.

29. Michael J. Puett, "The Ethics of Responding Properly: The Notion of Qing in Early Chinese Thought," in Halvor Eifring ed., *Love and Emotions in Traditional Chinese Literature* (Leiden: Brill, 2004), 42.

30. A.C. Graham, *Studies in Chinese Philosophy and Philosophical Literature* (Singapore: The Institute of East Asian Philosophies,1986), 60.

31. Ibid., 61.

32. Ling Hon Lam, *The Spatiality of Emotion in Early Modern China* (New York: Columbia University Press, 2018), 2, 5.

33. For "conceptual personae" in philosophers and their relationship with non-human existences, see Gilles Deleuze and Félix Guattari, *What is Philosophy?* trans. Hugh Tomlinson and Gram Burchell (New York: Columbia University Press, 1994), 73.

34. Xu, *Shuo wen jie zi*, 216.

35. Confucius et al., *The Book of Rites*, ed. Dai Sheng, trans. James Legge (Beijing: Intercultural Press, 2013), 104.

36. Immanuel Kant, *The Metaphysics of Morals*, trans. Mary Gregor (Cambridge, UK: Cambridge University Press, 1991), 40.

37. For some Chinese composite characters' separability and the possibility of structural analysis, see Qiu Xigui, *Wenzi xue gaiyao* [A General Outline for Chinese Philology] (Beijing: Shangwu yinshu guan, 2013), 10–11.

38. Andrew Beatty, *Emotional Worlds: Beyond an Anthropology of Emotion* (Cambridge, UK: Cambridge University Press, 2019), 248.

39. Antonio Damasio, *Descartes' Error: Emotion, Reason, and the Human Body* (New York: The Penguin Group, 1994), 159.

40. Gilbert Ryle, *The Concept of Mind* (Chicago: University of Chicago Press, 2000), 84–85.

41. For the use of "mood" to translate *qing* as appearing in ancient Chinese poetry, see Zhang Longxi, *The Tao and the Logos: Literary Hermeneutics, East and West* (Durham, NC: Duke University Press, 1992), 153–55.

42. Bertrand Russell, *A History of Western Philosophy* (New York: Simon & Schuster, 1972), 573.

43. Ruth Benedict, *The Chrysanthemum and the Sword: Patterns of Japanese Culture* (Boston: Houghton Mifflin Company, 1989), 100–1.

44. For this pattern and the modern attempts to interpret Confucianism in terms of its transcendental principles and its "rational" characters in the Weberian sense, see Michael J. Puett, *To Become a God: Cosmology, Sacrifice, and Self-Divinization in Early China* (Cambridge, MA: Harvard University Asia Center, 2002), 1–29. For the "religion to philosophy" theory, see Puett, *To Become a God*, 83, 105.

45. Michael Puett, "Ritual Disjunctions," in *The Ground Between: Anthropologists Engage Philosophy,* Veena Das et al. eds. (Durham, NC: Duke University Press, 2014), 220.

46. Ibid., 223.

47. The Shang belief in and sacrificial performance to *di*, the supreme spiritual being, meets the minimum definition of a "religion" proposed by E. B. Taylor: "the belief in Spiritual Beings," yet the Shang religion would fail to meet another higher standard: "judgment after death." Edward Burnett Taylor, *Primitive Culture* Vol.1 (Mineola, NY: Dover Publications, Inc., 2016), 424.

48. Marshall Sahlins, *Culture and Practical Reason* (Chicago: University of Chicago Press, 1976), 6.

49. Paul Radin, *Primitive Religion: Its Nature and Origin* (New York: Dover Publications, Inc., 1957), 34–35, 74–75. According to Robert Bella's definition of, the term "primitive religion" has several dimensions: It is oriented to a single cosmos; it is concerned with "the maintenance of personal, social, and cosmic harmony and with attaining specific goods—rain, harvest, children, health—as men have always been;" and it has not yet attained the "overriding goal of salvation" nor "world rejection" for which a full-fledged religion is known; and people's vision of life after death is shadowy and vague. See Robert N. Bella, *Beyond Belief: Essays on Religion in a Post-Traditionalist World* (Berkeley: University of California Press, 1991), 23.

50. George E. Marcus and Michael M.J. Fischer, *Anthropology as Cultural Critique: An Experimental Moment in the Human Sciences* (Chicago: University of Chicago Press,1999), 61.

51. Max Weber, *The Religion of China*, trans. Hans H. Gerth (New York: The Free Press, 1964), 156.

52. A.R. Radcliffe-Brown, *Method in Social Anthropology*, M. N. Srinivas ed. (Chicago: University of Chicago Press, 1958), 124–125. Radcliffe-Brown argues that it is appropriate to translate *Li* as "ritual."

53. Ibid., *Structure and Function in Primitive Society* (New York: The Free Press,1965), 157–58.

54. João Biehl, "Ethnography in the Way of Theory," in *The Ground Between*, 95, 104.

55. Arthur Kleinman, "The Search for Wisdom," in *The Ground Between*, 135.

56. Michael Lambek, "Introduction," in *Ordinary Ethics: Anthropology, Language, and Action*, Michael Lambek ed. (New York: Fordham University Press, 2010), 3–6.

57. For the questioning of the ahistorical anthropological approach to the lineage system in southeast China, mainly embodied by the study of Maurice Freedman, see Allen Chun, "The Lineage-Village Complex in Southeastern China: A Long Footnote in the Anthropology of Kinship," in *Current Anthropology* 37, no. 3 (June 1996): 429–50, with comments on and the comments and critiques of Chun by Johan Clammer, Patricia Ebrey, David Faure et al., as well as the response of Allen Chun. I agree with Chun's historical-ideological approach to revisit the ritual practice of Chinese lineages but want to add that true feelings among the members are another important aspect in Chinese lineage groups.

58. Li Anzhai, *Yi-li yu Liji de shehuixue yanjiu* [A Sociological Study of *Ceremonials and Rites* and *Records of Rites*] (Shanghai: Shanghai shiji chuban jituan, 2005), 3, 8.

59. Mayfair Mei-hui Yang, *Gifts, Banquets, and Favors: The Art of Social Relationship in China* (Ithaca, NY: Cornell University Press, 1994), 67. Yang also discusses the etymology of the character *Li* and its meanings. See Yang, *Gifts, Banquets, and Favors,* 227.

60. Wang Mingming, *Cunluo shiye zhong de wenhua yu quanli: Min Tai sancun wu lun* [Culture and Power from the Perspective of Villages: Five Theses on the Three Villages of Fujian and Taiwan] (Beijing: sanlian shudian, 1997), 66–68, 72–73, 169–73. The villages under Wang's investigation have their specific geographical and cultural traits, but the term *renqing* is very commonly used in Chinese social life, and in this sense, it is safe to say that the *renqing*-related practices in this region as Wang depicts epitomize Chinese culture in general.

61. Durkheim, *The Elementary Forms of Religious Life*, trans. Carol Cosman (Oxford, UK: Oxford University Press, 2001), 11.

62. Ibid., 160.

63. Carl Gustav Jung, *Psychology and Religion* (New Haven, CT: Yale University Press, 1966), 31.

64. Ibid., 36.

65. Ibid., 51.

66. In this study, I use the term "Confucianism" instead of "Ruism" for several reasons (1) While "'Confucianism' itself is highly confused" as an equivocal term, Ruism is no less ambiguous. The Eastern Han (25 AD–220 AD) dictionary *shuo wen jie zi* [*Explication of Words and Characters*] by Xu Shen glosses Ru as "being soft and gentle; it is how people call *shushi*" without referring to Confucius. See Xu, *Shuo wen jie zi*, 159. But the word *shushi* in ancient Chinese could broadly mean both Confucian scholars and Daoist priests, as well as any diviners and sorcerers; (2) By using "Confucianism," I mean a set of doctrines of ethics and a way of life consciously endorsed, promoted, and theorized, if not invented, by Confucius in a reflective way, and assume the practices before him were pre-Confucian, shamanistic beliefs and ritual art; (3) Confucianism is a unifying concept that encompasses the disputing "Ruist" factions after the death of Confucius, because all these factions shared the worship of Confucius as a sagely teacher; (4) "Neo-Confucianism" has

become an internationally accepted terminology, and it is difficult to replace it with "Neo-Ruism."

67. Martin Palecek and Mark Risjord, "Relativism and the Ontological Turn within Anthropology," *Philosophy of the Social Sciences* 43, no. 1 (2012): 3–23.

68. James George Frazer, *The Golden Bough, A New Abridgement* (Oxford, UK: Oxford University Press, 1994), 376.

69. Ibid., 498, 533, 581, 605.

70. Bronislaw Malinowski, *A Scientific Theory of Culture and Other Essays* (Chapel Hill: The University of North Carolina Press, 1944), 191.

71. Catherine Bell, *Ritual: Perspectives and Dimensions* (Oxford, UK: Oxford University, 1997), 29.

72. Mathew Desmond, "Relational Ethnography," *Theory and Society*, no. 43 (2014): 547–79.

73. Marshall Sahlins, *Stone Age Economics* (London: Routledge, 1972); Tim Ingold, *The Perception of the Environment: Essays on Livelihood, Dwelling, and Skill* (London: Routledge, 2000).

74. Mustafa Emirbayer, "Manifesto for a Relational Sociology," *American Journal of Sociology* 103, no. 2 (1997): 302.

75. Claude Lévi-Strauss, *Structural Anthropology* (New York: Basic Books, 1963), 300.

76. Clifford Geertz, *The Interpretation of Cultures* (New York: Basic Books, 1973), 168.

77. Bell, *Ritual*, 35, 41.

78. Graham, *Disputers of the Tao*, 7.

79. Daniel A. Bell and Hahm Chaibom, "The Contemporary Relevance of Confucianism," in *Confucianism for the Modern World*, Daniel A. Bell and Hahm eds. Chaibom (New York: Cambridge University Press, 2003), 7.

Chapter 1

Li and *Qing*: Sacrifice, Ritual, and Emotion Before Confucius

China has a long history of ritualism before Confucius. When Confucius was born in 551 BCE, he was brought into the Spring and Autumn period (771–476 BCE) which was the early part of the Eastern Zhou Dynasty. Prior to this, Western Zhou Dynasty (1045–771 BCE) had established solid political control and ritual institutions in northern China's plains, the prototype of "China," or the Central Realm, *zhongguo*, a geographical term with the cultural self-awareness of the ruling elites. The dynasty before Zhou, the Shang Dynasty, had left its large quantity of written records as inscriptions on oracle bones and bronze ritual vessels. This background reminds us that Confucius in his time was facing a civilization that already had 1,000 years of written history and continuous institutional building and breakdown, and it could be traced further back through mythologies about a wide range of legendary culture heroes. Modern archeological excavations and research continues to reveal the details of the pre-textual life of China, and all these may help understand the intellectual foundation of Confucius's concerns and inquiries in a time of crisis, known as *Li huai yue beng*—the lapses of decorum and etiquette and the corruption of music. It is arguable that the pre-Confucian belief in the ghosts of ancestors and the power of a supreme being and the associated religious feelings of reverence and awe can be seen as a sort of natural religion.[1]

What makes early Chinese culture distinct, however, was not the priority given to ancestor worship, as many believe, but other important facts: first, there were a complex set of ritual objects and vessels; second, all the practices and materials, as well as human emotions, were reflectively observed, collected, and recorded. It was textualization and final canonization with critical thinking, not the voluntary ritual actions of paying obeisance, that brought early Chinese culture to a higher level of rationalization, yet this textual reorganization and rationalization process retained and legitimized

1

human emotions and even sexual drives as we see in the *Book of Odes*. The records show that the relationship between the Shang rulers and the divine powers was not always harmonious but full of tensions and it was more like a "give-and-take" relationship of exchange, pacification, and coercion with the living's purpose of winning the support of the deified ancestors.[2]

However, whereas the Shang rites as recorded in the oracle bone inscriptions were state political rites, most of the Western and Eastern Zhou rites that were endorsed or detailed by Confucius were interpersonal and private rites. Festivals were "both worship and play" and included both "sacred and secular elements," and these were manifested in the *Book of Odes*.[3] When Confucius attached unprecedented importance to family funerals, the death of his students, and the prolonged mourning period for dead parents, as we will see in chapter 3, he was not concerned for the instrumental purposes in political rituals but the non-instrumental expression of genuine affection. Confucius's intellectual contribution was his switching of focus from state ritual ceremonies, which he still took seriously as an official, to interpersonal relations and his adding of emotional dimensions to make rituals more humane and secular.

RITUAL IN THE EARLIEST "CHINA"

Recent archaeological excavations found that in the Taosi site located in today's Shanxi Province there had emerged the prototype of the ritual systems, *Lizhi*, prominent in the Three Dynasties: Xia, Shang, and Zhou. According to the archaeologists, the Taosi culture of around 2000 BCE had produced nonpractical sacrificial vessels including painted porcelain plates and stone-made percussion instruments. They conclude that the Chinese ritual system centering on social distinction and hierarchy had emerged in the period of Longshan culture, which spans from 3000 BCE to 2000 BCE and of which Taosi was a part. The Taosi ritual vessels, however, were distinct compared with Shang bronze vessels in that they were known as "pre-bronze vessels." [4] It was only after the Taosi community had disappeared for over one hundred years that bronze vessels appeared in the Erlitou site near today's Luoyang of Henan Province.[5] The archeologist Xu Hong found that the early society as reflected in the Taosi findings had become complex because there are whole sets of food vessels, wine vessels, musical vessels (instruments), and weapons.[6]

The culture of *Li* and *yue*, rites and music, which Confucius accentuated and elevated to a philosophical-religious ground, had been entrenched in practice during the Erlitou period (1900–1500 BCE), when rites and music worked as linkage points that tied the northern Chinese chiefdoms on the

Central Plains together to form an (early) "state complex."[7] Because of the lack of direct written evidence, the Xia dynasty remains a mystery, and cautious archeologists such Xu Hong decline to identify the cultures in an archeological sense, which he studied, with the Xia "dynasty." For him, the historicity of Xia was an "unprovable" construction based upon the textual sources of much later times.[8]

Another important Chinese ritual vessel with symbolic meaning, jade objects also appeared in the Taosi period, although it was most prominent in southeastern Chinese Liangzhu culture (3400–2250 BCE). The American anthropologist Berthold Laufer, who visited China in 1901–1902, noted in his study of the ritualist use of jade in Chinese history that it is said that jade was known to the legendary culture hero and sage ruler the Yellow Emperor, Huang-ti [Huangdi].[9] For the archaeologist Li Xueqin (1933–2019), the extensive use of carved jade ornaments in tombs underscored the sharp social stratification caused by labor division.[10] Archaeologists usually see the use of jade ritual vessels, also notable in the Hongshan culture (4700 to 2900 BCE) as an expression of primitive religious sentiments and political authority. Archaeologist Su Bingqi (1909–1997) points out the earliest jade vessel discovered in China was completed in 6000 BCE, and the jade vessel's social function had long surpassed common ornaments. Instead, it served as a sample of the ruling elites' "virtue," *de* with added social awareness. He also argues that jade vessels could not be produced without the division of labor, and more importantly, ritualistic jade vessels would not have been needed in the first place if there had not been a social distinction.[11] The direct link between jade and shamanism can be found in a Han dynasty quote from philologist Xu Shen: "The magical (*lingwu*) serves the spirits with jade."[12]

The architecture of the pre-textual "state complex" also reflects ritualistic features. In 1983, a "Goddess Temple" was excavated near the Hongshan cultural site along with porcelain ritual vessels; in 1987, the relic of an altar was found in the Liangzhu culture. With an area of 400 square kilometers, the alter was believed to have served the purpose of offering sacrifices to heaven and earth. In the northwest Chinese Qijia cultural area, altar-like stone circles were found, along with the bone of oxen, sheep, and bones for divination purposes. Evidence of the earliest human sacrifice also appeared in the Yangshao (5000–4000 BCE) cultural area, the core region of early China.[13]

THE SHANG DYNASTY: SHAMANISM, DIVINATION RITUAL, AND EMOTION

A solid historical dynasty, the Shang was verified by and well-known for its oracle bone inscriptions. A Chinese word *wu* was identified in the oracle bone text with a connotation of dancer-shaman, who in the beginning were mostly women. The historian and philologist Xu Zhongshu (1898–1991) defines *wu* as an ancient social group that controlled sacrifice, dance, medicine, and writing, all related to religious rituals and proto-science and technology. They were officers of divination who were in charge of tortoiseshell, *bu*, and its ceremonial use, as well as *shi*, divination stalks. *Wu* presided over divinations and judged the cracks on the burned ox shoulder bones or tortoise shells; they were also people who grasped the script inscribed on shells and bones to record divination and other events.[14] Li Xueqin provides information about a shaman's tomb as early as 4000 BCE and suggests that shamans or shaman groups emerged because of the complications of sacrificial rituals.[15] The philosopher Li Zehou, however, points out that *wu* was more than a primitive group of masters of ceremony, but cultural agents who carried China's great tradition until it achieved the transition from *wu* to *Li*, or, in my translation, from shamanism to ritualism. For the eminent paleographer Tang Lan (1901–1979), *wu* diviners of the Shang dynasty invented the Eight Trigrams.[16] Yet for Li Zehou, the most salient phenomenon was not what the *wu* diviners did, but how they transformed shamanistic activities into more advanced ritualist and ceremonial institutions that all group members had to follow, and the process of systematizing, perfecting, and stabilizing this system was completed by the Duke of Zhou, the cultural idol worshipped by Confucius, [who] was said to have "created rites and composed music."[17] *Wu* could be the king, or the political leader with indisputable authority and influence, usually possessing shamanistic magical power and charisma, and *wu* was also the etymological origin of sages and kings.[18] As we will see in chapter 3, the Duke of Zhou had the combined traits of shaman and ruler in his capacity as a royal regent.

The Shang Dynasty had several cultural characteristics pertaining to the later development of Chinese religious thought and the rise of Confucianism: (1) It had a strong political orientation based upon a lineage system. The prominence of clans and lineages in which Confucius and his contemporary thinkers grew up can be traced back to the Yangshao period, and that led to ancestor worship; [19] (2) The modern virtual reconstruction of the "Xia," or Erlitou in the archaeological sense, and the Shang palaces hint at strong mobilizing power by the state over laborers and the moral authority of the ruler, and the social distinction and hierarchy was very visible; (3) Shamans or religious figures who engaged in divination, rainmaking, magic healing, etc., played a major role in assisting the political ruler and served as intermediaries between the human world and the supernatural world;[20] (4) The divination records in the oracle bone inscriptions show that the Shang rulers and the diviners prayed to their supreme High God, *di*; (5) Frazer and Malinowski's interests in agriculture as mentioned in chapter 1 will apply to

China because the Yangshao culture is "a culture of millet farmers and pig breeders who manufactured red pottery impressed with cord-marks or painted with a wide variety of animal and geometric motifs";[21] (6) A sophisticated system of bronze food vessels had been made for the Shang royal house, and 28 types of cooking, drinking, and serving instruments have been identified by modern Chinese archaeologists, each having its ancient name.[22] In this state-centered cultural milieu, *Li* as state sacrificial ritual served more religio-political than communal purposes to reinforce the absolute power of the ruler and the cultural dominance of *wu* elites, but it was also extended to regular interpersonal relations.

The fundamental agricultural character of early China placed emphasis on plants, animals, and food and its serving, rendering eating and feasting sacrosanct, which was to be reflected in Confucius's attitude toward food and feasting and the codification of the banqueting rituals. During the Shang Dynasty, food and eating had been unsurprisingly often "directly implicated in the negotiation of social status and relationship of power."[23] Shang art featured faces and bodily parts of animals, mainly tigers, cattle, and birds.[24] Sacrificial rites were also related to specific trees and each of the Three Dynasties had its own sacred tree. For the Shang it was a cypress.[25] Animals played a significant role in Shang ritualism. Statistics show that the Shang court used a total of twenty names to indicate a variety of sacrificial animals with gender differentiation in its weekly offering to the ancestors.[26] The hunted or domesticated animals to be slaughtered as offering linked man to the supernatural powers, but at the same time, men and animals were also united and there was rising feeling between men and domestic animals such as horses, cattle, sheep, pigs, and dogs.[27]

The ritual itself reflected a triad of divination, sacrifice, and feasting in the worship of Shang ancestors.[28] And it was in Shang dynasty feasting that people developed the formal etiquette between hosts and guests, which the Confucian canon *Yi-Li* [*Ceremonials and Rites*] records in great detail. One of the twenty-eight food and drink vessels, the bronze *jue* cup, was used in the elite ancestor libation ceremonies during the late Shang to offer wine to the spirit of a grandfather or at ancestral temples and altars.[29] Yet, the use of *jue* was not limited to the sacrifice. At the feast, the host must have the *jue* cup washed after he drank from it, and then he filled it again and invited the guests to enjoy wine.[30] Here, one important phenomenon is that the post-sacrifice feast became a social event in which the participants needed to consume the food and wine that was symbolically presented to the spirits, and they also used this opportunity both to establish the host/guest social distinction and to enhance their emotional ties by showing mutual respect.

As we discuss in later chapters, it took many centuries for the ancestral sacrifices to diffuse to the grassroots level of Chinese society. In the

Shang dynasty, the ancestral sacrifices were a quintessential royal affair and addressed to dynastic ancestors. Or, at least, the oracle bone inscriptions said little about the life of nonelites. David N. Keightley records seventeen topics of royal divination as recorded in the decoded oracle bone inscriptions. His research shows that except for the divination for consulting the supernatural powers in warfare and hunting, the administering of sacrificial rituals, *Li* itself needed a divine opinion about auspicious dates, a particular kind or number of sacrificial victims, or if a particular ritual will be appropriate.[31] This shows that ritual itself is subject to the divine will, as interpreted by the diviner.

During the divination process, the objects of the offerings and prayers, however, were multiple: the supreme High God, *di*, animistic Nature Powers, High Ancestors, etc., and the king played a pivotal role because most of the texts were about his plans, activities, and choices. It is notable that for the king, it was also a process of inner moral feelings, *qing*, because no doubt he would experience worry, fear, and respect.[32] These feelings can qualify as "religious sentiment," as William James calls it, with "religious fear" and "religious awe" among them, along with "religious love" and "religious joy."[33] Human emotions at a sacrificial ceremony were stimulated by music, which was believed to have the function of touching the inner heart of the participants and making them feel the order of things.[34]

In praying and performing sacrifices, the rulers did not treat the various supernatural beings the same way. Interestingly, there were never sacrificial offerings made to the High God, but they were presented to ancestors.[35] This was perhaps because the Shang rulers did not see the High God as a personified being, but they treated their ancestors *as* if they could be invoked and ought to descend to enjoy the food and wine symbolically. Yet evidence shows that in the following Zhou dynasty, hundreds of oxen were killed to offer sacrifice to Heaven, tian, which replaced the supreme position of the High God. Modern anthropological studies have provided an important perspective in distinguishing the act of performing sacrifice to animist and traditional gods and deities, and the ritual dedicated to one's own ancestors. For the former, the offerings are given and feastings are provided to maintain "good relations" with the deities such as "God of Water," and these rituals are more utilitarian or negative to prevent harm to the people, while offerings to one's family ancestors are made of personal feelings.[36] In some ceremonies, ancestors are invoked to witness the division of a family and its property, and family shrines are built in each house's middle room to store ancestors' wooden spirit tablets with inscribed names, which is always accompanied by offerings of food, incense tripods, candlesticks, and other artifacts.[37] Based upon my personal experience of performing a sacrifice to my grandparents' tomb, ancestral sacrifice is fundamentally intimate and emotional, and it is not an "exchange of favors."[38]

FROM SHANG THEOCRACY TO ZHOU RITUALISM

The Shang Dynasty was a kin-based theocracy that created a "patrimonial proto-bureaucratic mix"[39] and it was to yield to a more secular Western Zhou dynasty in 1045 BCE. The neologism that did not exist in Shang oracle bone inscriptions emerged in Zhou documents frequently, *min*, commoners, and *de*, moral virtue, although "commoners" were usually the target of disciplining and penalization under the Zhou rule of royal lineal rites.[40] Besides the prominence of *min* and *de*, the Marxist historian Hou Wailu (1903–1987) found other significant new concepts that marked the Shang-Zhou cultural and political transition. The first was the conceptual pair *de*, moral virtue, and *xiao*, filial piety; the former was directed to *tian*, heaven or cosmological forces, and the latter was to ancestors.[41] Hou also noted the rise in the Western Zhou of the distinct social class *shi*, which as an identity with self-imposed social roles later loomed large in the discussions of Confucius and Mencius. The *shi* were at first warriors of Western Zhou, then in the first part of Eastern Zhou, for instance, Spring and Autumn, they were intellectual elites who might assume civilian positions such as mayor, *yizai*, which was the title of at least seven of Confucius's students.[42]

Shang spiritualism continued in the Zhou. Famous for his founding of the political concept "Mandate of Heaven," the early Western Zhou royal regent Duke of Zhou assisted the young King Cheng with admirable moral virtue, and he was believed to have institutionalized rites and music. Remembered and worshiped by Confucius for this cultural accomplishment and his achievement as a statesman and political thinker, the Duke of Zhou was also a shaman-priest who prayed to the spirits for the health of the young King Cheng when he fell sick. The text of the prayer was archived and later discovered by King Cheng after he became an adult. King Cheng was moved to tears upon reading the text and recalled the Duke of Zhou, who was then in exile.[43] There was also continuity between Yin-Shang religiopolitical rituals and early Zhou rituals. According to the *Book of Documents*, *Shangshu*, the Duke of Zhou said, "Let the king at first employ the ceremonies of Yin, and sacrifice in the new city, doing everything in an orderly way, but without display." In one ceremony, the Duke of Zhou sacrificed a bull, a ram, and a boar to the spirit of the land.[44]

Aristocratic education to cultivate future scholar-official, also *shi*, who fit the elite ideal, had been institutionalized in Western Zhou. Early education included homeschooling from six to nine years old, and boarding school education started at ten, when music was an important subject. The role of music in cultivating moral sentiments is not unfamiliar to modern Western thinkers. As Ludwig Wittgenstein points out, "It has sometimes been said that what music conveys to us are feelings of joyfulness, melancholy, triumph, etc. . . . it seems to say that music is an instrument for producing in us sequences of feelings."[45] At the Zhou aristocratic academy, teenagers after fifteen focused on music and archery, and after completing the capping rite, *guanli* at twenty, they would be full-fledged adults, and only after this they could learn the whole set of rituals. The aristocratic college of the Western Zhou was named "*piyong.*"[46] *Piyong* was not only a school but also the site for aristocratic students to practice archery and hunting, which was expected to train their military skills, social etiquette, and provide birds and animals offered in sacrifice.[47] The school was also the space for an important social event at the time known as "*xiang yinjiu Li,*" or district libational rites, which Confucian scholar-officials in the eighteenth century attempted to restore, which we will discuss later. In the Western Zhou, the district libational rites served two purposes: to show respect for local senior citizens and to discuss state affairs.[48] Another ritual building in the Western Zhou was the Hall of Illumination, *mingtang*, where the Duke of Zhou received feudal lords and offered sacrifice to High God--the term *ming* meaning 'illuminating the high and the low.'"[49]

The Confucian canon *Yi-Li*, or *Ceremonials and Rites*, which for some modern scholars was written by Confucius, or by the Duke of Zhou and edited by Confucius, is a detailed account of the methods of *Li*.[50] Among the seventeen chapters, five had the word *shì* in the chapter title. In these chapters, the narrative did not center on the highest political authority or the ruler's ceremonial relationship with Heaven or his ancestors, and it was also not always about the hierarchical relationship between high and low. Instead, the descriptions were often about *shì* scholars' life and sometimes their equal and reciprocal social interactions among themselves. For instance, in the chapter titled *shì xiangjian Li,* "the rites of the scholars' meeting," there was not only a regulation about how a *shì* scholar should be received by a duke who possessed a social rank one grade higher than himself, but also how a scholar should meet another scholar and how a duke should visit another duke, while the main point here was about what gift, also *Li*, to present and how to do it. To be more precise, at the former's first visit, one scholar should present a hunted pheasant to another scholar if it was in the winter and wind-dried pheasant meat if it was summer. What they should say to each other and how the gifts would be given and taken were also set forth.[51] According to the *Yi-Li*, the King and foreign ambassadors used jade ornaments as gifts and exchanged them as part of the protocol.[52]

The *Yi-Li* emphasizes children's moral obligations to parents and pointed out that this defines not only the distinction between humans and non-humans, but also a social hierarchy. Birds and beasts know their mothers but not fathers, and uncouth barbarians living outside of the cities never cared about respect for their parents, it says. According to the book's logic, the worship of parents/ancestors extended along with the status of the worshipper: urban citizens knew their fathers should be respected; dukes and scholars worshiped their grandfathers; feudal lords extended the respect to their great-grandfathers; and the King, or the "Son of Heaven," could trace [all the way back?] to his primogenitor.[53]

In ceremonies to express filial piety, an impersonator of the dead, *shī* (in modern Chinese the same character means "corpse" only but in ancient Chinese it means both dead body and the living impersonator), was used in both funerary rites and ancestral sacrifices to establish the ceremonial link and relationship of continuity between the dead and the living. The *Yi-Li* records how and when the son and daughter-in-law should wail and stamp their feet, how the Master of Ceremony, *zhu*, should assist with receiving the impersonator by washing his hands, and how the *shī* was worshiped.[54] The young impersonator, often assumed by the grandson of the dead man,[55] ate *as if* the ancestors descended to enjoy the feast.[56] Using the *shī* impersonator to act out the feeling toward the dead and acknowledge the origin of the living is a symbolic act of visualization and metonym in the ritual process to project memory, emotion, and imagination.[57]

Based on fieldwork, the modern anthropologist Lin Yaohua (1910–2000) argues that the worship of ancestors as a ritual was a mix of love and fear based on the belief that the omnipotent ancestral spirits might protect or punish the living people or simply play tricks on them. Although the custom of "establishing an impersonator" was prohibited after the Qin Dynasty (221– 206 BCE), Lin points out, Eastern Han Confucians still defended the custom as an expression of sorrow and yearning and said the worshippers would be pleased when the impersonator was eating food, because they envisaged they were feeding their ancestors.[58] This phenomenon of establishing the impersonator in the deceased man's grandson in sacrifice and its lingering influence in fact reveals "mimesis" in an anthropological sense, in that the imitation and analogy became a representation and an expression that involves copying, and the imitator was put in contact with the world of the imitated.[59] It manifested the continuity of the vertical familial relationship while the loss was irrevocable.

Food culture related to the agricultural character of the Chinese civilization continued to develop in the Zhou, and animals were treated as the objects of hunting and artifacts of ceremonial sacrifices. The archaeological finding shows that in the Shang Dynasty, the Chinese had ritualized the kitchen knife, *dao*, and the cutting board, *zu*, used as burial objects as a pair.[60]

The Zhou ritual of ancestor worship took the form of communal meals in the ancestral temples, and it was full of emotions and rational considerations. Eating the meals played the social role of reaffirming the ties of the living people to create corporate solidarity. The Zhou King's menu was recorded, and he ate pork and lamb daily, which is called *shaolao*, the small barn, and when he ate pork, lamb, and beef on the first day of each lunar month, it was called *dalao*, the big barn.[61] When the three animals were used in sacrifice, hundreds of them would be slaughtered, but the hierarchy remained the same: oxen were used to Heaven and God of Grains, *ji*, and sheep and boar were used to the hundred spirits, the water, and the earth.[62]

Western Zhou was a time of divination and "shamanism," while "shamanism" is usually used in a loosely defined way, "spirit-medium" may be an accurate English term to translate *wu*.[63] And the practice of the spirit-mediums did not conflict with trance and possession. In modern Chinese usage, *shǐ* still means "history" while *wu*, often implies supernatural beliefs and magical practices. It is notable that "head shaman" [*siwu*] was recorded as an official position in the Western Zhou court, whose duty was to lead other shamans, male and female, to dance when there was a draught, while a Grand Scribe was the Zhou court minister in charge of institutions and laws, and Small Scribes [*xiaoshǐ*] were officials who recorded important events in feudal states.[64] The leading paleographer Qiu Xigui uses the collective term *wushǐ* to indicate early Chinese cultural elites and suggests that they developed primitive pictographic symbols in a systematic writing script.[65] More meticulous studies of the meaning of the ancient Chinese characters by Li Ling shows that *zhu* and *zong* mean "diviners" and "sacrifice performers," official positions in the Western Zhou court and they epitomized the the shamanistic culture.[66] Modern Chinese writer Lu Xun argues that shamanism was a deep-rooted Chinese belief but the group later split into two subgroups: one was still wu, or spirit-mediums, and the other group turned into *fangshi*, who were dedicated to alchemy and the search for immortals. In the Qin and Han dynasties, deities and immortals became prevalent beliefs of the Chinese and the shamanism was revived in the Late Western Han period.[67] These specialists, *fangshi*, "scholars of [esoteric] techniques," were intellectually closer to the legendary culture hero, the Yellow Emperor and Daoism than Confucianism.[68] In the second century BCE, the shaman went to welcome the descending gods of river or mountain, accompanied by bells, drums, strings, and flutes.[69]

Yet, one salient social change along with the rise of *shì*, warriors/scholars in the Shang-Zhou transition was the rise and consolidation of *shǐ*, royal scribes and later historians, who had assumed official posts since the Late Shang.[70] The royal scribe became a formal official title in the Western Zhou court, where they worked as "close historiographers of King, assuming the offices of sacrifice, calendar establishment, divination, and event record."[71] Grand Scribe/Historian of the Han Dynasty, or *taishǐ*, were primarily chroniclers while they were "also consulted on ritual matters" and "they carried out divinations or interpreted those conducted by others and omens and prodigies generally."[72] Despite the all-encompassing character of their job, the scribe's fact-based record-keeping for the royal archives was the most distinct Chinese cultural characteristic which embodied the budding rational Chinese humanist thought during this period.

In the elite consciousness, more rational sociopolitical concerns and secular "humanism" rose in the Western Zhou, when "prayers for rain were gradually replaced by irrigation. . . and man and his activities were given greater importance."[73] This trend reached a culmination as embodied in the thoughts and cultural, political, and educational activities of Confucius. In the late imperial Qing Dynasty (1644–1911), the Statute on Ritual dealt with "sorcery" under the subcategory "Sacrifices," in which sorcerers were associated with *wu* and "evil arts," *xieshu,* with a disparaging tone, for the Qing state saw these practices as delusions of the people and menace to its political order.[74] To be sure, shamanism never disappeared in Chinese society and I had a village shaman to tell my fortune in 2017, and the shamanistic repertoire of prophecy, fortune-telling, possession, exorcism and interpretation of dreams permeated Chinese history and society, including modern non-Han ethnic communities.[75]

RITUAL AND EMOTION IN POETRY: *BOOK OF ODES*

Among the Six Classics of Confucianism, the *Book of Odes*, sometimes translated as *The Book of Songs* or more literal *Classic of Poetry*, was an anthology of 305 poems selected and edited by Confucius. There are three types of poems: the *feng*, airs, which were folksongs collected from the grassroots level; the *ya*, the major and minor odes that reflected nobilities' life, feelings, and their historical consciousness, and the *song* (not the English word "song" but a Chinese pinyin spelling), liturgical hymns. Michael Nylan points out that Western Zhou officers gathered verses from the feudal states because folk poetry was at the time regarded as the spontaneous expression of public sentiments.[76] Edward L. Shaughnessy, pays more attention to the liturgical dimension of the *Book of Odes.* For him, some political poems under the subsection title *Zhou Song* were liturgical prayers chanted (and danced and acted) by the celebrants of ritual, and the Chinese *"song"* here is translated as liturgies. These poems were prayers addressed to the ancestors and the use of first-person plural pronoun *wo* along with the second-person personal pronoun *er* indicate a direct link between the sacrifice-chanter and the ancestor. I want to point out that the four-character solemn, ceremonial use of language in the liturgical hymns continued into the twenty-first-century eulogy in the annual celebration of Confucius's birthday.

Marcel Granet provides a most tenable way to examine the *Book of Odes* from the perspective of ritual-emotion relations, Western Zhou people's relationship with their dwellings and the plants and animals, rivers and mountains, and gender division and interaction. Granet suggests the folksongs collected in the anthology had seasonal ritual origins, originating from certain local festivals. He believes that "emotions" gave rise to the periodical gatherings of the local people living within the boundaries of certain feudal states such as Zheng and Chen, and the rituals cemented the bond between individuals and groups.[77] Informed by Western observations of southwest Chinese non-Han ethnic groups such as Miao and Lolo since the 19th century, Granet finds their festival assemblies, excursions, and love-song contests between young men and women comparable to those recorded in the *Book of Odes*.[78] The songs in the *Book of Odes* were not only emotional and expressive but also symbolical in widely borrowing the rustic imageries of plants such as flowers, cherries, reeds, and animals such as hawk, crow, fox. And the use of a wild goose as a ceremonial present in marriage ritual was recorded in one song, which shows ancient Chinese moralization of the bird for its coordinated, harmonious seasonal migration.[79]

Besides the agricultural-seasonal origins of the festivities in some songs recorded in the *Book of Odes*, some odes were not the prayers *per se* but "about" the ritual itself, which describes the beginnings of a different type of ritual.[80] For instance, sentences such as "There are blind drummers, there are blind drummers/ In the court of Zhou," and "Our guests arrive and stop/ Long viewing their performance"[81] were written from the perspective of an on-site observer and they departed from the liturgical text itself. The third-person depiction is more telling in this poem of the liturgical section: "So they appeared before their lord the king/To get from him their emblems. . . . Then they showed them to their shining ancestors/Piously, making offering/That they might be vouchsafed long life." These were self-conscious poem compositions. Shaughnessy's distinguishing of poems of the liturgical text and the records of the liturgical process, and his attention paid to the performers-audience relationship is thus very meaningful in revealing the change of perspective. It shows that rituals in the Western Zhou had a performing character with the King himself as the performer, and there were already elite poets who wrote about ritual.

With a very broad range of motifs and genres, the *Book of Odes* includes "folk songs, songs of the nobility, ritual hymns, and ballads on significant events in the history of the Zhou people."[82] Confucius, regarded as a serious and schematic editor of the anthology who allegedly deleted some and kept others until the 305 worthy pieces were kept and published, placed great emphasis on the study of these poems as essential to both human moral education and political training. Stephen Owen aptly captures the book's bent on reflecting human emotions and particularly what we call "negative emotions" in this study and the causes: "the reasons behind the suffering are quite clear: desertion by a lover, misgovernment, the hardships of forced military service."[83]

Most of the poems about love were written from women's perspective. Here is a stanza of a sentimental poem in the "Minor Odes" section of the *Book of Odes*:

> The drums and the bells blend their sound;
>
> The waters of the Huai weep on.
>
> Sad is my heart and wretched[84]

The word *qing* and the concrete words about various emotions appeared frequently. In a poem whose title is translated by Arthur Waley as "Hollow Mound" included in the folksong subsection "Airs of Chen (Feudal State)," there is a stanza:

> Truly, a man of feeling[*qing*],
>
> But very careless of repute.

Based on Arthur Waley's English translation, I found numerous words he used to translate the equivalent classical Chinese words used in the *Book of Odes* to describe concrete human feelings and I found many of them were about negative emotions: wrath, bitterness, melancholy, fear, pain, sadness, grief, anguish, spite, distress, sorrow, and pitiful, while there are also many that are positive: happiness, merry, pleasure, joy, gaily, pleasant, reverence, and love. According to my calculation, sadness and grief were the two keywords that appeared most frequently in Waley's translation, but in the Chinese original, "sadness" and "grief" as used by Waley can be one word that was very often used in Chinese poetry, prose, and verbal language from ancient times to the present, *you*.

Fish is important imagery and object of human gaze in the *Book of Odes*. Not a few of the songs in the chapters "The Minor Odes" and the "Airs of the States" depicted "Fish nets we spread," "fish trap by the bridge," "fish caught in the trap," and how fish "[i]n their multitudes they leap."[85] Some songs hinted that the caught fish would be used in noblemen's feast, since there was mention of the "wine" of "[o]ur lords."[86] Anthropologist Mary Douglas posits that "Bringing fish out of the water or the forest into the village is an act surrounded with precautionary ritual."[87] While in the Western Zhou based *Book of Odes,* the authors did not show empathy to fish, which carries ritualist meanings, in Eastern Zhou thinkers' writing, animals became more like an object to which the thinkers projected their own emotions and imagination, as we will see in chapter 2.

Why does the *Book of Odes* contain so many poems about human feelings, romance, and sex? If Confucius handpicked these poems and edited them, or at least he did not reject them, then why did Confucius think these emotional poems and words valuable? First, the Chinese language already had many words to express positive and negative human feelings by the end of the Western Zhou and before Confucius was born, and second, Confucian scholars, if not Confucius himself, took common men and women's moral and personal feelings seriously thus they, if not "he," kept them in the anthology—it is in this sense that we can again be convinced that the Zhou dynasty was a time for the maturity of Chinese humanism at least in elite cultural consciousness. Of course, emotionalism is not the complete picture even in the *Book of Odes* because many other poems are political or ritualistic. Yet the combination of all these in one edited volume is, of course, quintessentially Confucian.

One core debate in the tradition of Confucian classical studies was whether Confucius authored or edited these classics. For the staunch supporter of Confucius's sagely status Pi Xirui(1850–1908) of the late nineteenth century, if the classical studies cannot highlight Confucius's authorship of the Six Classics, then Confucius, who failed to get a sage-king position in his political career, would not receive the honor that he deserved.[88] It is not my intention here to engage in this age-old debate, but I found the modern Confucian philosopher and researcher of Chinese philosopher Feng Youlan's (Fung Yu-lan, 1895–1990) opinion valuable. Identifying himself with Confucianism and researching its history, Feng proposed his own innovated Confucian theory. Growing up in a cultural milieu where the old classical studies had been dormant and studying under John Dewey at Columbia University, Feng held both "emotion" and "rationality" toward Confucianism. For him, "Confucius was neither the author, commentator, nor even editor of the classics," because "Confucius never had any intention of writing anything himself for future generations."[89]

What is pertinent to my study here is that Feng argues the Six Classics, including one missing classic about music, "had existed before Confucius."[90] Late Qing Confucian scholar of classical studies Zhang Taiyan (1869–1936) had preceded Feng in arguing that the *Shi*, the *Shu*, the *Li*, and the *Yue* had existed prior to Confucius's time.[91] Feng's stance and his insistence on Confucius's true identity as only a "private teacher" helps disenchant Confucius and particularly dispel his aura as a religious founder but want to stress that Confucius was an avid reader and learner of these received texts, which symbolized a significant intellectual turn of Chinese thought. Richard J. Smith reminds us that "the Confucian classics contain a number of references to dream divination" and "rich in dream accounts."[92] Recent historical studies show that the relationship between Confucius and the *Book of Changes* is still controversial.[93] If Confucius did not write or edit these classics, then the deep interest in dreams is but an important part of Chinese culture, and Confucius himself was subject to this influence.

CONCLUSION

When Confucius said he only transmitted but not created, he was correct. There had been an entrenched, marvelous Zhou cultural tradition before he was born. From the bronze-age cultural sites to the "civilized" Zhou dynasty, the intellectual world of early China evolved from shamanism and the animistic beliefs in the High God and multiple gods and spirits to a more humanistic and moralist concern about interpersonal relations and human emotions. It was the early Western Zhou royal regent, the Duke of Zhou, who laid down the rule of rites and music, which Confucius endeavored to restore. Recording history and current affairs became a more important job of the Zhou royal scriber who laid the foundation for the increasingly rationalized Confucian high culture, which was now carried on by a rising scholar class. In the Western Zhou, the education for the young aristocratic scholars was not only ritualistic but also like an all-around liberal arts education with a sense of political mission combined with secular moral virtues such as filial piety.

Ancestor worship was at first a pre-philosophical ritual practice in early China of the royal lineage. During the time of Confucius, there had developed a sophisticated system of etiquette originating in the sacrifices and post-sacrifice banquets, and the use of utensils, grains, and animals. I agree that "the core of the ancient Chinese religion is ancestor worship," as Ping-ti Ho (He Bingdi, 1917–2012) argues.[94] However, students of Chinese culture should not assume ancestor worship is unique to China or to Confucianism. As I discussed in the introduction, African tribes also have their ancestor worship rituals. The phenomenon of worshiping a wise man (*wakan* in north American tribes) who knows the spirits and a shaman who can cure, ritual practices led by a master of ceremonies, use of musical instruments as part of the ritual, and even ancestor worship existed in Native American tribes, north or south.[95] And the use of sacrificial meat of small pigs and fish was prevalent among Hawaiian natives in the eighteenth century.[96] In southwest Chinese Yi ethnic communities, ancestors are worshipped, but their spirits are not always considered benign and protective, because they may "cause sickness in their descendants."[97] The code of etiquette that separates boy and girls at certain age, similar to the Chinese gender etiquette sanctioned by Confucianism, existed in the Samoan tribes of the early twentieth century.[98] The seasonal character of the rites might not be unique either. In Russian composer Igor Stravinsky's orchestral concert work "The Rite of Spring" (1913), there are sections that reflect a tribe's "Evocation of the Ancestors and "Ritual Action of the Ancestors."

In my view, it was textualization that made Shang China distinct from tribes without scripts for writing provides a fixed, inscribed, and "a permanent form . . . external to the human voice," and a text becomes a "structure of meaning"[99] open to interpretation. The professionalized scholars, *shi*, who were engaged in this process were self-conscious "experts" and "professional producer of discourse" in the sense of Pierre Bourdieu.[100] Their selection of the songs and compilation of the *Book of Odes* grasped both "the means of an art and the feeling for life that animates it," as the anthropologist Clifford Geertz paraphrases the artist Matisse. And Geertz himself emphasizes that "to study an art form is to explore a sensibility."[101]

NOTES

1. We may sometimes use the term "primitive religion" in the Weberian value-free sense. See Evans-Pritchard, *Theories of Primitive Religion*, 2, 18.

2. Puett, *To Become a God*, 41, 43, 63, 65–66.

3. Robert Redfield, *The Folk Culture of Yucatan* (Chicago: The University of Chicago Press, 1941), 270. The book demonstrates many similarities between the festivals, worships, and ritual experienced of the Yucatan Maya people and ancient Chinese, despite the Catholic influence in the communities of Yucatan.

4. Xu Hong, *Heyi zhongguo: gongyuan qian 2000 nian de zhongyuan tujing* [How China Came in Being: The Landscape of the Central Plains around 2000 BCE] (Beijing: Sanlian shudian, 2016), 10–13.

5. Ibid., 23

6. Ibid., 15.

7. Ibid., 159.

8. Ibid., 33.

9. Berthold Laufer, *Jade: A Study of Chinese Archaeology and Religion* (New York: Dover Publications, Inc., 1974), 22.

10. Li Xueqin, *Zhonggguo gudai wenming qiyuan* [Origins of Ancient Chinese Civilization] (Shanghai: Shanghai kexue jishu wenxian chubanshe, 2007), 289.

11. Su Bingqi, *Su Bingqi wenji* [Collected Essays of Su Bingqi] (Beijing: Wenwu chubanshe, 2010), 181.

12. Gábor Kósa, "The Shaman and the Spirits: The Meaning of the Word 'Ling' in the Jiuge," *Acta Orientalia Academicae Scientiarrum Hungaricae* 56, no. 2 (2003): 286.

13. Li Xueqin, *Zhongguo gudai wenming shijiang* [Ten Essays on Ancient Chinese Civilization] (Shanghai: Fudan University Press, 2005), 47, 51.

14. Xu Zhongshu, *Xu Zhongshu qian Qin shi jiangji* [Xu Zhongshu's Lectures on Pre-Qin History] (Tianjin: Tianjin guji chubanshe, 2008), 55–56.

15. Li, *Zhongguo gudai wenming qiyuan*, 289.

16. Tang Lan, *Zhongguo wenzi xue* [The Science of Chinese Characters] (Shanghai: Shanghai shiji chuban jituan, 2005), 44–45. The English translation of the book's title is based on the author's own suggestion of the character of his discipline.

17. Li Zehou, *Shuo wushi chuantong* [On the Tradition of Shamans and Historians] (Shanghai: Shanghai yiwen chubanshe, 2012), 56–59.

18. Wang Jiafan, *Zhongguo lishi tonglun* [A Comprehensive Study of Chinese History] (Beijing: sanlian shudian, 2012), 33–34.

19. Kuang-Chih Chang, *Art, Myth, and Ritual: The Path to Political Authority in Ancient China* (Cambridge, MA: Harvard University Press, 1983), 112.

20. Ibid., 47.

21. Kuang-Chih Chang, *Shang Civilization* (New Haven, CT: Yale University Press, 1980), 338.

22. Ibid., 23–24.

23. Katrinka Reinhart, "Ritual Feasting and Empowerment at Yanshi Shangcheng," *Journal of Anthropological Archaeology,* no. 39 (2015): 77.

24. Chang, *Shang Civilization*, 209.

25. Kuang-Chih Chang, "Sandai Archaeology and the Formation of States in Ancient China: Processual Aspects of the Origins of Chinese Civilization," in *The Origins of Chinese Civilization*, ed. David N. Keightley (Berkeley: University of California Press, 1983), 501.

26. Adam C. Schwartz, "Shang Sacrificial Animals: Material Documents and Images," in *Animals Through Chinese History: Earliest Times to 1911*, ed. Roel Stercks (Cambridge, UK: Cambridge University Press, 2019), 36.

27. David N. Keightley, *The Ancestral Landscape: Time, Space, and Community in the Late Shang China, ca.1200–1045 B.C.* (Berkeley: University of California Press, 2000), 109–11.

28. Ibid., 79.

29. Ibid., 85.

30. Xu, *Xu Zhongshu qian Qin shi jiangji*, 292.

31. David N. Keightley, *Sources of Shang History: The Oracle-Bone Inscriptions of Bronze Age China* (Berkeley: University of California Press, 1985), 33.

32. Wm. Theodore de Bary and Irene Bloom, *Sources of Chinese Tradition, 2nd ed. Vol.1 From Earliest Times to 1600* (New York: Columbia University Press, 1999), 8.

33. William James, *The Varieties of Religious Experience: A Study in Human Nature* (Penguin Books, 1982), 27.

34. Léon Vandermeersch, *Les Deux Raisons de la Pensée Chinoise Divination et Idéographie* [The Two Rationalities in Chinese Thought: Divination and Ideograph] Chinese translation by Jin Siyan, *Zhongguo sixiang de liangzhong lixing: biaoyi yu zhanbu* (Beijing: Beijing daxue chubanshe, 2017), 39.

35. Li Feng, *Early China: A Social and Cultural History* (Cambridge, UK: Cambridge University Press, 2013), 99.

36. Francis L. K. Hsu, *Under Ancestor's Shadow: Kinship, Personality and Social Mobility in China* (Stanford, CA: Stanford University Press, 1967), 23.

37. Ibid., 50, 115.

38. Joseph A. Adler, *Chinese Religious Traditions* (Upper Saddle River, NJ: Prentice Hall Inc., 2002), 28.

39. David N. Keightley, "The Late Shang State: When, Where, and What?" in *The Origins of Chinese Civilization*, 558.

40. Hou Wailu, *Zhongguo gudai shehui shilu* [Essays on Ancient Chinese Society] (Shijiazhuang, Hebei jiaoyu chubanshe, 2003), 79–81.

41. Ibid., 214.

42. Ibid., 200.

43. Edward L. Shaughnessy, *Before Confucius: Studies in the Creation of the Chinese Classics* (Albany: State University of New York Press, 1997), 122.

44. *Book of Documents,* trans. James Legge (Middletown, DE: Dragon Book, 2016), 195, 203.

45. Wittgenstein, *Major Works*, 307.

46. Yang Kuan, *Xian Qin shi shi jiang* [Ten Essays on Pre-Qin History] (Shanghai: Fudan daxue chubanshe, 2008), 230–32.

47. Ibid., 238–39.

48. Ibid., 238.

49. Pi Xirui, *Xiao Jing Zheng zhu shu* [Classic of Filial Piety, annotated by Zheng Xuan and explicated by Pi Xirui] (Beijing: Zhonghua shuju, 2016), 81.

50. Peng Lin ed., *Yi-Li* [Etiquette and Rites] (Zhengzhou: Zhongzhou guji chubanshe, 2011), 4–5. The authorship of *Yi-Li* is an old and moot question in Chinese classical studies focusing on whether Confucius wrote it or just edit it. Contemporary scholar and modern translator Peng Lin argues it was a book compiled by the students of Confucius. In my opinion, the content of the Western Zhou ritual methods recorded in this manual were at least endorsed by Confucius, even if he did not write them.

51. Ibid., 64–65.

52. Ibid., 246.

53. Ibid., 300.

54. Ibid., 388–89.

55. Ibid., 351, 389, 408.

56. Lothar Von Falkensausen, *Chinese Society in the Age of Confucius (1000–250 BC)* (Los Angeles: Costen Institute of Archaeology, 2006), 47, 67, 71.

57. For the use of symbols in ritual process, see Victor Turner, *The Ritual Process: Structure and Anti-Structure* (Ithaca, NY: Cornell University Press, 1966).

58. Lin Yaohua, *Yixu de zongzu yanjiu* [A Study of the Lineage at Yixu] (Beijing: Sanlian shudian, 2000), 233, 245.

59. Rane Willerslev, *Soul Hunters: Hunting, Animism, and Personhood Among Siberian Yukaghirs* (Berkeley: University of California Press, 2007), 9–10, 26.

60. Li Xueqin, *Zhongguo dudai wenming yanjiu* [Studies in Ancient Chinese Civilization] (Shanghai: Huadong shifan daxue chubanshe, 2009), 221.

61. Ibid., 68.

62. Shaughnessy, *Before Confucius*, 36.

63. Edward L. Davis, *Society and the Supernatural in Song China* (Honolulu: University of Hawaii Press, 2001), 2.

64. For the ritual duty of *wu* and *shi* in the Western Zhou, see Li Xueqin ed., *Zhou Li zhu shu* [Annotations and sub-annotations of *Rites of Zhou*] (Beijing: Beijing daxue chubanshe, 1999), 687–93. This is a modern edition with the annotation of Zheng Xuan of the Eastern Han Dynasty and Jia Gongyan of the Tang Dynasty. *Shi* also participated in the performance of ritual, but their main job was to check ritual books to make sure the procedures were correct. Sun Yongdu, Meng Zhaoxing, *Zhongguo lidai zhiguan zhishi shouce* [A Manual of Chinese Official Titles in the Past Dynasties] (Tianjin: Baihua wenyi chubanshe, 2006), 157–58.

65. Qiu, *Wenzi xue gaiyao*, 34.

66. Li Ling, *Zhongguo fangshu kao* [An Examination of the Early Chinese Craft of Medicine, Astrology and Divination] (Beijing: Dongfang chubanshe, 2001), 7, 13.

67. Lu Xun, *Lu Xun xueshu lunzhu* [Academic Writings of Lu Xun] (Hangzhou: Zhejiang renmin chubanshe, 1998), 29, 218.

68. Mark Edward Lewis, *Sanctioned Violence in Early China* (Albany: State University of New York Press, 1990), 168.

69. Arthur Waley, *The Nine Songs: A Study of Shamanism in Ancient China* (San Francisco: City Lights Books, 1973), 9.11. Again, as mentioned in the introduction, since *fangshi* overlaps semantically with the term *ru* yet the group engaged in alchemy and other mythical techniques, I do not think "Ruism" is a more accurate term to replace "Confucianism."

70. Ping-ti Ho, *The Cradle of The East: An Inquiry into the Indigenous Origins of Techniques and Ideas of Neolithic and Early Historic China 5000–1000 B.C* (Hong Kong: The Chinese University of Hong Kong Press, 1975), 297–98.

71. Lu Huiliang and Yu Li eds., *Xi Zhou jinwen ying yi* [English Translation of Western Zhou Bronze Inscriptions] (Beijing: Yuwen chubanshe, 2011), 261. Compared with the short sentences in Shang oracle bone inscriptions, Western Zhou bronze inscriptions are usually full paragraphs of narrative about the process of a noble feudal lord receiving appointment, which was symbolized by receiving a bronze vessel from the king.

72. G.E.R. Lloyd, *The Ambitions of Curiosity: Understanding the World in Ancient Greece and China* (Cambridge, UK: Cambridge University Press, 2002), 9.

73. Wing-Tsi Chan, *A Source Book in Chinese Philosophy* (Princeton, NJ: Princeton University Press, 1963), 3

74. Philip Kuhn, *Soul Stealers: The Chinese Sorcery Scare of 1768* (Cambridge, MA: Harvard University Press, 1990), 85–86.

75. Guo Wu, *Narrating Southern Chinese Minority Nationalities: Politics, Disciplines, and Public History* (Singapore: Palgrave MacMillan, 2019), 187–200; Erik Mueggler, *The Age of Wild Ghosts: Memory, Violence, and Place in Southwest China* (Berkley: University of California Press, 2001), 199–200.

76. Michael Nylan, *The Five Confucian Classics* (New Haven, CT: Yale University Press, 2001), 79.

77. Marcel Granet, "Introduction," in Marcel Granet and E.D. Edwards, *Festivals and Songs of Ancient China* (New York: E. P. Dutton, 1932), 7–9.

78. Ibid., 140–41.

79. Ibid., 97–98.

80. Shaughnessy, *Before Confucius*, 186–87.

81. Ibid., 183.

82. Stephen Owen, "Foreword," in *The Book of Songs: The Ancient Chinese Classic of Poetry*, trans. Arthur Waley. Edited and Additional Translations by Joseph R. Allen (New York: Grove Press, 1996), xv.

83. Ibid., xxii–xxiii.

84. Arthur Waley, *The Book of Songs,* 193.

85. Ibid., 37, 81, 145.

86. Ibid., 144.

87. Mary Douglas, *Implicit Meanings: Selected Essays in* Anthropology, 2nd edition (London: Routledge, 1999), 54.

88. Pi Xirui enunciated this in the preface to his review of Confucian classical studies. See Pi Xirui, *Jing xue tong lun* [A General Survey of Confucian Classics] (Beijing: Zhonghua shuju, 2017), 1.

89. Fung You-lan, *A Short History of Chinese Philosophy: A Systematic Account of Chinese Thought from Its Origins to the Present Day*, ed. Derk Bodde (New York: The Fee Press, 1976), 39–40.

90. Ibid., 40.

91. Zhang Taiyan, *Guoxue jiangyi* [Lectures on National Learning] (Shenyang, Wanjuan chuban gongsi, 2015), 46.

92. Richard J. Smith, *Fortune-tellers and Philosophers: Divination in Traditional Chinese Society* (Boulder, Co: Westview Press, 1993), 246–47.

93. Liang Cai, *Witchcraft and the Rise of the First Confucian Empire* (Albany: State University of New York Press, 2014), 79.

94. Ho, *The Cradle of The East*, 324.

95. James R. Walker, *Lakota Belief and Ritual* (Lincoln: University of Nebraska Press, 1991), 68–69.

96. Marshall Sahlins, *How "Natives" Think: About Captain Cook, For Example* (Chicago: University of Chicago Press, 1996), 43–44.

97. Liu Xiaoxin, "The Yi Health Care System in Liangshan Chuxiong," in *Perspectives on the Yi of Southwest China*, ed. Stevan Harrell (Berkeley: University of California Press, 2001), 277.

98. Margret Mead, *Coming of Age in Samoa: A Psychological Study of Primitive Youth for Western Civilization* (Perennial, NY: 2001), 32.

99. Brian Stock, *Listening for the Text: On the Uses of the Past* (Philadelphia: University of Pennsylvania Press, 1996), 102, 108.

100. Pierre Bourdieu, *Distinction: A Social Critique of the Judgement of Taste*, trans. Richard Nice (Cambridge, UK: Harvard University Press, 1984), 461.

101. Clifford Geertz, "Art as a Cultural System," *Comparative Literature* 91, no. 6 (1976): 1477–78.

Chapter 2

Ritualism and Emotion in Pre-Qin Confucianism and the *Zhuangzi*

This chapter examines the textualization and institutionalization of sacrificial and death rituals ranging from the time of Confucius to the pre-Qin thinker Xunzi. Additionally, it investigates how early China's *shì* scholars took part in ritual actions and understood the role of ritual propriety in cementing social distinctions and controlling excessive emotions. After the fall of the Western Zhou in 771 BCE, the Eastern Zhou was reduced to a small domain, leaving its royal house with only symbolic authority that operated under the guidance of Heaven. The *shì* group that worked as officials, advisors, and experts now had a number of members who lost their employment and became "itinerant scholars," *youshì*. The *youshì* found a heightened sense of intellectual freedom and creativity with their newfound ability to travel, sojourn, and seek political employment at their leisure. These scholars engaged in independent inquiries into various secular issues such as the status of the monarch in political life, yet almost none of the feudal lords fulfilled their high ideal for a wise ruler.[1] They also wrote about how personal sentiment and sociopolitical rites could be reconciled with rationality. A shared inclination among Confucian thinkers was an emphasis on ritual and the proper expression of one's true feelings. They tried to employ rational decision-making whenever conflict arose between Confucian morality and codified ritual proprieties. Utilizing an anthropological perspective helps us revisit how Confucius treated sacrificial meat and how Mencius treated animals.

One key intellectual turning point during the process of deliberation and debate amongst Confucian scholars arose during a discussion of the origins of *qing*. They tried to build a sequent, and organic emanation to connect what it meant to be human, with ritual propriety. As an example, the Guodian bamboo slips that reflect the trend of thought between Confucius and Mencius assert that "ritual arises from the affections." The last pre-Qin Confucian scholar, Xunzi, meticulously analyzed the dynamics between emotion and ritual as a social function, which can be regarded as a proto-anthropological study. As a more radical intellectual rebellion to the Confucian attempt to balance ritual, emotion, and reason, Daoist thinkers challenged both ritual and emotion through implicit logical reasoning.[2]

THE *BOOK OF CHANGES*

Since the Western Han Dynasty (206 BCE–9 CE), Confucian scholars canonized the received texts and established the Six Classics: the *Yi*, or *Book of Changes*, the *Shi*, or *Book of Odes*, which we discussed in chapter 2, the *Shu*, or *Book of History*, the *Li* which we discussed under its title *Yi-Li*, "*Ceremonials and Rites*," and the *Yue*, *Music*.[3] Exegesis, emendation, and authentication of these classics gradually became a separate field among Confucian scholars, and this thread continued to the nineteenth century.

Confucius's own conversations with his students and interlocutors were recorded in *Lunyu*, the *Analects*, in which he weighed in on how an ideal society should be governed, stating that "effective rule should rest not on brute force but ultimately on some kind of consent."[4] As a political thinker, Confucius "decoupled the relations between the supernatural and ritual."[5] If we only focus on the political engagements of Confucius and other like-minded *shi* scholars,' their sociopolitical orientation can become undeservingly simplified. Yet, if we treat the texts of the Classics as an object of study, viewing them not as products of Confucius,' but as texts that had existed before him, then we have a better way to grasp the meaning of these received texts as manifestations of a more general ancient Chinese way of looking at the world, which is far beyond politics and governance. These texts were appropriated by Confucianism, just as the pre-Confucian rituals of sacrifice, guest reception, and life passage were also appropriated by it. In addition, modern studies of ancient Chinese texts show that prior to the Western Han, the texts were circulated and discussed as single pieces, and the edited book versions of *Zhuangzi, Xunzi,* and *Han Feizi* did not appear until mid-Western Han.[6]

One of the Six Classics, the *Book of Changes* originated from the Eight Trigrams based on the yin/yang dichotomy, a method of divination attributed to the legendary culture hero Fuxi. The combination and multiplication of the trigrams produced sixty-four trigrams, but its textualized judgments were attributed to King Wen of Western Zhou, the father of the Duke of Zhou. Modern researchers believe that Confucius and his students perhaps wrote the extension of the *Book of Changes* in the form of the separate "Great Commentary," *dazhuan*, sometimes known as "Ten Wings," *shiyi*, because of the number of existing pieces. The Great Commentary, even with its unknown authorship, has been subject to politicization and moralization, sufficing to reflect the intellectual and the humanistic bent of the *shi* scholars who were contemporaries of Confucius and his disciples. It is thus accurate to say that the textualization and continuous addition of meaning to the esoteric sixty-four trigrams marked the transition of Chinese high culture from divination to philosophy.[7] Confucius himself did not reject the "prayers and divinations" contained within the work, but he placed them behind the ideal of "virtue and propriety."[8]

I will focus on how the pre-Confucian judgment text in the *Book of Changes* and post-Confucian extension elaborated upon rites and emotions. One hexagram called *lü*, treading, was interpreted before Confucius as "Treading upon the tail of tiger/It does not bite the man/Success." The word *lü*, however, has another neglected meaning: gait. Early Qing Confucian scholar Huang Zongxi (1610–1695) comments that the Duke of Zhou demonstrated his sagely quality through his gait, *bulü*.[9] Both have the connotation of bodily movement. Modern research shows that the hidden meaning of this sentence was about the "right way of conducting oneself," and "This shows the difference between high and low, upon which composure, correct social conduct, depends."[10] The imagery of gently treading on the tail of the tiger without inviting disaster reflects the idea that "one's purpose will be achieved if one behaves with decorum."[11] The description here is already very close to *Li*, hierarchical social conduct which also honors decorum and produces harmony. The semantic connection between *lü*, treading, and *Li*, was revealed in the *Xugua*, one of the ten chapters allegedly written by Confucius, in which the author asserted that "Ritual means treading and practicing [*Li zhe lü ye*]" and proceeded to suggest that treading and practicing "brings about harmonious conduct."[12] In *Xici*, the essays that explained the *Book of Changes*, *lü*, as a ritual action, was valued as the "basis of moral virtue."[13] The definition of *Li* here was not an "*explicit* (italicization original)" denotation provided in a modern dictionary but a brief, "philosophical" connotation that captures the concept's distinctive feature and ought to be understood as a defi*nit*ion "*in use* (italicization original)," as A. J. Ayer notes.[14] This assertion shows the articulator's personal commitment to the knowledge about the relation of ritual to treading/practicing.[15] Since the Chinese language lacks plural inflection, the "mass noun" *Li*, be it sacrificial rituals or a corpus of codes and rules, was concretized to be a visible action that can express its meaning.[16]

Another judgment is *Dui*, which is equivalent to another character *yue*, joyousness. The pre-Confucian interpretation elaborated on this word by presenting an ideal person who can achieve genuine joy by having "firmness and strength within," while looking "yielding and gentle" on the outside.[17] There are two layers of meaning here: the first is that the ideal personality of the ruler or gentleman is the combination of the two oppositional qualities, which coexist because of the demarcation of the inside and the outside. Second, attaining a genuine sense of joy can free oneself from bias and prove instrumental for elites wishing to prosperously lead and influence the people.[18]

Compared with the pre-Confucian text, the "Great Commentary" is bolder in its discussion of human emotions. In one passage, it alluded to the sages with popular imagery of Confucius's time by saying that "The feelings of the holy sages reveal themselves in the judgment."[19] One chapter in the Great Commentary argues that the ancient sages' thoughts and emotions, *qing*, were embedded in the judgments of the *Book of Changes.*[20] It is notable that the Great Commentary was composed with a historical perspective by contemporaries of Confucius, who explored the motivation of former sages in the *Book of Changes* and speculated on the time of the rise of the divination method as in the late Shang period.[21] From its citing of Confucius's words, we can deduce some pieces were written by his students. The reflective researchers of the *Book of Changes* in Confucius's time inherited the original text's emphasis on the treading-ritual trope and expanded the joyous feeling discussed in the text to the "sages." As we will see later, joy was an important moral feeling that Confucius pursued.

HOW CONFUCIUS BALANCES THE RITES, EMOTIONS, AND RATIONALITY

On the premise that Confucius, an erudite statesman and teacher, may or may not have influenced the "classics" himself, I will examine the remarks and actions of Confucius toward ritual and its tension with emotion, as recorded by his disciples in various received texts. The *Analects, Lunyu*, the *Family Talk of Confucius* [*Kongzi jiayu*], and the *Book of Rites, Liji*, are the three works that record the conversations, monologues, and interactions between Confucius, notable figures, and his students. All three are written in third person with sentences frequently beginning with *ziyue*, "The Master said." Since the Western Han dynasty, the *Analects* had been studied by Confucian students and it was selected to be canonized as one of the "Four Books" along with the *Mencius* and two chapters from the *Book of Rites* that focused on sociological concerns. The remaining portion of the *Book of Rites* can be considered an interpretive expansion of the *Yi-Li*, which was akin to a list of technical ritual steps and details. Archaeological findings in the late twentieth century authenticated the *Family Talk of Confucius,* after having been deemed a forgery for centuries. Additionally, records in the *Family Talk* overlapped with the canonized *Book of Rites.*[22] James F. Peterman's approach to the *Analects* may apply to other received texts that contain conversations and narratives: they might be fictional or semi-fictional texts. What remains pertinent is not the validation of authorship, whether that was the real Confucius, Mencius, or Zhuangzi, but its meaning and whether the narrative, even as "philosophical novel," reflected the prevalent worldviews and perceptions of the time.[23]

According to these records, Confucius engaged with his private sacrificial rites with sincerity and commitment. He took to heart the use of imagination to show his genuine emotion to the ancestral spirits: "Sacrificial as if present" is taken to mean "sacrifice to the gods as if the gods were present." The Master, however, said, *"Unless I enter into the spirit of a sacrifice, it is as if I did not sacrifice."* (The *Analects*, 3–12. Italicization original in the translation)[24] Here, Confucius used the trope *ru,* "as if," which we encountered in the last chapter, to legitimize the power and efficacy of emotional imagination that overcomes the suspicion of the existence of the spirits themselves. When Confucius exalts the legendary sage ruler Yu, he emphasized that Yu "ate and drank the meanest fare while making offerings to ancestral spirits and gods with the utmost devotion proper to a descendant." *(The Analects,* 8–21) He also thought the impersonator assumed by the dead man's grandson was a must. If the grandson was too young, then he must be held by someone at the sacrificial rite.[25]

Through the lens of historical anthropology, the *Analects* provides ample evidence to illustrate how Confucius treated food and eating as part of rites. In his daily life, Confucius treated eating as a ritual action: "He did not eat food that was not properly prepared, nor did he eat except at proper time. He did not eat food that had not been 'properly cut up,' nor did he eat unless the proper sauce was available." These were all beyond the basic necessities of life. A more important phenomenon was how Confucius treated official political rituals. First, the received text reveals the fact that the post-sacrificial meat would be distributed to the attendees, which I would call a "meat-sharing" ritual; second, Confucius assisted with his lord's sacrifice; and third, Confucius took the sacrificial meats back home to eat; and fourth, when eating at home, Confucius still observed the ritual codes: "He did not keep his portion of the sacrificial meat for more than three days. Once it was kept beyond three days [,] he no longer ate it." (The *Analects,* 10–9) On another occasion, Confucius's sanctification of sacrificial meat is exemplified by the fact that "Even when a gift from a friend was a carriage and horses—since it lacked the solemnity of sacrificial meats—he did not bow to the ground." (The *Analects,* 10–9) This hints at the proper bodily movement Confucius employed when receiving sacrificial meat after a ceremony. When Confucius himself asked for dried meat from his students as compensation for his teaching, or "gift," to fulfill their obligations, he must have seen in dried meat the spiritual value of it as a "ritual object," or *Liwu,* whose contemporary use will be discussed in the epilogue of this book again.

The *Family Talk* records that when Confucius served the Lu State as the Minister of Justice, he partook in the state *zha* sacrifice to the "one-hundred-gods," which was inherited from the Zhou rite system.[26] Since the Lu State was the vassal state enfeoffed to the Duke of Zhou's son, it inherited many Western Zhou rites, laws, and institutions, and that was partially why Confucius felt a special spiritual connection with the Duke of Zhou. To be sure, these public and political rituals for Confucius were more formulaic than emotional, compared with the private funerals and mourning in which he was engaged. However, Confucius's solemn attitude toward meat, an edible sacrificial object, deserves more attention. The narratives in the *Analects* and *Family Talk* both show that the post-sacrifice feast was not fully secular and communal, and the shared meat was considered sanctified because it had gone through the ritual process.[27]

When limited financial resources threatened the adequacy of the sacrificial rites, Confucius prioritized rationality and emphasized the importance of sincere respect. In response to an inquiry from a student named Ziyou, Confucius stated that, "For the sacrificial rites, I would rather see inadequate rites with surplus respect than see inadequate respect with surplus rites."[28] Sacrificial rites also related to another important Confucian value: filial piety. When questioned about filial piety by a student named Fanchi, Confucius replied, "When your parents are alive, comply with the rites in serving them; when they die, comply with the rites in burying them and in offering sacrifices to them." (The *Analects*, 2–5) For Confucius, one must fulfill a sequence of actions linked to the rites, in life or death, to honor the principle of filial piety. The basis of these sequential actions is nothing but affective emotion. Unsurprisingly, a true expression of it was expected from the ruler at a funerary rite,

The Master said, "What can I find worthy of note in a man who is lacking in tolerance when in high position, in reverence when performing the rites and in sorrow [*ai*] when in mourning?" (The *Analects*, 3–26)

True feelings didn't necessitate an excessive or exaggerated display: "The Master said, "To offer sacrifice to the spirit of an ancestor not one's own is obsequious." (The *Analects*, 2–24) As Roel Sterckx points out, through all the food-related activities of sacrificial offerings, private eating, and banqueting, Confucius saw "[t]he art of proportioning and self-cultivation."[29]

The existence of the afterworld and the perception of the spirits had become a topic of Confucius's dialogues and contemporaneous scholarly inquiries. The *Analects* recorded a famous dialogue in which Confucius was confronted with questions about spirits, life, and death. When asked by Jilu about how to serve the spirits and gods, Confucius said, "You are not able even to serve man. How can you serve the spirits?" Then Jilu pressed him with a question about death. Confucius's reply was, "You do not understand even life. How can you understand death?" (The *Analects*, 11–12) These excerpts from the *Analects* may, at first glance, lead the reader to view Confucius as evasive and defensive in relation to death rituals. However, upon closer examination, two insightful messages can be evoked: firstly, the context and circumstances of the situation must be taken into account. This is an individual conversation between Confucius and Jilu, with the goal of a heightened appreciation for life at its end. Secondly, in Confucius's subconsciousness, the lifeworld is prioritized if there must be a choice; he himself pit "life" and "death" against each other while Jilu only asked about "death."

Another pertinent Confucian discourse on life and death can be found in the *Family Talk*, in which Confucius was asked by Zilu about whether the dead can perceive. This time, Confucius was visibly less evasive:

> If I say the dead people have perceptions, then I will worry the filial sons and grandsons would mourn the passing of the dead by hindering the life of the living; yet if I say dead people have no perceptions, I will worry the unfilial sons abandon their dead parents. Ci (Zilu's first name), you don't need to know whether the dead have perceptions or not. This is not an imperative issue right now, and you will know it in the future."[30]

If we combine the two dialogues and pay particular attention to the second and less discussed one between Confucius and Zilu, then we could reasonably conclude that Confucius, as with his students, was also puzzled by the question of life and death. He was uncertain about the existence of an afterworld, which seems appropriate, given that the *shi* scholars of Eastern Zhou had chipped away at the shamanism and animism of the Shang dynasty. On top of that, the pre-Buddhist Chinese high culture had not developed a solid belief in the afterworld and the reincarnation of the soul. Given this vacuum in Chinese high culture, Confucius wisely utilized a strategy in which he took all the death and sacrificial rites seriously but emphasized the potent effects of true emotion and imagination. At the same time, as a rational, critical scholar, he was acutely aware of his own influence as an intellectual authority and the social consequence of his articulation, thus he chose not to give a clear-cut answer to the question. Of course, only with Zilu, one of his favorite students, did he express his genuine concern and introspection—this practice should not be unfamiliar to any modern professors.

Confucius was an emotional person who treated other people's feelings as entirely natural and understandable, and he used the word *le*, joy, on many occasions. Michael Nylan aptly points out the nuance between pleasure and joy in English, the former being more related to bodily processes and the latter more with religious ecstasy.[31] However, Nylan's reflection may not apply here, given that *le* as used by Confucius may often be better understood as a kind of scholarly self-contentment. Confucius admitted that the age of a man's parents would make him feel both rejoice, *xi*, and fear, or dread, *ju*. Both feelings here are moral sentiments since they differ from a person's reaction to the vision of an object or an animal, although they are conflicting: one is pleasant and the other unpleasant. I disagree with D.C. Lau's translation of *ju* as "anxiety" for I believe the normal feeling of a person when thinking of parents' aging is "fear" or "trepidation" (of their deaths as a definite threat) rather than a vague anxiety about the unknown. Yang Bojun's modern Chinese rendition with the composite word *kongju* [fear, dread], captures this emotion.[32] Here, Confucius rationalized the existence of emotional ambivalence toward one's parents' longevity, yet this ambivalence reflects a deep affection for them.

Moral sentiments could also be caught in legal-ethical dilemmas. According to Confucius, when the father stole a goat, the son ought to "cover up" for the father and vice versa. (The *Analects*, 10–9) Regardless of intentionality and motivation, benevolent affections did not overrule law and punishment, but families would be absolved of the obligation to mutually testify throughout the litigation. The dilemma was undoubtedly difficult to resolve, in light of the Confucian prioritization of moral sentiment and the very special and loving relationship of father and son. In a situation where starvation was motivating animal theft, less severe punishment would have undoubtedly been considered.[33]

The ideal gentleman, *junzi*, for Confucius, should transcend negative and debilitating emotion. When asked about the definition of an ideal gentleman, Confucius exclaimed that he should attain the ability to eliminate worries, *you*, and fears, *ju*. This inner tranquility, excluding existential and legitimate fear, when imagining parents' future death, was based upon a clear moral conscience: "The Master said, 'If, upon self-examination, a man finds nothing to reproach himself for, what worries and fears can he have?'" (The *Analects*, 12–4) In another conversation, Confucius proposed three qualities for the ideal gentleman, one who is wise, *zhi*, benevolent, *ren*, and courageous, *yong*, and he said, "The man of wisdom is never in two minds, [*huo*]; the man of benevolence never worries[*you*]; the man of courage is never afraid [*ju*]." (*The Analects*, 9–29) In Confucius's moral distinction of gentlemen and petty-minded men, *xiaoren*, constant anxiety, *qiqi*, is the hallmark of a petty-minded small man: "The gentleman is easy of mind, while the small man is every full of anxiety." (The *Analects*, 7–37)

While considering the ways of diminating "anger, worry, fear, despair, or other undesirable affections," William James proposes two methods: using an opposite affection to overcome the negative feelings, or exhausting oneself "with the struggle that we have to stop."[34] These two ways suggested by William James both have to force people, while Confucius's approach is more natural, with a focus on self-examination and introspection as a means to the good life that accords with the *Li*. Confucius also understands the challenge of conquering negative feelings, whose indulgence can be motivated by one's economic condition: "It is more difficult not to complain of injustice when poor than not to behave with arrogance when rich." (The *Analects*, 14–10)

Although Confucius seldom used the word *li*, or rational principle/reason, he attempted to control emotions with ritual propriety and reason to maintain proper balance in his life. According to the *Book of Rites,* when Zilu, with whom Confucius shared his agnostic view of the perception of the dead himself died, Confucius wailed in public, and he bowed to the people who came to condole with him, which was seemingly at odds with the perception that he was one who "disliked those who wailed in the open fields."[35] For Confucius, proper space seemed to be important and one should take rational action and avoid wailing in any places. Unlike the older and more technical *Yi-Li, Ceremonials and Rites*, *Liji*, the *Book of Rites*, provides guidance on how to regulate and control one's grief after the death of a parent,

The rites of mourning are the extreme expression of grief and sorrow. The gradual reduction of that expression in accordance with the natural change (of time and feeling) was made by the superior men, mindful of those to whom we owe our being. (*Tan'gong*, 136) [36]

Confucius himself cautioned against unrestrained grief, while simultaneously falling prey to it when he wailed for his disciple Zilu's death in his courtyard, however, he remained steadfast with his reason in the following anecdote:

> There was a man of Bian who wept like a child on the death of his mother. Confucius said, "This is grief indeed, but it would be difficult to continue it. Now the rules of ceremony require to be handed down, and to be perpetuated. Hence the wailing and leaping are subject to fixed regulations. (*Tan'gong*, 67)[37]

Confucius's comment was rational enough in that he believed *Li*, the "rules of ceremony," as translated by James Legge here, was an institution that would be passed down to the future generations and thus an individual's emotion should be subject to this large scheme. While the Confucian endorsement of a filial three-year mourning period may seem foreign and unnecessary to a modern reader, a clearly defined period of three years signaled that even the most traumatic feeling of losing one's parents should cease at a certain point.[38] Again, this testified to the rational Confucian creed about when to start and when to stop and how *Li* should control *qing*.

The justification of controlling one's emotion and borrowing certain methods to express it was what distinguished civilized people of the Central Realm from uncivilized people beyond its boundary. In one scenario, two students of Confucius watched a mourner demonstrating a child's affection to the dead parent as spectators, while the mourner seemed to display his emotions through bodily movements. The two rational Confucian *shì* scholars on the spot, Youzi [Master You or Youruo] and Ziyou, however, watched the spectacle peacefully and analytically. Youzi was skeptical of the entire ritual performance by questioning, "I have never understood this leaping in mourning and have long wished to do away with it. The sincere feeling (of sorrow) which appears here is right, (and should be sufficient.)" Compared with Youzi's emphasis on true feeling over ritual acting, Ziyou defended the bodily movements as indispensable elements of the mourning process that served as mediums to convey the feeling of mourners. He explained, "To give direct vent to the feeling and act it out as by a shortcut is the way of the rude Rong and Di," but "[t]he method of the rules. When a man rejoices, he looks pleased; when pleased, he thereon sings; when singing, he sways himself about; swaying himself about, he proceeds to dancing; from dancing he gets into a state of wild excitement, that excitement goes on to distress; distress expresses itself in sighing; sighing is followed by beating the breast, and beating the breast by leaping. The observances to regulate all these are what are called the rules of propriety." (*Tan'gong*, 164) Ziyou admitted that wrapping the dead body and ornamenting the coffin was done to minimize people's natural disgust of corpse.

This dialogue, which can be read as a mini-fiction about ethnography, has a theatrical effect and philosophical significance: the omniscient "narrator" of the entire story writes about two young Confucian scholars who watched someone in mourning self-dramatize. The two "fieldworkers," unmoved, debated the value of the public ritual performance of the mourner as their "human subject."[39] One scholar thought it was unnecessary, and the other defended it as proper *Li*, suggesting that the correct use of multiple mediums and objects to express emotions set civilized men apart from barbarians. Even for the modern philosopher Ludwig Wittgenstein, ritual action's role in expressing emotion is self-evident. When commenting on anthropologist James Frazer's *Golden Bough*, Wittgenstein remarks, "When I am angry about something, I sometimes hit the ground with a tree with my cane. But surely I do not believe the ground is at fault or the hitting would help matters. 'I vent my anger.' And all rites are of this kind."[40] Here Wittgenstein adumbrates the relation of rites to emotion in a legible way.

While public wailing is legitimized as an essential means to express sorrow at a funeral, modern scholars have found a gender difference based upon their field observation: while both men and women wail at funerals, only women, especially the wife and the daughter-in-law are socially expected to mourn continuously and loudly.[41] This modern anthropological study reminds us that Confucius's emphasis on self-cultivation through the exercise of self-control and sense of proportion was also gendered, and a Confucian gentleman was expected to learn how to both express his emotion and control his emotion, while women were allowed greater flexibility to express their grief. Confucian mourning rites had long "emphasized the importance of female roles" in the patrilineal family, and women's participation ensured a funeral's success.[42]

THEORIZING *LI* AND *QING* ON
CHU STATE BAMBOO SLIPS

Confucius in his dialogues talked about *ren*, kindness or benevolence and *Li*, ritual propriety with much greater frequency than the issues of human nature and human emotion by referring to the terms *xing* and *qing*. Within Chu State bamboo slips purchased from Hong Kong in 1994 and housed in the Shanghai Municipal Museum, Confucius was recorded as saying "When music was lost, emotions dissipated." [*yue wang li qing*] Another quote is decoded as "Emotion means love." [*qing ai ye*][43] It is notable that in both classical and modern Chinese language, *xingqing* and *qingxing* are two kindred composite words used often interchangeably, meaning one's natural disposition.

After the death of Confucius, the question of the intrinsic disposition of man, whether he was naturally good or evil, loomed large in the intellectual debate between Confucian thinkers Mencius and Xunzi of the Warring States period. One theory suggests that Youzi, the previously mentioned Confucian student who defended the funeral ritual, was the intermediary figure and the link between Confucius and Mencius, who contributed to the Guodian bamboo texts' focus on the relationship between nature, emotion, and fate, placing an equal emphasis on ritual and music, the human mental state, and emotional expressions.[44] These bamboo texts were excavated from the Chu state tombs in 1993 at Guodian, an ancient Chu State site in south China and interned around 300 BCE.[45] These texts point to an intellectual transition from Confucius to Mencius-Xunzi which brought the concept *qing* into metaphysical discourse and delineated the relationship of human nature, emotions, and ritual propriety.

The texts on the Guodian bamboo strips have one prominent feature. They contain parts corresponding to the received Daoist classic *Daode jing* and some are equivalent to the Confucian Book of Rites, *Liji* chapters, with strips seemingly a mix of both schools.[46] The texts appear to reflect a Daoist conception of the world and its influence on Confucian way of thinking.

For instance, "*sheng*," to give birth to or to breed, the biological imagery of emanation, appeared in the bamboo texts with both Daoist and Confucian inclinations. The Daoist phrase was *taiyi sheng shui*, "The Great Unity Gives Birth to Water," and the Daoist-influenced Confucian expression was "Ritual is born from solemnity; music arises from fullness. When ritual is replete and music is deficient, there is stress; when music is replete and ritual is deficient, there is dissipation."[47] This sentence utilized typical Confucian terminology of "ritual" and "music," but the logic and imagination is Daoist in that it constructs a relationship of ascending emanation by invoking the character *sheng*, which is part of the composite character *xing* after combining with the "heart-mind" radical, *xin*. Following a similar logic, the text asserts that "The affections, *qing*, are born of [human] nature; ritual is born of the affections; gravity is born of ritual; reverence is born of gravity; yielding is born of reverence; the sense of shame is born of yielding; discipline is born of the sense of shame; integrity is born of discipline. [48]

The Guodian tomb texts thus build a hierarchical order and emanating sequence that place human nature as the original cause, somewhat like the seeds of a plant, and human emotions grow out of it, which precipitate the rites. This imagery legitimized affective emotions as a natural outgrowth of human nature and, more importantly, the very foundation of the rites. It affirms "our basic need for emotional expression stemming from our various encounters with the world around us."[49] Similar imagery appears when the text states that "The desires, *yu*, are born of [human] nature." We can speculate that in the mind of the author(s) of these texts, both affective emotions, *qing*, and desires, *yu*, organically grow out of human nature. In a comparative perspective, Bengali religious thought, as another non-Western way of thinking, shares a similar interest in tracing the source of emotion and a similar belief in the controllability of human emotions.[50]

The Guodian texts admired human affections. One strip text says, "In general, true affections in a person are something to delight in. If one does so with true affections, though he may transgress, this is not to be deplored."[51] The emphasis on "true" feeling reminds us of a similar point made by Confucius, where he suggested that a gentleman should attempt to transcend undeniable negative feelings to elevate himself to higher moral ground. As we will see later, however, the "true man" transformed into a Daoist ideal personality, compared with the self-controlled Confucian "gentleman."

Another important theoretical contribution of the Guodian texts was its elucidation of the interplay among human nature, the affections, and the heart-mind, *xin*. The heart-mind, *xin*, which was discussed by Mencius, was defined by the bamboo strip texts as having "no fixed inclinations," but "depends upon external things to arise." As a result, "[i]n general, yearning (for external things) makes extreme use of the heart-mind."[52] For *shi* scholars, human nature comes via mandate, with one strip text in the section titled *"xing zi ming chu"* arguing that "the most difficult thing in learning is the search for the [authentic] heart-mind. If one follows the lead of what is to be performed, one will be close to attain it."[53] In the understanding of some Warring States period scholars, human heart-mind has an original tranquil state, awaiting external things to arouse it. However, the goal of moral learning is to search for, or restore, the authentic heart-mind.

As we will discuss in later chapters, the recovery of the original heart-mind or the unsoiled human nature was a key concern of Chinese thinkers in later dynasties. Scott Cook finds one passage on the human chain reactions after the feelings are aroused bears a striking resemblance to a passage in the *Tan'gong* chapter of the *Book of Rites*, which I quote. While in the *Book of Rites*, the passage assumed the form of a dialogue between two Confucian disciples Ziyou and Youzi, appearing in the bamboo strip as an independent passage that seems out of place. Again, it is assumingly just an innocuous theatrical fable that illuminates the main point about the sequence of emotional expressions and the importance of various mediums.

Scott Cook argues that this internal/external division was identical to the description of the external stimulation of inner, tranquil human nature in the chapter on the social function of music in the *Book of Rites*.[54] The canonized *Book of Rites* exhibited an aura of politicization not shared by the bamboo slip texts. First, the passages from the *Book of Rites* cited by Cook attached more importance to "regulation" while the bamboo text emphasized genesis: "Ritual arises from the affections";[55] second, the *Book of Rites* seems to think the people, *min*, which had the connotation of commoners who were to be disciplined and penalized by the rulers, "lack any constancy in terms of sorrow, happiness, joy, or anger"; and third, it was the sagely "former kings" who created ritual and propriety, *Li*, based upon human nature and its affections.[56] Scott Cook is correct in asserting that the authors of the bamboo slip texts were first generation disciples of Confucius, holding the opinion that "there is both good and bad in human nature," unlike Mencius and Xunzi who debated about this issue from two oppositional stances.[57]

REINTERPRETING MENCIUS, ZHUANGZI, AND XUNZI'S APPROACHES TO EMOTION AND RITUAL

My reading of Mencius as recorded in *Mengzi* again focuses not on his political philosophy but on his concern with human emotions, human-animal relations, and the various scenarios where ritual failed. For me, dysfunction does not entail inefficacy, because the ritual masters, performers, and spectators of a death ritual or ancestral sacrifice all knew the rituals would not have any real efficacy on the dead, and the function was to comfort the living. The "as if" imagining shows how the rites linked the living with the dead through invoking affections in mind-heart. The real dysfunction occurred when the *Li* rules and moral codes conflicted with exigencies.[58] These exigencies reflect *qing* in the sense of emotion-situation.

In *Mengzi*, there were four types of relational and situational exigencies that required one to act virtuously. In the first situation, Mencius showed his extension of emotions toward families to non-human animals. In the famous dialogue between Mencius and Duke Xuan of Qi, Mencius extolled the feudal lord for being rueful to the sacrificial ox who was fearful and trembling and sparing it. Mencius commented that he knew the duke "could not bear the suffering of the ox," and suggested this moral feeling was a common trait of a "gentleman": "Gentleman cannot bear to see animals die if they have seen them living. If they hear their cries of suffering, they cannot bear to eat their flesh."[59]

There are four layers of meaning here: (1) In the Chinese cognition during the Warring States period, as with that in ancient India, animals as sentient beings [*youqing*, literally, "those who have feelings"] would fear death, though Buddhism entirely prohibited animal sacrifice;[60] (2) Animal's trepidation due to ritual killing might trigger human sympathy through sensory experience because the duke was stricken by the ox's frightened appearance;[61] (3) The experiences of seeing and hearing would serve as the medium of this stimulation and imagination, and thus Mencius explained why "gentlemen keep their distance from the kitchen"—without being affected by visualizing and hearing the violence, one's mind-heart would not be aroused, then they could act "as if" nothing happened even if someone still needed to slaughter the animal. There is "some hypocrisy" from a modern point of view;[62] (4) Occasionally, rituals would fail after human sympathy was given primacy, which motivated the pardoning of large ritual animals. It is notable that an ox was the sacrificial animal specific to the rank of the King of the Zhou (Son of Heaven) and the feudal lords under him, including Duke Xuan of Qi.[63]

Mencius showed emotional empathy to domesticated, non-threatening animals like an ox, for when he mentioned the historical merit of the Duke of Zhou, he emphasized that the Duke of Zhou drove wild animals such as tigers, leopards, rhinoceros, and elephants far away, which "greatly delighted" the world. The elephants were not life-threatening, but their forest habitat must be cleared for farming.[64] If we reexamine Mencius's narrative regarding human-non-human relations, the fate of the elephant in north China and his attitude, and Confucius's reaction to the fire of stable, then the Confucian value of ecology has an overall anthropocentric and pragmatic inclination.

The remaining three cases centered on morally right actions embedded in inter-human relations. In the second, hypothetical relational scenario in the *Mengzi*, one man suddenly saw a baby was going to fall into a well. Again, the sight instantly triggered the spectator's intuitive feelings of fear and compassion (The *Mengzi, 4A17)*. Mencius put particular emphasis on the feeling's character as an unconditional, "categorical" reaction because it was "not because one sought to get in good with the child's parents, not because one wanted fame among one's neighbors and friends, and not because one would dislike the sound of the child's cries. "[65] I argue that as with Immanuel Kant, Mencius tried to identify a specific human mental and moral condition where feelings and potential subsequent actions are detached from any utilitarian considerations.

In the third hypothetical, contingent situation, Mencius was asked about whether a man should save his drowning (elder)sister-in-law [*sao*] because physical touching between adult men and women is indecorum. Mencius's reply was that to pull her out of water is "discretion," *quan*, literally meaning measuring the weight, although the no-touch rule is "ritual." (The *Mengzi*, 4A17).[66] We may say that the two men were put in the same situation when they were compelled by the Kantian categorical imperative, and their salvations were morally self-sufficient in themselves without external purposes. Of course, the third case displayed intricacy with the fact that the man had fulfilled the objective necessity of saving a life by breaching decorum and daily moral constraints.

In the fourth, still a hypothetical yet more complicated situation of an ethical dispute, the ancient legendary sage, king Shun's father, committed the crime of homicide. Mencius, when asked, replied that Shun could have had his father apprehended by the Minister of Crime to show the respect of the law, but as a private person he could quit and flee with his father, "joyfully forgetting the world." (The *Mengzi*, 7A35) In this moral dilemma related to kinship, Mencius imagined a way to reconcile Shun's public position as ruler and upholder of *Li* and his private feeling, *qing*, as a son, and Shun made a wise decision to resolve the problem.

In all the four disparate situations, Mencius legitimized the expression of true human ethical sentiments transcending the bounds of regular ritual propriety by using one's free will to choose what to do. In two of the stories, the sister-in-law and Shun's father suggest using discretion and permitting necessary and inevitable ritual dysfunction to accommodate situation-emotions related to family ties when one made a judgment. Spontaneous choices manifest moral value. In the *Analects*, Confucius demonstrated his attitude toward the living animal and humanity when faced with the situation of choosing between the two. When hearing about a stable catching fire, Confucius was concerned about the injury of people but "did not ask about the horses." (The

Analects, 10–17) We might also say that Mensius's imagery of the younger brother-in-law's rescuing his sister-in-law was limited and metaphorical because, in real life, a man needs to save a drowning adult not with a hand, but by throwing himself into the water to catch her. In this scenario, however, the physical contact between these in-laws would not be so simple as holding and pulling a hand.

Chinese philosophers' attitudes toward animals were intriguing. Bryan W. Van Norden makes the provocative claim that Zhuangzi, the Daoist thinker, might have used a cook and ox butcher's story as an intentional jab at Mencius, in which the ox was not the object of sympathy but mere human excellence in butchering.[67] In this fable, the same act of immolation as appeared in the *Mengzi* gained a different meaning. Zhuangzi dismissed the ritualist purpose of slaughtering a sacrificial ox and transcended the moral dilemma stemming from killing animals by starting the piece with "The cook was carving up an ox for King Hui of Liang." The story details the process and the main point is with the grasp of the Way, *dao*, the cook could cut up thousands of oxen without damaging the knife. With the Way as the supreme goal, the Daoist thinker Zhuangzi dismissed both ritual propriety and human compassion in his writing, perhaps to challenge the Confucian standpoint of Mencius. In this context, the sacrificial ox was only used to lure the spirits of the descending ancestors, and the role of the butcher was like a rational sage-advisor.[68]

Another occasion where the book *Zhuangzi* challenges the sanctity of ritual propriety is in the chapter titled "The Great Source as Teacher," *Da zongshi*, where three of the Daoist scholars were friends but one day one of them died. Before his burial, Confucius, who often appeared in the *Zhuangzi* as an antithesis, sent his disciple Zigong to pay his respects. Zigong, however, found the two mourning friends were singing and playing instruments. Confused, Zigong asked them if it accorded with ritual propriety to sing at a corpse, and the two friends replied, "What does this fellow understand about the real point of ritual?"[69] Daoist scholars again jeered at Confucian scholars' adherence to ritualism. A direct assault on Confucian ritualism also comes from another Daoist classic *Dao de jing*, or the *Book of the Way*, which dates to around 375 BCE, had already inveighed against "ritual rule" as "turn[ing] loyal trust to deceit" and "leading to disorder."[70]

Zhuangzi's way of thinking was rational and schematic rather than being detached and "carefree," or "anti-rational" as scholars think.[71] In another parable in the book, Zhuangzi continued to take issue with the weeping ritual at the corpse, sanctioned by Confucians. In this famous story written in the third person, Zhuangzi's wife died, and Master Hui went to offer his condolences and he found Zhuangzi beating a basin and singing. Zhuangzi explained to the confused Master Hui that, "When she first died, how could I not be melancholy? But I reflected on her beginning and realized that she was originally unborn. Not only was she unborn, originally she had no form. . . . If I were to have followed her weeping and wailing, I think it would have been out of keeping with destiny, so I stopped."[72] This parable illustrates that Zhuangzi, or the articulator of the nihilist worldview, underwent a logical reasoning process and he made a rational choice. In the story, or, the "plot," "Zhuangzi" at first felt an intense emotional experience of grief by instinct and he knew well the proper death rituals of weeping and wailing. Nevertheless, he gave a second, reflective and artificial thought about the formless existence of his wife before and after her death, concluding that life and death were but the same thing in destiny. The story, of course, does not tell the reader how Master Hui, the spectator of the scene, responded to Zhuangzi's acting, speech, and his reasoning, because it was nothing but a rational sophistry designed to debunk orthodox Confucian emotionalism and ritualism. This was similar to the anecdote about how the two Daoist friends mocked Zigong, and how the Way, or *Dao*, transcended ritual and sensitivity to the suffering of an ox.

From the point of view of the anthropology of emotions, Zhuangzi's seamless transition from grief to self-dramatized public singing reveals that self was malleable through a cognitive process.[73] One can debate whether feeling grief at one's wife's death is universal or culture-specific, but the public showing of sad facial expressions is a required signal of one's proper mood at another's death and singing was prohibited, but Zhuangzi chose to disregard the norm and stop performing the ritual act, exposing that routine death rituals and the expected mode of expression could be put under personal scrutiny.[74] Other scholars have noticed that the term *li*, the naturalist-rational component in my trio, emerges with great frequency in the Outer and Miscellaneous Chapters of the *Zhuangzi*.[75] It is arguable that Zhuangzi, who epitomized southern Chinese radical skepticism, was more anti-ritual and anti-emotion than anti-reason.[76] Depicting singing and playing an instrument rather than adhering to the Confucian rite of weeping at the funeral and recording the verbal explanation was just a designed Daoist strategy of challenging Confucian ritualism.

Another famous parable is about how Zhuangzi debated with Master Hui about how he knew the "joy of the fishes" while Master Hui doubted his knowledge. The last sentence of the story goes:

> "Let's go back to where we started," said Master Chuang, "When you said, 'How do you know what the joy of fishes is?' you asked me because you already knew what the joy of fishes is?' You asked me because you already knew that I knew. I know it by strolling over the Hao (River)."[77]

Here Zhuangzi treats the fish as sentient beings who share the human feeling of "joy," and more importantly, their joy is perceptible to him. It is notable that the initial refutation of Master Hui was "You're not a fish, how do you know what the joy of fishes is?"[78] Here Master Hui only questioned Zhuangzi's epistemological ability of knowing the joy of fish, but not the assumption about the joy of the fish themselves. In other words, Master Hui did not deny the possibility of fish feeling happy but was questioning Zhuangzi's ability to discern it. Zhuangzi made the claim because of his confidence in rationally equating humans and non-humans, and the imagery of joyful and jumping fish greeting King Wen of the Zhou had already appeared in the *Book of Odes*, and the poem was quoted in the *Mengzi*.[79] The personification and humanization of fish was a common trope of his time.

Xunzi was a Confucian thinker who appraised all past philosophers including Zhuangzi and any who might be intellectually connected with Zhuangzi, as I mentioned in chapter 1. Xunzi's emphasis on the significance of poetry and music, and music [*yue*]'s semantic resemblance of joy [*yue*] is underscored by Paul Rakita Goldin.[80] Famous for his insistence on evil as the default state of human nature, challenging Mencius's upshot about the intrinsic goodness of human nature, Xunzi was also the first theorist of ritual and emotion through his composition of a chapter titled "A Discussion on Rites." Mencuis seldom systematically discussed the rites and their relationship with emotions, except when he employed parables to illuminate the priority of human emotions. This was especially the case when one has to use discretion, but Xunzi studied the rites and emotions more like a modern social scientist who distances himself from the object of study.

Xunzi elaborated on the definition, origins, foundations, functions, and goals of the rites. He linked the origin of ritual first to inborn human desires and asserted that rituals are created to set limits and degrees to the human seeking of satisfaction of desires. For Xunzi, the artificial creation of ritual was attributed to the ancient sage kings who hated disorder and established the code of conduct to "train men's desires and to provide for their satisfactions."[81] Moreover, "ritual principles" should guide statecraft: "So if ritual principles are not applied in the state, then its fame and accomplishment will not be become known."[82] Xunzi pitted "rituals" and "laws" against each other and argued that if the ruler relied upon laws rather than rituals, he would become a dictator, not a true king.[83] But for the sage kings, the ultimate purpose of creating rituals and asking people to follow them was to "nourish" [*yang*] and enrich people. Here Xunzi also invoked the syntax "A *zhe* B *ye*" by saying "*Li zhe yang ye*" to highlight the economic function of *Li*.[84] For Xunzi, ritual was intrinsically rational because it was an extension of Nature's patterns and organizing principles, or *li*.[85]

Xunzi theorized the metaphysical foundations of the rites as composed of three bases: "Heaven and earth are the basis of life, the ancestors are the basis of the family, and rulers and teachers are the basis of order."[86] Given this triad of cosmology, ancestor cult, and political and cultural authority, performing the rites allowed one to serve Heaven above and earth below, and honor the ancestors and exalt rulers and teachers. In line with logical reasoning, Xunzi's articulation was closest to a modern argument based upon premises, reasoning, and conclusion. Xunzi denied the efficacy of non-emotional, instrumental ceremonies of praying for rain, seeing them as only ornaments in the eyes of educated "gentleman" but as a supernatural miracle for commoners.[87] For Xunzi, ritual dysfunction or failure was self-evident on these occasions because weather patterns remain unimpacted by sacrifices. And thus, for Xunzi, the praying for rain ritual no longer maintained its earlier sacrificial and quasi-religious values for a rational scholarly gentleman like himself. Bringing anthropology into the study of Confucianism, Xunzi's negation of the meaning of the utilitarian sacrifices that were "directed toward particular ends"[88] was comparable to Émile Durkheim's distinction of magic and religion. Xunzi can be regarded as an ancient anthropologist who was trying to distinguish magic from higher religious belief. Yet at the same time, Xunzi was self-reflective enough to know his own identity as an intellectual elite whose rational ability buttressed his privileged social status, which contrasted starkly with the status of commoners. He believed that a full and beautiful expression of the natural feelings of joy and sorrow could only be handled by a "gentleman" "of thorough moral training and practice."[89]

A significant theoretical contribution of Xunzi was his discussion of the relationship among nature, *xing*, emotions, *qing*, and the mind, *xin*. This sequence had been discussed in the bamboo slips excavated in 1993, which only found recognition long after Xunzi textualized and published his discussion. In the section of *Xunzi* titled "Rectifying Names," Xunzi focused on naming. i.e., definition. Using nature, emotions, and the mind as examples, he argued that the nature of man was formed at the time of a person's birth, which responded to external stimulations through the senses but was not socially trained, and nature contained within itself emotions such as "[t]he likes and dislikes, delights and angers, griefs and joys of the nature." In the third stage, when the emotions are aroused, "the mind makes a choice from among them, and this is called thought [*lü*]."[90] In this legible theoretical formulation, intrinsic human nature was the basis, and emotions were the natural results of its response to external stimulations, while the mind made rational choice from amongst these sentiments. Compared with Xunzi's postulation about humanity's intrinsic evil and the subsequent political guidance, this nature-emotion-mind trio was more academic than ethical.

Unlike Zhuangzi, who mocked Confucian death rituals, particularly the spectacle of public weeping and leaping, and pretended that his wife's life and death were all the same, Xunzi took death rituals seriously. He inherited the "as if" imaginative tradition in earlier Confucianism and emphasized the importance of correct treatment of the dead. "The dead man is treated *as though* (italicization added) he merely changed his dwelling," he said, "and it is made clear that he will never use these things. This is all done in order to emphasize the feelings of grief."[91] Here, Xunzi implicitly balanced rites, feelings, and rationality. For him, funerary rites, which should not be abolished, were performed only to express the feelings of grief effectively and legitimately, although the mourners' recognized that none of the ornaments and sacrifices would be utilized by those who passed. In the process, the mourners invoked emotional imaginations to comfort themselves with the notion that the dead merely changed dwellings.[92] He also defended the three-year mourning period, which the pragmatic and consequential thinker Mozi had rejected, as "a form set up after consideration of the emotions involved, because at such a time the pain of grief is most intense."[93]

As with Confucius, Xunzi separated political rituals from family death rites. The latter for him was not made to limit human desires; rather, they "originated in the emotions of remembrance and longing for the dead"[94] as positive emotional and mnemonic devices. As a ritual expert, Xunzi believed rituals stem from emotions, and this theory was in line with the assumption in the Guodian bamboo slip texts. I disagree with the claim that Xunzi's assessment of *qing* was consonant with his assessment of evil human nature, *xing*.[95] As we will discuss in later chapters, the "situation-emotion as the basis of ritual" thesis, as I would call it, would reappear in the late imperial Qing dynasty as a positive theory.

Xunzi might be a "religious philosopher" or "proto-Marxist and proto-scientific" thinker based on his cosmology and perception of Heaven, or *tian*.[96] Yet we might also see him as a rationalistic proto-social scientist in ancient China who "studied" proto-political philosophy, proto-anthropology, and proto-psychology, while being influenced by his self-identity as a Confucian gentleman. One way of rethinking the possible intellectual connection between Xunzi and Zhuangzi, two disparate thinkers, is to consider that both inherited the scholarship of Zixia, one of Confucius's students, by studying under Zixia's followers. This genealogy was affirmed by the Qing dynasty scholar Zhang Xuecheng (1738–1801).[97] Contemporary historian and archaeologist Li Xueqin argues that Zixia was the only student who heard Confucius's teaching of the art of poetry, and in the "Preface to the Classic of Poetry," allegedly authored by Zixia, there was an explicit discussion on how songs and dances function as the expression of emotion after its arousal: "The emotions were aroused from within but manifested themselves first in speech; when speech is insufficient, people let out a sigh; when sighing is not enough, people sing, but when singing is still inadequate, people dance with their arms and feet."[98]

One strain of Xunzi's ideology evolved into the school of Legalism that emphasized law, order, and penalty. For legalist thinkers, human natural dispositions and emotions could be perilous for violating ritual. Shang Yang (390–338 BCE), the political advisor to the Qin state who was accountable for its agricultural prosperity, military strength, and administrative efficiency, wrote in his influential political treatise *Shangjun shu* [Book of Lord Shang] that "The nature of the people is to seek food when they are hungry, to seek respite when they toil, to seek joy when they are embittered, to seek glory when they are humiliated: this is the people's disposition. In seeking benefit, the people lose the standard of ritual, in seeking name (= repute), they lose the constant of their nature."[99] In the *Spring and Autumn Annals of Lü Buwei* [*Lü shi chunqiu*], completed during the Warring States period and close to the time of the Qin dynasty (221–207 BCE), the authors wrote a chapter titled *Qingyu*, "Emotions and Desires" in which there was an assertion that "Men are born with greed and desire. Once one has a desire, one would have an emotional impulse, *qing*, and once there is emotional impulse, one must put it under control."[100] Although the book was an intellectual fusion of multiple schools, this reflected the Confucian understanding of the legitimacy of *qing* and the necessity of confining it within boundaries.

CONCLUSION

Although *li*, rationality or rational principle, had not received full-fledged deliberation and expounding during this period as it did in the Song dynasty, Confucians had shown the tendency of balancing daily rationality with its emphasis on ritualism and human emotions. Confucians defended ritual actions and cherished ritual objects as proper and indispensable external expressions of human emotion, philosophically analyzing emotion as a human mental state and analytical framework. Confucians also dealt with the tension between ritual and emotion in some concrete circumstances of the lifeworld and attempted to resolve the dilemma by allowing temporary ritual failure. They engaged in debates with Daoists, and Zhuangzi purposefully scorned Confucian insistence on the necessity of ritualism.

Classical Chinese philosophy distinguishes itself from ancient Greek philosophy in the following ways: Chinese culture did not develop the Greek-style conception of an immortal soul, which can be traced back to Pythagoras.[101] In Chinese culture, "*hunpo*," the linguistic equivalence to the "soul" was never a substance that "determine[s] action and truth" with its "three components: perception, intellect, and desire."[102] When a man dies, according to Chinese folk culture, the cloud-like "*hun*" associated with *yang*, was supposed to ascend to Heaven, while the *po* stayed underground. But for pre-Qin thinkers, the key issue was not the nature of the soul but the appropriate forms of ritual.[103] Plato's discussion about the three parts of the soul, "the divine, the human, and essentially irrational and subhuman,"[104] is not contingent upon where they would arrive at, but their character and function. Plato also talked about enjoyment and physical pleasure, and the need for restraining feelings.[105] Yet, compared with Confucius's agnostic attitude toward the spirits and Xunzi's recognition of death ritual's actual role of emotional comfort, the immortality of the soul persisted in Plato's worldview and Plato's thesis on the dichotomy of the body and the soul, particularly the distracting character of the body also did not exist in China.[106] For both Plato and Descartes, the "mind" and the "soul" were interchangeable terms, both being ontologically separable from the body,[107] while for the Chinese, mind-heart differs from the *hunpo* of the dead.

Another feature of the Greek classical Theory of Ideas is the Principle of Sublimity and the participating Ideas in the principle belonging to a "superior world of Being," not the "inferior world of Becoming."[108] The sequence of nature, emotions, and rites as discussed in the Chu bamboo slips showed, however, a process of growing and becoming, which marks the Chinese biological-agricultural way of understanding the human world. China's Heaven, tian, is closer to the Supreme Being in the native American belief system, but it became secularized and politicized as a means of selecting the proper ruler, the Son of Heaven, penalize him, and show him signs of displeasure. Additionally, the ruler has to maintain his connections with Heaven through sacrifices, sanctioned by the state and Confucian classics. Pre-Qin Chinese had a hierarchical grading scale to "arrange all animals according to their degree of 'perfection'" as Aristotle did.[109] For Mencius and Zhuangzi, oxen and fish could trigger a feeling of empathy, yet when the king could not bear to witness the trepidation of the sacrificial ox and thus pardoned it, he replaced it with a goat which was considered a lower animal. And Mengzi was not opposed to it.

A final distinction was the attitude toward myth and ritual. The Chinese concept of *Li*, as a virtue with hybrid connotations of both ritual activity and social etiquette, which Mencius combines, has the least clear equivalence in Western culture.[110] Animal sacrifices existed in Greek pagan religious practices, and in Greek thought there were also ideas of virtue, good sense, and the importance of music and rites; they were also not without concern for affections, emotions, and passions, *thymos*. However, since the sixth century BCE, when Confucius, not a Master of Ceremony but an idiosyncratic prophet, began to "transmit" the ritual-emotional tradition in a more rational way, the Greek culture achieved a breakthrough in which the supernatural agents, myth, and concerns with ritual were all liquidated to usher in a positivistic age of intellectual revolution.[111] Confucianism was more rationalized than Shang shamanism, but it retained or appropriated the earlier ritual practices and romanticized the institutions before Confucius. Its core concerns never broke with the ritualist and mythical traditions of the past, but ancestral sacrifices were sanctified by Confucianism as an indispensable means of maintaining and perceptualizing an ethical family relationship, emotional bonds, and delivering affective memory. In addition, the agricultural and lineal characters of the Chinese civilization rendered the rituals invariably entangled with complicated kinship relations and sophisticated preparation and treatment of animals, cooked food, liquor, and serving utensils. At the same time, relational and situational human emotions and their control and balance, often with sociopolitical connotations, occupied a central place in pre-Qin Confucian thinking.

NOTES

1. Liu Zehua, *Xianqin shiren yu shehui* [Pre-Qin Scholars and Society] (Tianjin: Tianjin renmin chubanshe, 2004), 19–27.

2. Hans H. Panner, "Rationality, Ritual, and Science," in Jacob Neusner et at eds., *Religion, Science, and Magic: In Concert and in Conflict* (New York: Oxford University Press, 1989), 15.

3. The Classics concerning rituals are also known as *Three [Texts about] Rituals [san Li]* after the Han Dynasty: *Ceremonials and Rites [Yi-Li]*, *Book of Rites [Liji]*, and *Rites of Zhou [Zhou Li]*. Among the three texts, *Yi-Li* was more detailed and technical, *Liji* was more interpretive and philosophical, and *Zhou Li* was more about the idealized ancient politics and institutions. Due to *Zhou Li*'s essential character as a book of Western Zhou institutions and offices, I will not focus on it in this study.

4. Youngmin Kim, *A History of Chinese Political Thought* (Medford, MA: Polity Press, 2018), 28.

5. Ibid., 30.

6. Du Zexun, *Wenxian xue gaiyao* [A General Outline of the Studies of Ancient Chinese Texts] (Beijing: Zhonghua shuju, 2001), 448.

7. This transition is a consensus among recent Chinese researchers as reflected in the editorial remarks of a new version of the *Book of Changes*. See *Zhouyi* [Book of Changes from the Zhou] (Beijing: Zhonghua shuju, 2015), 1–4. There is also an opinion that the Commentary was written in an extended time span from the Warring States to the Han.

8. *I-Ching The Classic of Changes,* trans. Edward L. Shaughnessy (New York: Ballantine Books, 1996), 25.

9. Huang Zongxi, *Ming ru xue an* [Intellectual Biographies of Ming Confucian Scholars] e-book (Yiya chubanshe, 2018)

10. Richard Wilhelm, *The I Ching* or *the Book of Changes*, trans. Cary F. Barnes (New York: Bollingen Foundation Inc, 1967), 44.

11. Ibid.

12. Ibid., 436.

13. *Zhouyi*, 294.

14. A.J. Ayer, *Language, Truth and Logic* (London: Penguin Books, 1946), 48–49.

15. For the assertive proposition and its connotation, see Scott Soames, *Rethinking Language, Mind, and Meaning* (Princeton, NJ: Princeton University Press, 2015), 18–19.

16. For the features of Chinese language and definition and their influence on Chinese philosophical thinking, see Chad Hansen, *Language and Logic in Ancient China* (Socoro, MN: Advanced Reasoning Forum, 2020), 32–33, 75. However, I disagree with Hansen's assertion that Chinese philosophy "lacks a preoccupation with meanings as expressed in definitions." See Hansen, *Language and Logic in Ancient China*, 58. For me, the definition of *Li* through the syntax structure "*zhe . . . ye*" here conveys a meaning that emphasizes action and practice.

17. *The I Ching* or *the Book of Changes*, 224. *Zhouyi*, 238.

18. My interpretation here considers the original text, the modern Chinese explanation, and the English-translated German interpretation of Richard Wilhelm.

19. *The I Ching* or *the Book of Changes*, 327.

20. *Zhouyi*, 284.

21. Ibid., 294–95.

22. For this new finding and the reassessment of its value, see the preface to the *Kongzi jiayu*. Wang Guoxuan, Wang Xiumei ed. (Beijing: Zhonghua shuju, 2016).

23. James F. Peterman, *Whose Tradition? Which Dao? Confucius and Wittgenstein on Moral Learning and Reflection* (Albany: State University of New York Press, 2015), 83, 87.

24. For the English translation of the *Analects*, I use D.C. Lau's authoritative English translation in combination with the leading mainland Chinese specialist of the book Yang Bojun's modern Chinese rendition of the meaning. Both are included in *Chinese-English Edition, Confucius, The Analects* published by Zhonghua shuju [Zhonghua Book Company] in 2008.

25. Confucius et al., *The Book of Rites*, 90. Here the title *The Book of Rites* is the English rendition of *Liji*, one of the three components of the *Li* compendium, which I translate literally as *Records of Rites* in this book.

26. Ibid., 276.

27. For the scholarly debate about whether the sacrificial feast and meat-eating in history was sacred or secular, see Maria-Zoe Petroppoulou, *Animal Sacrifice in Ancient Greek Religion, Judaism, and Christianity, 100 BC—AD200* (Oxford, UK: Oxford University Press, 2008), 14.

28. Wang Guoxuan, Wang Xiumei eds., *Kongzi jiayu* [Family Talk of Confucius] (Beijing: Zhonghua shuju, 2016), 346. English translation is mine.

29. Roel Sterckx, *Food, Sacrifice, and Sagehood in Early China* (Cambridge, UK: Cambridge University Press, 2011), 43.

30. Ibid., 81.

31. Michael Nylan, "Lots of Pleasure but Little Happiness," *Philosophy East and West* 65, no. 1 (2015): 198.

32. *Chinese-English Edition, Confucius, The Analects* (Beijing: Zhonghua Book Company, 2008), 66–61. Heidegger also thinks that as a "mood" which for me is another appropriate rendition of *qing*, specific anxiety should be called fear. See Simon Critchley, *Continental Philosophy: A Very Short Introduction* (Oxford, UK: Oxford University Press, 2001), 97–98.

33. For a discussion of animal theft in rural Greece and its justification rhetoric, see Michael Herzfeld, *The Poetics of Manhood: Contest and Identity in a Cretan Mountain Village* (Princeton, NJ: Princeton University Press, 1985), 20–21.

34. James, *The varieties of Religious Experience*, 212.

35. Confucius et al., *The Book of Rites*, 35.

36. Ibid., 38.

37. Ibid., 29.

38. See the record of the *Classics of Filial Piety*, in *Liji/Xiaojing* [Book of Rite/ Classics of Filial Piety], eds. Hu Pingsheng, Chen Meilan (Beijing: Zhonghua shuju, 2007), 277.

39. For an analysis of the three layers of the relationship, see James Clifford and George E. Marcus eds., *Writing Culture: The Poetics and Politics of Ethnography* (Berkeley: University of California Press, 1986), 88.

40. Ludwig Wittgenstein, *The Mythology in Our Language: Remarks on Frazer's Golden Bough*, trans. Stephan Palmié (Chicago: HAU Books, 2018), 54.

41. Hsu, *Under Ancestor's Shadow*, 160.

42. Bret Hinsch, *Women in Early Imperial China* (Lanham, MD: Roman & Littlefield Publishing Inc., 2006), 147–48.

43. Pu Maozuo ed., *Shanghai bowuguan cang Chu zhu shu Kongzi shilun, zigao, Lubang dahan* [Collection of the Shanghai Museum: Chu State Bamboo Books: Confucius on Poetry, Zigao, Great Draught in the Lu State] (Shanghai: Zhongxi shuju, 2014), 12, 32.

44. He Yixin, "Rujia xinxing zhixue de zhuanchu—Lun ziyou de sixiang chuangzao ji qi daotong diwei" [The Rise of the School of Heart/Mind-Nature of Confucianism: The Intellectual Innovation of Ziyou and His Orthodoxy Status"], *Fudan xuebao shehuikexue ban* [Journal of Fudan University: Social Sciences] no. 4 (2020): 105–17.

45. Scott Cook, "Introduction," *The Bamboo Texts of Guodian: A Study and Complete Translation* (Ithaca, NY: Cornell University East Asia Program, 2013), 5.

46. Ibid., 14.

47. Ibid., 835.

48. Ibid., 850.

49. Ibid., 676.

50. June McDaniel, "Emotion in Bengli Religious Thought: Substance and Metaphor," in Joel Marks and Roger T. Ames eds., *Emotions in Asian Thought: A Dialogue in Comparative Philosophy* (Albany: State University of New York Press, 1995), 53.

51. Scott Cook, *The Bamboo Texts of Guodian: A Study and Complete Translation.*, 674.

52. Ibid., 724.

53. Ibid., 673.

54. Ibid., 679.

55. Ibid., 714.

56. I think Scott Cook's translation of the term *min* as "humans" renders it identical with another word *ren* which was translated as "humans." For me, *ren* are generic humans, but *min* carried a political connotation in ancient Chinese texts mean subjects of the kingdom who were to be penalized or to be protected. See Hou Wailu, *Zhongguo gudai shehui shilun*, 82–83.

57. Scott Cook, *The Bamboo Texts of Guodian*, 684–85.

58. Michael David Kaulana Ing, *The Dysfunction of Ritual in Early Confucianism* (Oxford, UK: Oxford University Press, 2012), 59.

59. *Mengzi with Selections from Traditional Commentaries*, trans. Bryan W. Van Norden (Indianapolis, IN: Hackett Publishing, 2008), 9.

60. Chen Huaiyu, *Dongwu yu zhongguo zhengzhi zongjiao zhixu* [Animals and the Politicoreligious Order in Medieval China] (Shanghai: Shanghai guji chubanshe, 2020), 77.

61. Ibid. Bryan W. Van Norden quotes Zhu Xi and emphasizes that the King "saw the ox's frightened appearance" and then changed his mind.

62. Ibid., 10.

63. Oxen are the sacrificial animal of the King of Zhou and his feudal lords and goats are for the sacrifice of their ministers. For the explanation of this system, see Chen Li, *Baihutong shu zheng* [The Annotated Treatise of the White Tiger Hall] (Beijing: Zhonghua shuju, 1994), 81. Chen Li was a Qing Dynasty scholar and the *Treatise of the White Tiger Hall* was an authorized explication of Confucian theories and systems completed in 79 BEC in the Eastern Han.

64. Mark Elvin, *The Retreat of the Elephants: An Environmental History of China* (New Haven, CT: Yale University Press, 2004), 11.

65. *Mengzi with Selections from Traditional Commentaries*,46. Bryan W. Van Norden notes here that Mencius does not say that every human would act to save the child.

66. In traditional Chinese culture and rural society, a woman and her husband's older brother avoid each other because of social taboo, but between a woman and her husband's unmarried younger brother there have more freedom and the elder sister-in-law, who has a different appellation from younger sister-in-law in Chinese is sometimes considered as a mother figure. For this different treatment, also see Hsu, *Under Ancestor's Shadow*, 62.

67. *Mengzi with Selections from Traditional Commentaries*, 10.

68. Sterckx, *Food, Sacrifice, and Sagehood in Early China*, 51.

69. *Zhuangzi: The Essential Writings with Selections from Traditional Commentaries*, trans. Brook Ziporyan (Indianapolis, IN: Hackett Publishing, 2009), 46.

70. Laozi, *Dao De Jing The Book of the Way*, trans. Moss Roberts (Berkeley: University of California Press, 2001), 106.

71. This standard way of understanding Zhuangzi as a philosopher who stood out because of his carefree attitude toward the world can be found in Jeeloo Liu who

accepts the conclusion of A.C. Graham on this issue. See Jeeloo Liu, *An Introduction to Chinese Philosophy* (Malden, MA: Blackwell Publishing, 2006), 156, 179.

72. Zhuangzi, *Wandering on the Way, Earliest Tales and Parables of Chuang Tzu*, trans. Victor H. Mair (Honolulu: University of Hawaii Press, 1994), 169.

73. For the study of anthropology of emotions on the universality, biological character, and cultural specificity of emotions and the social construction of emotions, see William M. Reddy, *The Navigation of Feeling: A Framework for the History of Emotions* (Cambridge, UK: Cambridge University Press, 2004), 37–38.

74. *The Book of Rites* stipulates that "When one sees at a distance a coffin with the corpse in it, he should not sing." Confucius et al., *The Book of Rites*, 35.

75. Curie Virag, *The Emotions in Early Chinese Philosophy* (Oxford, UK: Oxford University, 2017), 148.

76. For the geographical variation of ancient Chinese thoughts and the argument that Confucianism was an Eastern Chinese trend of thought while Daoism, including the *Daodejing* and *Zhuangzi*, were Southern Chinese way of thinking, see Meng Wentong, *Jingxue jueyuan* [Tracing the Origins of the Classical Studies] (Shanghai: shiji chuban jituan, 2006), 37, 141.

77. Zhuangzi, *Wandering on the Way, Earliest Tales and Parables of Chuang Tzu*, trans. Victor H. Mair, 165.

78. Zhuangzi, *Wandering on the Way, Earliest Tales and Parables of Chuang Tzu*, 165.

79. Bryan W. Van Norden's translation of *Mengzi* (Book 1A3.1) renders the sentence in the *Book of Odes* as "The King was at the Spirit Pond/Oh, it was full of jumping fish." See *Mengzi with Selections from Traditional Commentaries*, 3. Qing dynasty Chinese scholar Jiao Xun annotates this quoted sentence in the Mengzi by emphasizing the fish were "jumping joyfully," *yu nai tiaoyue xiyue*, when King Wen was at the Pond. See Jiao Xun, *Mengzi Zhengyi* [A Critical Annotation of *Mengzi*] (Beijing: Zhonghua shuju, 1987), 47.

80. Paul Rikita Goldin, *Rituals of the Way: The Philosophy of Xunzi* (Chicago: Open Court, 1999), 78.

81. *Hsun Tzu Basic Writings*, trans. Burton Watson (New York: Columbia University Press, 1963), 89.

82. Ibid., 86.

83. Ibid., 86.

84. Xiao Gongquan (Kung-Chuan Hsiao), *Zhongguo zhengzhi sixiang shi* [A History of Chinese Political Thought] (Shenyang, Liaoning jiaoyu chubanshe, 1998), 100–1.

85. Kurtis Hagen, *The Philosophy of Xunzi, A Reconstruction* (Chicago: Open Court, 2007), 49.

86. *Hsun Tzu Basic Writings*, 91.

87. Ibid., 85.

88. Edward J. Machle, "Xunzi as a Religious Philosopher," in *Ritual and Religion in the Xunzi*, eds. T. C. Cline and Justin Tiwald (Albany: State University of New York Press, 2014), 31.

89. *Hsun Tzu Basic Writings*, 102.

90. Ibid., 139.

91. Ibid., 105.

92. Ibid., 104.

93. Ibid., 105.

94. Ibid., 109.

95. For this analogy, see Aaron Stalnaker, *Overcoming Our Evil: Human Nature and Spiritual Exercises in Xunzi and Augustine* (Washington D.C.: Georgetown University Press, 2007), 62.

96. For modern scholars' debate on how to define Xunzi and his thoughts, see Michael R. Slater, "Xunzi on Heaven, Ritual, and the Way," in *Philosophy East and West* 68, no. 3 (2018): 887–908.

97. Zhang Xuecheng, *Wenshi tongyi* [A General Discussion on Literature and History] (Shanghai: shanghai shiji chuban jituan, 2008), 27.

98. Li, *Zhongguo dugai wenming yanjiu*, 365.

99. Yuri Pines, "Social Engineering in Early China: The Ideology of the Shangjunshu Revisited," in *Oriens Extremus*, no.55 (2016): 7.

100. Guan Xianzhu et al. eds., *Lü shi Chunqiu Quanyi* [Complete Modern Translation of the Spring and Autumn Annals of Lü Buwei] (Guiyang: Guizhou renmin chubanshe, 1997), 51.

101. Russell, *A History of Western Philosophy*, 32.

102. Aristotle, *The Philosophy of Aristotle: A Selection with an Introduction and Commentary by Renford Bambrough*, trans. J.L. Creed and A.E. Wardman (New York: Penguin Group, 2011), 385.

103. Mark Lewis, *Early China* (Cambridge, UK: Harvard University Press, 2007), 199.

104. Dougal Blyth, "The Ever-Moving Soul in Plato's Phaedrus," *American Journal of Philosophy* 118, no.2 (1997): 210.

105. Plato, *The Republic* (London: Penguin Books, 2007), 41, 207, 350.

106. For a discussion on Plato's metaphysics on the soul, body, and the Forms, see Shelley Kagan, *Death* (New Haven, CT: Yale University Press, 2012), 69–97.

107. Sarah Broadie, "Soul and Body in Plato and Descartes," *Proceedings of the Aristotelian Society*, no.101 (2001): 295–308.

108. Anthony Kenny, *Ancient Philosophy* (Oxford, UK: Clarendon Press, 2004), 53.

109. Arthur O. Lovejoy, *The Great Chain of Being: A Study of the History of an Idea* (Cambridge, MA: Harvard University Press, 2001), 58.

110. Lee H. Yearly, *Mencius and Aquinas: Theories of Virtue and Conceptions of Courage* (Albany: State University of New York Press, 1990), 36–37.

111. Jean-Pierre Vernant, *The Origins of Greek Thought* (Ithaca, NY: Cornell University Press, 1982), 87, 103, 107.

Chapter 3

The Rise of Rational Principle and Diffusion of Rites in the Tang and Song Dynasties

The development of Confucianism reached intellectual heights in the Tang-Song period under the two centralized imperial governments. Three forces drove the reshuffling of Confucian textual classics and practices: the state, the thinkers, and the grassroots-level society. The most prominent intellectual achievement of this period was the philosophizing of rational principle as a transcendental, cosmological being and the invention of the neologism "Heavenly principle." The *Li-qing-li* triad was entrenched through Zhu Xi's theoretical elaborations, which allowed the cosmological-rational principle's supremacy to coexist with legitimized human emotions and their expression as family rituals. Despite the incessant assaults on the Cheng-Zhu School of Principle from the Ming Dynasty through the twentieth century for its ethically oppressive character, Neo-Confucianism uplifted Chinese philosophical thinking to an ontological level to the inquiries into the relations of men and heaven while paying adequate attention to implementing the ritual system at the grassroots level.[1] In the meantime, in Zhu Xi's theoretical schema, "[r]itual is associated with being and substance (coherence as *ti*) rather than action and function (*yong*)"; that is, ritual gained its ontological status.[2]

DEFENDING CONFUCIAN RITUALISM IN THE TANG DYNASTY

Before the Tang Dynasty (618–907), Confucianism had undergone three major transitions. In the Western Han Dynasty, Confucianism was established as the imperial ruling ideology, and the Five Classics were standardized and canonized after Emperor Wu as a repository of ancient wisdom. The classic concerning *Li* was composed of three parts: the more technical *Ceremonials and Rites*, the more interpretive and philosophical *Book of Rites*, and the *Zhouli* [*Zhou Rites*], which was an institutional study of the Zhou ritual-based political system. Neither Mencius nor Xunzi, however, thought Confucius was the author or editor of these texts.[3] With the orthodox classics' canonization and entrance into the imperial college curriculum, classical studies arose as a discipline with the glossing of the pre-Qin meaning and the authentication of the texts as its core. This was the first transition. The second transition in the post–Western Han intellectual world was the prevalence of shamanistic Daoist practices, belief in the afterworld, and the later arrival of Buddhism in the Eastern Han. The third trend was the rise of metaphysics after the fall of the Eastern Han Empire among radical scholars. These three trends all led to the gradual loss of the rigor of Confucianism and its attraction among intellectual scholars who were seeking the meaning of life and existential interpretation of the world.

Despite the Qin Dynasty's enmity toward Confucian doctrines and scholars, animal sacrifice persisted as a part of local ritual action. In the Qin Dynasty, the heart, kidney, and limbs from the corpses of the sacrificial animals were used in state and village sacrifices, and communal feasting usually followed a village offering.[4] In the Qin Dynasty, offerings from the state sacrifices would be considered government property.[5] The property character of the sacrificial meat might help explain the secular aspect of its distribution to Confucius and the way Confucius treated it.

In Eastern Han philological studies, the semantic connection between *lü*, treading and practicing, and *Li*, which had been revealed in the *Xugua* chapter of the *Book of Changes* (one of the ten chapters allegedly written by Confucius, in which the author asserted that "Ritual means treading and practicing"), was picked up. Philologist Xu Shen of the Eastern Han dynasty copied this proposition as an interpretive explanation in his semantic study *Explication of Words and Characters* [*Shuo wen jie zi*], that "Ritual means treading and practicing."[6] As mentioned earlier, Xu explained *Li*'s purpose as serving gods and acquiring their blessing. Here Xu attached importance to the religious character of *Li*, but "treading and practicing" as a verb and action and bodily movement was used to explain what "ritual" must entail in the lifeworld. The emendation to *Li* that *Li* is tantamount to both *ti*, body, and *lü*, by another Eastern Han master of classical studies, Zheng Xuan (127–200), reflected the consensus of his time. A modern anthropological interpretation of Zheng Xuan's emendation emphasizes Zheng's reference to *Li*'s imagery as a complete, integral, and appropriate human body.[7]

Buddhism spread to China in the Western Han via the transportation route later known as the Silk Road. But it was first accepted by the Chinese as a sacrificial rite, and it relied on the budding religious Daoism for its propagation. Buddhist doctrines in China borrowed the nonaction philosophy of Daoism and acquiesced to the Daoist Yellow Emperor-Laozi belief, and contemporary people did not distinguish the two beliefs. Modern eminent specialist of Buddhist history Tang Yongtong (1893–1964) insisted that Buddhism in Han China was but "a kind of Daoist techniques."[8] Chinese Buddhism in later years accentuated universal Buddhist nature. On the one hand, it emphasized "emotion," *qing*, as a trait of human Buddhist nature not possessed by nonhumans, but, on the other hand, it advocated cutting off love and hatred, pain, and happiness to achieve the (Buddhist) principle, *li*.[9] The decline of Confucianism triggered the metaphysical interest in *xuanxue* among Wei-Jin scholars who opposed the rites and identified themselves with Daoism.[10] Chinese scholars had turned inward since the middle period of the Eastern Han, becoming more individualistic, less pragmatic, and less bound by the Confucian ritualism.[11] By the Sui-Tang dynasties, Buddhism had gained independence from religious Daoism, centering on its own organized monks and Chinese-language sutras.[12] The predominance of Buddhism set the stage for the attempt to revive Confucianism as a response to Buddhism, Daoism, and the overly scholastic tradition of Han Confucianism, and the overarching theme during this period was the relations between the human world and the cosmos and the moral relations among people themselves.

Under the third Tang emperor Gaozong, the central government organized the compilation of an *Annotated Tang Code* [*Tang Lü shu yi*] led by Prime Minister Zhangsun Wuji. Although rarely used as source material for the study of Confucianism, the book reflected the deep influence of Confucianism in its attempt to combine law and ritual and its philosophical discussion of human nature and human emotions. This legal codebook recognized that the seven human feelings—joy, anger, sorrow, fear, love, repulsion, and yearning—grow out of the human heart-mind, and thus they are *qing*. The code, however, distinguished the sages, equipped with upper-level intelligence, from the unenlightened lower class by their ability to control the emotions: the sages, after nourishing their nature, could let their feelings sprout, but the expressions all strike home, *zhongjie*, whereas the uneducated lower-class people, unable to follow their nature, let their emotions loose, and these emotions all "degenerated into (excessive) human desires."[13] According to Yuan dynasty scholar Ma Duanlin (1245–1322), the *Analects* and the *Mengzi* were emphasized as texts that grasped the sages' deep thinking and added to the subjects of the Civil Service Examination.[14] These two books later were chosen to be two of the *Four Books* by Zhu Xi. Yet it is notable that prior to the rise of Neo-Confucianism in the Song dynasty, there had been intellectual inquiries into different human abilities to control emotions and the relationship between normal emotions and excessive desires, and the lawmakers had entertained the alleged relevance between self-control and intelligence. There was also state promotion of certain ancient classics. In terms of material culture, Tang state ritual accepted tea as an offered drink and imperial gift.[15]

Mid-Tang poet and essayist Han Yu (768–824) made several contributions to the formal transition of classical Confucianism to Neo-Confucianism in his critical treatise *On the Origin of the Way*: 1. Despite Han dynasty scholars' inheritance of the legacy of Xunzi, Han Yu promoted Mencius; 2. He delineated a Confucian orthodox genealogy, the Way, from the Duke of Zhou to Confucius and then to Mencius, who had been famous for mysticism and intense interest in mind-heart and nature; and 3. With deep knowledge in Buddhism, Han Yu attacked Buddhism for distracting people from social responsibility. For our discussion in this study, Han Yu's discussion on nature and emotion was particularly salient although not strongly innovative compared with the polemics in the annotation of Tang Code. His real contribution was to enunciate that human nature and emotions are two contrasting concepts and to classify three kinds of nature. While nature has three hierarchical grades—good, neutral, and evil—it itself is inborn. However, the seven sentiments of joy, anger, sorrow, fear, love, repulsion, and yearning were but results of external arousal.[16]

Li Ao (772–841), a disciple of Han Yu, held a more negative view of human emotions than Han Yu. For him, emotion grows out of nature, which is what makes a sage a sage, but the seven emotions confuse and conceal people's intrinsic stable nature.[17] Feng Youlan believes that Li Ao identified the Buddhist teaching about the "original mind-heart," *benxin*, with "nature" and that thought emotions were but annoyances.[18] While Han Yu was also a poet, Li Ao dismissed poetry as so overladen with emotion as to hinder the work of nature. He wrote *Book on Restoring Nature* and brought scholars' interest to the more philosophical *Zhongyong* chapter in the *Book of Rites for its concern with the "Way of nature and fate."* For Li Ao, the relationship between nature and emotion is more than internal versus manifestation of external stimulations; it is also emanating and hierarchically reciprocal, for emotion is an outgrowth of nature and subject to the latter.[19] To be sure, the relationship between nature and emotion cannot be said to be new in Chinese thinking. In Eastern Han scholar Xu Shen's *Explication of Words*, he had already put these two characters together and said that nature is *yang* and emotions are *yin* and that emotions are pertinent to desire, *yu*.[20]

THE CHENG BROTHERS AND THE REINVENTION
OF *LI* AS RATIONAL PRINCIPLE

Confucianism followed its own internal logic of development. As Qian Mu points out, "Confucius did not talk about nature and the Heavenly Way, only Zhuangzi and Laozi later talked about the Heavenly Way, and Mencius and Xunzi began to talk about nature."[21] Natural dispositions, *xing*, and rational principle, *li*, loomed large in Song dynasty discussions on Confucian philosophy. The rekindling of the interest in rational principle can be traced back to the Northern Song (960–1127) scholars Shao Yong (1012–1077), Zhou Dunyi (1017–1073), and Zhang Zai (1020–1077). Shao Yong argues that, epistemologically, "perceiving things with things is what is called nature; perceiving things with my senses is what is called emotion. Nature is impartial and illuminating, and emotion is partial and darkening."[22]

Famous for "*qi*-monism," Zhang Zai recognizes that although *qi*, materialistic "matter" or " an organic pluralism,"[23] is to change, degenerate, integrate and disintegrate constantly, principle, *li*, has an order and is unerring as the foundation of *qi*.[24] Influenced by the cosmology in the *Classic of Changes*, Zhang Zai formulated his Heaven-*qian*-male versus Earth-*kun*-female dichotomy involving these six categories and thus elevated human moral ethics to the ground of ontology. Zhang Zai's reification of cosmology into the imageries of the father, mother, and monarch was completed in his famous treatise "Western Inscriptions," *Ximing*, by sacralizing the lineage law, *zongfa*, which looks "anti-democratic" for modern scholars.[25] Following Zhang Zai's logic, the religious emotion toward Heaven and Earth, which is not based on the senses, and the personal feeling of loving parents are identical, and people need to both moralize the cosmology and philosophize filial piety. The ritual theory of Zhang Zai traced rituals to their three origins: Heaven/Great Vacuity [*tian/taixu*], rational principle (Zhang asserted that "rituals come after rational principle" [*Li chuyu li zhihou*] and that "rituals can be created after rational principle is grasped" [*zhi li ze neng zhi Li*], and the human heart-mind and human emotions from the inside.[26]

It was the Cheng brothers, Cheng Hao (1032–1085) and Cheng Yi (1033–1107) of the Southern Song (1127–1279), who accentuated the metaphysical status of rational principle based on the supremacy of Heaven. The Cheng brothers reinvented the concept *li*, while in the received pre-Qin texts, the character was not found in the *Analects* or in the Daoist *Daodejing*.[27] However, there was also philosophical use of *li* as a secular rational principle, and in the interpretation of the *Book of Changes* Zhu Xi explains one of the book's values as being able to examine the principle, *li*, of the earth, and the term "principle of the earth," *dili*, is still the modern Chinese word for "geography." In the *Mengzi*, Mencius used it to mean the "standard of moral conduct." Xunzi connected "human nature" with the "principle of things."[28] For Warring State political thinker Han Feizi, "[t]he principle is the order of existence for each particular thing."[29] What is consistent here is that *li* means pattern, standard, and principle, and it is abstract and normative. But it was not until the Song dynasty that the term was picked up and given transcendental, metaphysical meaning as a concept independent from the material world, represented by the word *qi*, which means the gaseous substances, the flow of energy, matter, or any concrete existences compared with *li*.[30]

The Cheng brothers then created an ontological concept in the composite word *tianli*, Heavenly principle. For the brothers, the Heavenly principle entails a uniform and omnipotent natural tendency beyond human intervention. It is an eternal, unchangeable, and irrevocable being and cosmological law, which could be neither added nor reduced.[31] Semantically, Cheng Hao, the inventor of the terminology *tianli*, the Heavenly principle, used the familiar structure *zhe . . . ye* in a nominal sentence in classical Chinese to interpret the obscure term Heaven as *li*, meaning, Heaven means rational principle, literally.[32] The sentence structure and semantic meaning in this phrase is identical with *Li zhe lü ye*, "Ritual means treading and practicing," discussed in chapter 2. The *li* theory of the Song dynasty envisaged a structured and unified world in which unity was represented by the concept of *li*.[33] We have perhaps seen certain rigid, inflexible, and authoritarian traits in this imagination of *li*. Indeed, in the many centuries to come, this cosmological rational principle, after being entrenched in the Chinese social and family institutions as the absolute metaphysical-ethical order, became more oppressive than *Li*, ritual propriety.

Yet in the Song Dynasty's theoretical formulation, the concept "heart-mind," *xin*, was emphasized as an agent that commands [*tong*] the natural dispositions, *xing*, and the emotions, *qing*.[34] Again, natural dispositions were considered as a more stable essential principle of the heart-mind, while emotions (passions) are "the movement of the nature."[35] Eastern Han Dynasty Confucian scholars had confirmed that after a human being was born with both the *yin* and the *yang* vital energies, "five natural dispositions and six emotions" [*wu xing liu qing*] coexisted within him when he was born.[36] However, this proposition seems to contradict the notion in the Warring States bamboo slips that affective emotions grow out of natural dispositions as we discussed in chapter 2. It is likely that between the originating process from *xing* to *qing* and the notion of their inherent, synchronic coexistence lies a conundrum that ancient scholars did not address adequately.

The brothers' interest in the heart-mind's movement is a salient point. For them, the heart-mind has two conditions: when it is in motion or when it is motionless, however, the priority is given to the motionless psychological condition because only in this tranquil state can a human heart-mind achieve "interpenetration after resonance," *gan er sui tong*, all principles and all affairs in the world.[37] This seems to be a "psychological turn" of Confucian philosophers. For Cheng Yi, the sages in history had emotions too, but their emotions rise and decline with the concrete thing and will not linger.[38] When the emotions of "pleasure, anger, sorrow, and joy" are aroused, Cheng Yi reasons, the idealized sagely "tranquility," *zhong*, or "the state of absolute quiet," would certainly be disturbed.[39] Thus, ordinary Confucian students should pursue self-control and unperturbed quietism. Cheng Hao discussed the concrete negative feeling of "anger" and how it could be controlled by using rational judgment: "Among human emotions the easiest to arouse but the most difficult to control is anger. But if in time of anger one can immediately forget his anger and look at the right and wrong of the matter according to principle, he will see that external temptations need not be hated, and he has gone more than halfway toward the Way."[40] As staunch Confucians, the Cheng brothers refuted the Buddhist assumption that it is necessary to abolish the emotions and "all perception of external things."[41] In another scenario, they emphasized the importance of not transferring one's anger, which Confucius emphasized in the *Analects*: "A person who has sufficient control of himself to be angry with one man and not with others already has an exceptional awareness of moral principle."[42]

The Chinese *li*, although containing the connotation of reason and rationality, is not identical to rationality's meaning in the modern West. When commenting on Zhou Dunyi's writing, Zhu Xi added an attribute to *li* to make it clearer: "the rational principle of Heaven, Earth, and a myriad of things" [*tiandi wanwu zhi li*].[43] If we adopt the definition of Nicholas Rescher that "Rationality consists in the appropriate use of reason to resolve choices in the best possible way. To behave rationally is to make use of one's intelligence to figure out the best thing to do in the circumstances,"[44] then the rational principle for Zhu Xi was primarily *a prior* cosmological-moral principle rather than only a way to deal with daily affairs, particularly those concerning how to maximize one's benefits optimally. In other words, the narrow definition of rationality as "goal-efficient action" does not fit the Chinese *li*, but its less technical concern with the general "human flourishing" does.[45]

There are also aspects that render the Chinese *li* comparable if not identical to the Western notion of rationality. First, the Chinese *li* does have its practical, problem-solving aspect, and the Cheng brothers and Zhu Xi were often consulted about the best solution of mundane problems. Usually balancing human feelings, ritual propriety, and common sense, the answers they provided were rational even from today's point of view. Second, the Western concept that feelings are "generally not a matter of reasoning, but certainly not outside the province of reason"[46] shows a similar interest in the tension between rationality and emotion, as with Chinese thinkers, and the conclusion that rationality has such as broad domain to include the emotions is also close to the Chinese understanding of the relationship. Third, the Western notion that rationality must be autonomous and systematically self-sufficient is also similar to the song Chinese philosophers' emphasis on the supreme status of *li*, which subjugates more fluid *qi* and much more volatile sentiments and moods.[47] Fourth, Nicholas Rescher's argument about universal, uniform rationality with variations contingent on time and space corresponds to Zhu Xi's assumption about the uniformity of overarching *li* and its circumstantial and various application in concrete situations. For Zhu Xi, as for Zhang Zai, *li* is *a prior* force and the metaphysical foundation of the cosmos and the human world, and it is both naturalistic and ethical: "Before heaven and earth existed, there was after all only principle. As there is this principle, therefore there are heaven and earth" and "Principle itself has neither physical form nor body," Zhu Xi asserts.[48] But Zhu Xi also believes *li* has multifarious configurations in concrete situations, which Zhu Xi conceptualizes as *li yi fen shu*: "The principle is one, but the manifestations are always many."[49] Rescher refutes anthropologists' relativist argument about the diversity of rationality but insists that rationality itself is a uniform conception and that the tribal people studied by anthropologists did not have essentially distinct rationality of their own.[50] It is arguable that with the theorization of the uniform rational principle, *li*, Neo-Confucianism in the Song Dynasty constructed a cosmological, metaphysical foundation for Confucianism.[51]

ZHU XI'S DISCOURSE ON RITUAL, RATIONAL PRINCIPLE, AND EMOTION

Song Confucian philosophers' metaphysical thoughts were synthesized by Zhu Xi, who was known as the master of the intellectual School of Rational Principle, *lixue*. Zhu Xi's contribution was his comprehensive intellectual interests and a wide range of concepts on which he elaborated, including rational principle, *li*; Great Ultimate, *taiji*; the flow of energy/material force, *qi*; humanity, *ren*; righteousness, *yi*; equilibrium, *zhong*; and harmony, *he*.[52] Zhou Dunyi's reinvention of the concept "*taiji*" enabled Zhu Xi to link *qi* with *li*.[53] The current study will not elaborate on all these concepts but will focus only on how Zhu Xi perceived *li* and *qing* and will pay attention to how Zhu Xi promoted ritual practice at the lineage and communal levels.

The Confucian concept Heaven, *tian*, as used by Confucius, was annotated by Zhu Xi as the rational principle. The phrasing of Zhu Xi was *tian ji li*: Heaven is the principle, literally. The equivalence between *tian* and *li* was not new because the Cheng brothers had advanced the theory of *"tian zhe li ye,"* literally, Heaven is tantamount to/all about the principle, or Heaven has its norm and rules. But Zhu Xi's syntactical structure was more straightforward by using the word *ji*, "is." From the point of view of hermeneutics, Zhu Xi's annotation was a more personal interpretation than an explanation because "principle" was not a prevalent terminology of Confucius's time but a concept that Zhu Xi himself was promoting. To berate Zhu Xi for this distortion was fair enough in the Qing dynasty, but from a philosophical point of view, Zhu Xi deserved his credit for the creative interpretation.[54] However, the proposition "Heaven is principle" does not mean Zhu Xi accepts Cheng Hao's emphasis on his own terminology "Heavenly principle." Zhu Xi cautions that the concept "Heavenly principle" is too intangible to become a guide of doing the concrete things in front of one's eyes. Rational principle, for Zhu, can be sought only by heart-mind and through attending to daily affairs.[55] In daily life, Zhu Xi argues that the restoration of the rites, *Li*, would put people back into the substantial framework of rules and norms.[56] He points out that ceremonial rites also control and restrain people and make them more respectful and civilized, so that music is needed to give expression to human nature.[57]

Concerned about effective pedagogy, Zhu Xi saw the rites as instrumental to achieve the goal of moral self-cultivation, but the concept "Heavenly principle," which was fine with Zhu Xi himself, was too vague for young students to grasp. By connecting *Li* and *li*, Zhu Xi suggests that the highest principle, *li*, can be naturally approached by using one's heart-mind, *xin*, in the handling of daily affairs and through honoring ritual propriety, *Li*. Zhu Xi himself believed that the all-encompassing Heavenly principle in fact contains human desires that grow out of Heavenly principle.[58] At the same time, Zhu Xi established another equivalence between heart-mind, *xin*, and rational principle, *li*: "For me heart-mind and rational principle are one and the same [*wu yi xin yuli wei yi*]."[59]

The expression and regulation of emotion to make it more rational had become an implicit theme in the Song Neo-Confucianist's psychological turn. For Zhu Xi, human emotions are subject to this Heaven/principle/ heart-mind abstraction because he inherited the Cheng brothers' theory of "heart-mind commands nature and emotion" and affirmed this as a great theoretical breakthrough since the time of Mencius.[60] Between nature and emotion, the former was considered by Zhu Xi as the "unmanifested" "innate essence," while the latter the manifested, visible external expressions.[61] Another metaphysical focus was on the distinction between the emotions' dormant condition and their arousal, a thesis in the *Zhongyong* chapter of the *Book of Rites*. The pre-arousal, tranquil, and unbiased condition was named equilibrium, *zhong*. The arousal and expression of emotions for Zhu Xi was not entirely negative as long as they "strike home," *zhongjie*, and do not deviate, and this appropriate expression of emotions was named "harmony," *he*.[62] Wing-Tsit Chan focuses on the positive attitude toward emotion in Zhu Xi's thought. He points out that for Zhu Xi, the "principle of love," *ren*, which is regarded by Zhu as substance, is already preserved in the mind before feelings are perturbed.[63] By invoking the theory "*ren* is the principle of love,"[64] Zhu Xi also admitted that women are superior to men in terms of love, although women are inferior in terms of capability.[65] When replying to an inquiry, Zhu Xi aptly separated love, *ai*, from desire, *yu,* by saying the former means a general affection toward a thing but the latter entails grasp and acquisition.[66] In his annotation of the *Book of Odes*, as Zhang Longxi notes, Zhu Xi tempered the Han dynasty classicists' overly politicized and moralized interpretation that regarded many love songs included in the *Book of Odes* as political allegories, arguing honestly that these were true love songs that simply articulated human "emotions and natural dispositions when they were moved by things."[67]

There was an important dimension of Zhu Xi as a person in the lifeworld. Zhu Xi recognizes that sublime human affections and moral feelings such as respect and filial piety to parents are inherent in the human heart-mind despite the existence of some negative moods. In actual life, Zhu Xi himself was very human, and he could smile and could also get angry.[68] When asked by an interlocutor, Zhu Xi was quoted as saying, "Loving good and hating evil is human nature. It's part of human nature to love good and hate evil; to love or to hate without basis is partiality."[69] For Zhu Xi, the expression of emotion is natural as long as it is well grounded and kept within limits, but emotion without a rational basis might have a negative impact on one's cognition. Overall, however, Zhu Xi's demeanor was grave and movements were respectful; he began the day by worshipping ancestors and paid attention to the details of ritual observances.[70]

Zhu Xi made another significant contribution to Confucianism through his project of group annotation and the establishment of the *Four Books*, the *Analects*, the *Mengzi*, and the *Daxue* ("Great Learning") and *Zhongyong* ("Doctrine of the Mean"), the last two being chapters taken out of the *Book of Rites* to replace the Five Classics. The tradition of Chinese classical studies based on the state-sanctioned Confucian canons in the Western Han had lasted for more than one thousand years by the time of Zhu Xi, and the original Six Classics had also been reduced and modified to the Five Classics: the *Book of Changes*, the *Book of Odes*, the *Book of History*, the *Book of Rites*, and *Spring and Autumn Annals* [*chunqiu*], the last one being an alleged history of the Lu State written by Confucius in a succinct and esoteric way. Daniel K. Gardener is correct in questioning Zhu Xi's selection and reorganization of the old classics as reflective and schematic. By choosing only two chapters from among multiple chapters of the *Book of Rites*, Zhu Xi showed his visible "philosophical approach" because he determined that these two chapters were better explanations of the cosmos and the self-imposed sense of mission of the scholars, while the "Great Learning" chapter had received little attention prior to the ninth century until Li Ao paid attention to its value.[71] In the process of textual rearranging and annotating, Zhu Xi, inspired by the Tang-Song new tradition of focusing on metaphysics and moral ethics, chose not to include other chapters in the *Book of Rites* that focus more on the technical details of the rites and ceremonies.

Zhu Xi's canonization of the *Analects*, the conversational and anecdotal text that was not part of either Five or Six Classics, was indeed meaningful, although he advances his argument by creatively annotating the classics. Based on Zhu Xi's annotation of the *Analects* as analyzed by Daniel Gardener, I believe Zhu Xi successfully reconciled ritual, emotion, and rational principle, the three essential components in the Confucian conceptual triad. According to my reading of both Zhu Xi and Gardener's study of Zhu Xi's annotation of the *Analects* and *Mengzi*, Zhu Xi presented four essential upshots regarding this interdependent and reciprocal relationship.

First, to practice Confucian ritual propriety distinguishes a Confucian from a Buddhist who allegedly "plunge[s] into emptiness."[72] By asserting one's membership in the clan, ritual action is instrumental in Confucian scholars' battle against the prevalence of Buddhism in Tang-Song China.

Second, the ritual has its indispensable intrinsic value because it is an "external expression of the principle within him."[73] Hence, ritualism is more than a weapon used in partisan struggles; it is a necessary manifestation of the rational principle. Here we can recall Confucian students Youzi's and Ziyou's debate about why external mediums are needed, as discussed in chapter 3.

Third, the supreme rational principle, *li*, for Zhu Xi is higher than both ritual, *Li*, and music, *yue*, ontologically, and "ritual and music are governed by principle."[74] This fulcrum is, of course, consistent with Zhu Xi's vantage point as a master of the School of Principle. Zhu Xi also defines the rational principle inside the human heart-mind as nature.[75] He asserts, "*Xing* is *li*. When it lies in human heart-mind, it is called *xing*, and when it lies in things it is called *li*," and "*xing* is but the generic name of all rational principles."[76] According to the *xin tong xing qing* schema, the human heart-mind commands natural disposition (as the inner mental manifestation of rational principle) and emotion, and hence *Li-li* and *qing* are now coexisting within the human heart-mind.

Fourth, performing a ritual cannot be reduced to mere formality. It is a substantial process of self-cultivation to achieve true goodness and must be imbued with an inner spirit, which is the "feeling of reverence and the feeling of harmony."[77] Here, Zhu Xi connects positive emotions with ritual and regards emotion as the spiritual fundamentals of ritual performance. It should be pointed out here that "reverence" and "harmony" are two sublime inner moral experiences, and this type of emotion is not the same as moods such as anger or pleasure. Wing-Tsi Chan notes that, for Zhu, ritual propriety is congruent with human moral affections because "propriety is basically the principle of culture. As it is activated, it becomes deference and respect."[78] Also, these sublime feelings differ from passions, a term used more often in Western philosophical writing. In case there was a conflict between ritual and feeling in actual life, then, as with Confucius and Mencius, Zhu Xi would prioritize the actual feeling over ritual.[79]

Fifth, in his annotation of the *Mengzi*, Zhu Xi tackled the relationship between humans and animals when pondering the famous story about King Xuan of Qi pardoning the sacrificial ox. "The sound (of the animal) means whining when facing death," Zhu Xi commented, "With regard to the relationship between humans and birds-beasts, they are all creatures yet belong to different species. That's why humans consume them but treat them with ritual, and the mind-heart of compassion reaches out to wherever he sees and hears."[80] Here Zhu Xi affirmed the connection between human perceptions and their feelings, and, more significantly, he emphasized that people must treat animals with a ritual that reflects the animal's position as a creature in the world that deserves respect and sympathy from humans.

The ideal situation is, of course, the congruent combination of ritual and emotion, but in a special occasion when the ritual has to fail, one must use discretion to consider the concrete situation-emotion. I believe the expedient choice here is rational because it fits the principle of the highest goodness. Hoyt Cleveland Tillman's study of Zhu Xi also testifies to this point, "To Chu (Zhu in old pinyin spelling), the emphasis was on the warm and gentle feelings of commiseration with which people were endowed so they could love and benefit others."[81] In the theoretical framework of "heart-mind commands nature and emotion," Song Confucian philosophers' emphasis on the cognitive and emotional faculty of heart-mind already made the recognition of human feelings inevitable. When annotating the *Analects*, Zhu Xi encounters the story about how the father and the son refused to report on each other when either side committed misconduct, and his conclusion is that the free moral choice in mutual cover-up symbolizes the simultaneous culmination of "Heavenly principle" and "human emotion."[82]

Zhu Xi's Promotion of "Family Rituals"

Zhu Xi's metaphysics has been studied by many scholars. For my purpose in this book, I want to draw more attention to how his philosophical thinking was reflected in practice and how he restored and adapted ancient rites to facilitate proper moral relations at the family and communal levels. Zheng Zhenman, a contemporary Chinese scholar of historical anthropology focusing on Fujian province, points out that in this region, ancestral sacrificed arose as a new custom that challenged the old system as early as the Northern Song so much so that Emperor Huizong had to respond to it and he finally lifted the old limit on it.[83] After the Song, people in Fujian, Zhu Xi's native region, had developed three main sacrificial spaces: home, lineage-based ancestral offering hall, and grave site.[84] The state played a leading role in explaining and reforming the ritual system. For instance, three official historical records prior to the Song dynasty listed the "Five Rituals" allegedly belonging to the Western Zhou, but they all had different orders. According to the *Records of the Song* [Songzhi] compiled in the Yuan dynasty, the Song government reordered the five rituals as auspicious rites, *jili*; social rites, *jiali*; guest rites, *binli*; military rites, *junli*; and inauspicious rites, *xiongli*, by moving social rites ahead of guest and military rites.

Song emperors also reformed the state ritual system by giving the royal sacrificial "Hall of Illumination" (allegedly a Western Zhou legacy, as we discussed in chapter 1) higher status in both political life and textual recording.[85] This background is crucial for understanding the ritualist thought of Song dynasty thinkers. It was a typical phenomenon in ancient China that commoners' social practice prompted the adjustment of state policy, triggering more widespread practices, and, finally, the theoretical justification of philosophers who are involved in policymaking and secular and communal affairs resonated with the practice and the state policy.

In order for the entire society to fulfill the relational obligations, Neo-Confucian philosophers felt the imperative to spread this elite and scholarly practice down to commoners with large lineage groups.[86] As I mentioned in earlier chapters, sacrifice to the ancestors in the Zhou Dynasty was a royal and aristocratic activity, but in Song China, the rise of clans and lineage groups and Neo-Confucian cultural elites' conscious effort to construct the family and lineage as a ritual/moral entity also facilitated this major transition in Chinese history.[87] Also a promoter of Confucian ritualism, Cheng Yi suggested common people performing ancestral sacrifices based on righteousness, but for a while, even Zhu Xi thought it was a transgression. After his deliberation during the Southern Song, Zhu Xi made a concession by instructing that sacrificial land should meet the expenses of the offering hall, and he approved of offerings to founding and distant ancestors at the grave site, although Zhu still thought that too-distant ancestors should be excluded from the sacrifices in the offering hall. In an actual ancestral offering hall, the regulations stipulated that the offspring worship only up to four generations of ancestors.[88] In the orthodox Confucian understanding, the human soul is attached to the spiritual tablet placed in the ancestral hall after a man dies, and tombs are for burying the corpse only and thus irrelevant to sacrifice. Zhu Xi made a concession by endorsing sacrificial performance at the graveyard as an unauthorized popular practice because he believed it reflected the natural secular feeling of people despite its violation of ancient rites.[89] It is notable, however, that popular practice had long preceded the intellectual debate. As early as 1152 of the Northern Song, as source material shows, people already performed sacrifice at the ancestral graveyard by bringing "money, wine, and duck and geese."[90]

Cheng Yi gave emphasis to the significance of lineage sacrificial ceremonies in cultivating relationships and fostering clan solidarity. For one thing, sacrifices epitomize the affective bond between a man and his ancestors because a man needs to know his origin, and for the other, ritual actions were interpersonal, and the gathering itself, like a festival of reunion, allows "the feeling of blood relationship circulate[s]" among "kinsmen" as a collective through participation.[91] Here we may consider again the Chinese word *qingjing*, emotion-situation, in light of the modern sociological theory about "interaction ritual," which puts emphasis on "the situation . . . as a process by which shared emotions and intersubjective focus sweep individuals along by flooding their consciousness."[92]

Besides the codification of the state and the polemics of the elite thinkers such as the Cheng brothers and Zhu Xi, another force that shaped the liturgical practice at the grassroots level was religious Daoism. As early as the Han Dynasty, religious Daoism adopted a rite of passage that was very similar to a Confucian capping ceremony by requiring a qualifying ceremony when the Daoist monk reaches age twenty.[93] At the village level, popular cults and Daoist liturgy deeply influenced local life in southeastern China. Since the Tang dynasty, Daoist liturgists had been involved in local lineage members' rites of coming-of-age, marriage, and cult worship, and Daoism provided the liturgical framework to expand local cults. Together with the rise of Neo-Confucian cosmology and metaphysics, the Song dynasty also saw an outburst of Daoist revelation.[94]

Daoism did not overshadow Confucianism or supplant it at the communal level, but I want to underscore two things: first, Zhu Xi was born into a region where Daoist ritual and popular cults were prevalent and there might be a certain correlation between them; second, Confucianism itself as a higher-level ruling ideology accommodated Daoist practices at a local level, and the two did not conflict with each other. Daoist liturgists provided medical, geomantic, funeral, and other services to all Song dynasty local community members regardless of intellectual self-identity, as I experienced in 2012. Even Zhu Xi himself was deified by Daoist liturgy posthumously.[95]

The combination of folk customs with Buddhism since the Tang dynasty contributed to the extensive use and burning of "paper money" for the souls of the dead to use in the netherworld, and by the early Song dynasty, the paper-burning custom developed by the common people had been widespread in China. As Confucian scholars, Zhu Xi and his followers expressed "mixed feelings" toward the use of paper money, and he did not mention paper money in his *Family Rituals*.[96] However, just like how Confucianism appropriated the pre-Confucian rites and philosophized them, as I discussed in chapters 1 and 2, Confucianism eventually came to terms with the custom of burning mock money for the use of the spirits in the netherworld as not only an innocuous way of communicating with the dead but also filial children's attempt to satisfy the imagined sentient needs of the late parents and grandparents.

In this sociopolitical milieu where philosophers were not detached from politics and the lifeworld, Zhu Xi's attitude toward ritual was both polemical and practical. On the theoretical level, he legitimized ritual as subject to principle as an indispensable outward expression of emotion, while emotion itself must not be liquidated; on the practical level, Zhu Xi's political thought agreed with Confucius that ritual in political life should first limit the ruler's authority and the ruler is expected to treat his ministers with ritual because they collaborate with each other only based on reciprocal justice.[97] This fair treatment rested on the assumption that ritual means order, *xu*, and Zhu Xi went so far as to say that even bandits had their ritual to manage their internal relations.[98] Also on the practical level was Zhu Xi's concern about ritual details for the commoners to follow. With regard to death ritual, Zhu recognized that the common practice was to keep three days' fasting before eating rice porridge, and only after the burial is completed can the mourner eat sparingly. Zhu thought that this is a general rule that has applied to all people regardless of their social class.[99] When commenting on Mengzi's speech, Zhu also admitted that a great man such as Mengzi treated ritual in a flexible and case-by-case way as long as he follows principle.[100]

My textual analysis aims at revisiting the ritual practice envisioned by Zhu Xi through the lens of practice theory. Zhu Xi showed a detached, scholarly attitude toward ritual as reflected in *Zhu zi yu lei* [Classified Conversations of Zhu Xi], where he told the dialogue partners ancient rites had been lost, and what his contemporaries could do was nothing but forcing to create some rules. He also believed that rituals had been distorted by later generations compared with pre-Qin ancients.[101] Therefore, Zhu Xi knew fully that Confucians of his time were trying to "restore [the lost] rites," *fu-Li*, with the goal of teaching the rules and etiquette to learners more easily, because *li* is formless and intangible, *wu xing wu ying*.[102] He also emphasized the value of the more plain and technical *Yi-Li* version of the *Book of Rites*, just because it was a full account of things without interpretation. More important, Zhu

Xi realizes that *Yi-Li*, which for him was not a "book" written with a plan but were practices endorsed and written down by the sages, and those ritual actions were mostly "scholarly rites," *shì-Li*.[103] As for the use of an impersonator in sacrifices, Zhu Xi approved the view of Tang Confucian scholar Du You (735–812) that it was an archaic and barbaric custom that was not changed by the sages, but he said that modern "muddle-headed Confucians," *yuru*, were trying to restore an impersonator because they were foolish.[104]

Family rituals in ancient China included four rites of passages: initiations, weddings, funerals, and service to ancestral spirits. These Confucian rites as a cluster made up the cult of the ancestors and family. For Zhu, "When a man is about to die, the warm material leaves him and rises. This is called the *hun* rising. The lower part of his body gradually becomes cold. This is called the *p'o* falling."[105] A living person for Zhu is the concentration of vital energy, *qi*, and when *qi* dissipates after one's death, the person becomes a numinous being, *gui*, and thus ghosts and spirits, *guishen*, are nothing but a manifestation of *qi*.[106] It is this lingering *qi*, material force, or vital energy, that connects the ancestors and descendants at the sacrificial rites that require the true feelings of being honest and respectful from the worshippers to build the spiritual link.[107] In Zhu Xi's time, "home sacrifice," *jiaji*, had already been dedicated to the dead parents. The Southern Song poet Lu You (1125–1210), five years Zhu's senior, wrote a poem in which he wanted his children not to forget to report to his spirit in the future "home sacrifice," when the Southern Song might recover its lost territories in the north. A modern survey of the twentieth century shows that the private "home sacrifice" to a domestic altar is part and the culmination of the funeral itself rather than a future commemorative service, and in it a eulogy would be delivered.[108] Through the utterance of ritual words, home sacrifice was turned into a form of domestic cult that provided an opportunity of direct communication and expressing intense feelings between the living and the dead in a private, intimate, and emotional space. Zhu Xi compiled the accessible liturgical manual to instruct people about the correct way of conducting the rites in this domestic space.[109] According to Zhu Xi, the "offering hall," with a table-altar and four tablets, was a place within a home to perform the sacrifice, which was expected to be "set up [by a man of virtue] to the east of the main room of his house," and four generations of ancestors would be worshipped there, from great-great-grandfather down to the father.[110]

Zhu Xi accentuated his pedagogical agenda, focusing on how to more effectively communicate the ideas to the students and common, nonscholarly folks, and thus he clearly states his goal as laying down the "basis for rectifying personal relationship and principles and deepening kindness and love."[111] The book itself was written as a "manual for local magistrates to educate the people in their charge."[112] As with Xunzi, Zhu Xi can also be regarded as a self-reflective ancient social scientist who is aware of his own agenda and its artificiality and has engaged in textual criticism of the received ritual classics.

Focusing on *how* the ritual act should be performed, the manual defines the status-specific role of the participants in ancestral sacrifice held in an ancestral offering hall, when the appropriate descent-line heir and his wife act as presiding man and presiding woman but the presiding man's mother does not take part in the sacrifice.[113] The manual legitimizes the authority of parents in daily life: "Whenever parents make a mistake, the son must offer advice in a calm, pleasant, soft voice. Should the parents not take the advice, the son must be more respectful to them." The son also needs to manage his facial expression: "When a parent is ill, the son should look upset; he should neither amuse himself nor go to parties."[114] Through the rites of passages, children are taught about "the distinction of etiquette based on age and generation" and learn "modesty and yielding."[115]

Ritual actions are gendered. "Any young men from fifteen to twenty years of age may be capped, provided his parents are not in mourning for a period of a year or longer," the *Family Rituals* advises, but girls are pinned when they get engaged.[116] The capping ceremony of a young man should be presided over by his father or grandfather, the "presiding man," when either of them is the decent-line heir of the great-great-grandfather.[117] In the weddings section, a bride is required to serve parents-in-law food and wine, and she should eat what the mother-in-law left.[118] There is a hierarchical classification of mourning garments, depending on the relationship of the mourner with the dead and the mourner's gender and status in the clan: standard mourning supplemental mourning, reduced mourning, and duty mourning.[119]

The *Family Rituals* manual is consistent with Zhu Xi's notions of balancing ritualism, emotion, and rationality. When receiving information of the death of a parent and hurrying to the funeral, one should, as Zhu Xi suggests, first "[r]espond to the messenger by wailing, and then change clothes, and travel at a pace of one hundred *li* per day but avoid traveling at night." The advice here is "Although one is in sorrow, still act it prudently."[120] Here Zhu Xi suggests that following ritual code (*Li*) while controlling sorrow (*qing*) with volition means rationality, *li*. Concrete situation-emotion should be prioritized to avoid posing ritual dilemma. For instance, although three days was made the norm of death ritual, Zhu Xi allows unprepared poor people to extend the regular period.[121] As for the sacrificial objects, Zhu Xi listed incense, tea, wine, and food as gifts to the ancestors.[122] He accommodates non-Confucian popular cult: "Worship the god of earth to the left of the grave" to allow an emotional vent for the people.[123]

Practice theory applies to the study of ritual actions devised by Zhu Xi because it makes it possible to "focus more directly on what people do and how they do it" and "explore[s] how ritual is a vehicle for the construction of relationship of authority and submission."[124] Modern anthropology has understood sacrifice as "establishing or managing particular forms of (social) relations between humans and immaterial beings (gods, spirits, ancestors, ghosts)."[125] Then our question here should be how Zhu Xi wanted people to build this relationship and by doing what.

As an operating manual, Zhu Xi's *Family Rituals* exerted great influence on local culture through regularizing the ritual practice at the communal level and fleshing out the recognition of the power relations embedded in the ritual process. In Korea, Kim Jangsaeng (1548–1631), a Neo-Confucian philosopher born in the mid-sixteenth century, argued that Koreans could adopt and implement Zhu Xi's *Family Rituals* after adapting them to Korea's national customs by using discretional judgment. The concrete forms of Zhu's *Rituals* were changeable, but its spirit was not, Kim asserted.[126] As late as the 1990s, the extent of the reach of Zhu Xi's *Family Rituals* could still be felt in rural Fujian's lineage-based ancestral sacrifice method.[127] In the spring and summer, Zhu Xi would wear the ancient-style one-piece long linen robe named *shenyi*, which was recorded in the *Yi-Li*, and allegedly prevalent from the Warring States period to the Han dynasty. And he wrote a treatise on the material and measurement of this atavistic "deep garment," as literally translated.[128] Here the *shenyi* clothing was invoked as a symbolic artifact that carries on the cultural memory of orthodox Confucianism, although the accurate design of the *shenyi* had faded into oblivion in the Tang dynasty.[129] Zhu Xi's followers mimicked him in wearing the *shenyi* before they led their pupils to enter the Confucian learning hall to pay tribute to the image of Confucius.[130]

By examining the *Family Rituals* in the historical and social contexts, we find that what Zhu Xi engaged in was more than metaphysical contemplation; it was a combination of metaphysical conceptualization and proactive social practice. The reinvention and adjusted application of the ancient rituals in his time and space were regarded as an effective way to improve society. The practical character of Song Neo-Confucianism surpassed the Han Dynasty's scholastic glossing and emendation tradition and would continue to influence the Ming and Qing dynasties.

Contemporary Confucian scholar Shu-hsien Liu classified the configuration of Confucianism in the textual tradition and in the lifeworld into three strains: "Spiritual Confucianism," "Political Confucianism," and "Popular Confucianism." This threefold division reflects the multifaceted image of Confucianism and explains its internal contradictions. The first layer is the most metaphysical dimension, the second is political philosophy, and the third "emphasizes concepts such as family values, diligence, and education, and can hardly be separated from other beliefs in popular Buddhism and Taoism (Daoism), including, for example, various kinds of superstitions."[131] Liu points out elsewhere that the values and practices of popular Confucianism were formed following the Han dynasty.[132] After Zhu Xi declined to serve as an official ideological adviser, he assumed the image as an independent scholar-teacher and a man of great probity, and he stuck with his own missions of metaphysical contemplation, instructing, and coming to terms with as well as guiding and elevating community-based "popular Confucianism."

Modern philosopher Li Zehou is insightful in asserting that Zhu Xi's effort to elevate Confucianism to the level of a "transcendental, or *a prior*, rational ontology" was a failure because Zhu's "rational principle," "heart-mind," and "nature" can never be detached from empirical and concrete "emotion," "vital energy," and "desire."[133] Zhu Xi's downward popularization of the rites at the grassroots level of the commoners was another success. Anthropologist Wang Mingming asserts that Song thinkers' ideological justification and the state's promotion were the two prerequisites for the prevalent entrenchment of the lineage system.[134] Nevertheless, this rational design dominated social life. In the Song dynasty, the prevalent emotional needs and aspiration to see and to communicate with the dead family members were fulfilled by another set of ritual in which spirit-mediums summoned the dead, but the living families might have conflicting emotions like pain or fear when the rituals brought the dead back.[135]

CONCLUSION

In medieval China, Confucians continued to unravel the relation among ritual, emotion, and rational principle. Ritualism was entrenched through the establishment and spread of Zhu Xi's *Family Rituals*, which as a practical manual provided minute instructions about how to fulfill ritual obligations. Confucian philosophers Zhu Xi and the Cheng brothers engaged in the discussions on the proper sacrificial sites and helped the spread of sacrificial rituals at the village level. With the establishment of the lineage system as a stronghold of Confucian ritualism and emotional bonds, which was advocated by Song dynasty Confucians, Confucianism made inroads into the lifeworld of the villages. At this level, Confucian rituals coexisted with the popular practice of invoking the dead by spirit-mediums. At the same time, the Cheng brothers and Zhu Xi uplifted the redefined *li*, rational principle, to a cosmological and ontological height. By the Southern Song dynasty, Confucians had completed the rebalancing of the three core ideas with (heavenly) rational principle as the ideological anchor and ritualism as the norm of the lifeworld. The character of *li* as a transcendental essence was complemented by secular ritual, emotion, and moralism within a nexus of lineage relations. Under Song neo-Confucianism, however, the expression of individual human emotions was curbed, while ritual propriety and social and gender hierarchy gained more weight.[136] What separates Confucian philosophers from their Western counterparts, if comparable, lay in their attitudes toward the role of rituals despite an ontological commitment to Heavenly principle. Ritual for David Hume are perhaps the "ceremonies" that are associated with the "Roman Catholic religion," although he similarly argues that "love and hatred are always directed to some sensible being external to us."[137] While Rene Descartes argues that the "nobility of soul" serves as a remedy for emotional excesses,[138] Zhu Xi believes that family rituals can both express and guide emotions.

NOTES

1. Bryan W. Van Norden defines metaphysics as "the branch of philosophy that attempts to answer the question: What are the most fundamental types of things that exist?" See Norden, *Introduction to Classical Chinese Philosophy*, 164. Cheng-Zhu's reinvention of *li* as a prior universal force for me was a significant attempt to address a fundamental, metaphysical question that had been overshadowed by the past Confucian concern with daily life and the scholarly tradition of classical exegesis since the Han Dynasty.

2. Angela Zito, *Of Body and Brush: Grand Sacrifice as Text/Performance in Eighteenth-Century China* (Chicago: University of Chicago Press, 1997), 109.

3. Nylan, *The Five Confucian Classics*, 6, 20.

4. Charles Sanft, "Paleographic Evidence of Qin Religious Practice from Liye and Zhoujiatai," *Early China* 37 (2014): 330–31.

5. Robin D. S. Yates, "Slavery in Early China: A Socio-Cultural Approach," *Journal of East Asian Archaeology* 3, no. 1 (2002): 296.

6. Chen, *Baihutong shu zheng*, 93. Lü has several meanings in the Chinese language: shoes, treading, and practicing/implementing. The treading/practicing connotation and its recurring association with rites and the human body, *ti*, in multiple texts and annotations show *Li*'s essential character as bodily movements and actions.

7. Wu Fei, "Zheng Xuan 'Li zhe ti ye' shiyi" [An Explication of Zheng Xuan's Proposition "Ritual is Tantamount to Human Body], accessed September 16, 2020, https://www.rujiazg.com/article/19217. The Harvard-trained anthropologist Wu Fei also notes that the classical Chinese character for "body," *ti*, and that for *Li* are very similar.

8. Tang Yongtong, *Han Wei liang Jin nanbei chao fojiao shi* [A History of Buddhism in Han, Wei, the Two Jins and the Southern-Northern Dynasties] (Beijing: Kunlun chubanshe, 2006), 99.

9. Ibid., 613, 680.

10. Xiao, *Zhongguo zhengzhi sixiang shi*, 335.

11. Yu Yingshi, *Zhongguo zhishi ren zhi shi de kaocha* [An Examination of the History of Chinese Intellectuals] (Gulin: Guangxi shifan daxue chubanshe, 2004), 278–83.

12. Tang Yongtong, *Sui Tang fojiao shigao* [A Draft History of Sui-Tang Buddhism] (Beijing: Bejing daxue chubanshe, 2010), 255.

13. Zhangsun Wuji et al., *Tang lü shu yi* [Annotated Tang Code] e-book (Yiya chubanshe, 2019).

14. Ma Duanlin, *Wenxian tong kao* [A General Examination of Historical Source Materials] e-book (Yiya chubanshe, 2019).

15. Bret Hinsch, *The Rise of Tea Culture in China* (Lanham, MD: Rowman & Littlefield, 2016), 35.

16. Feng Youlan, *Zhongguo zhexue shi* [A History of Chinese Philosophy] (Shanghai: Huadong shifan daxue chubanshe, 1999), Vol. 2, 198–99.

17. Li Ao, *Fu xing shu* [A Treatise on Recovering Nature], accessed July 11, 2020, https://zh.wikisource.org/wiki/%E5%BE%A9%E6%80%A7%E6%9B%B8%E4%B8%8A.

18. Feng Youlan, *Zhongguo zhexue shi*, 200.

19. Tan Shaojiang, *Li Ao* [*Li Ao*] (Xi'an: Shaanxi shifan daxue chubanshe, 2017), 133.

20. Xu, *Shuo wen jie zi*, 216.

21. Qian Mu, *Song dai lixue san shu sui zha* [Random Notes on the Three Books of the Song Learning of Principle] (Beijing: Sanlian shudian, 2002), 100.

22. Cited in Li Zehou, *Zhongguo gudai sixiangshi lu* [Studies in Ancient Chinese Intellectual History] (Tianjin: Tianjin renmin chubanshe, 2004), 210.

23. The dispute here lies in that mainland Chinese philosophers and overseas Chinese researchers conventionally regarded Zhang Zai as a materialist philosopher and his *qi* "matter," while a Korean scholar argues that this materialist interpretation of Zhang Zai is inaccurate and *qi* is not a singular substance but an organic pluralism and generic traits of the human experience. See Jung-Yeup Kim, *Zhang Zai's Philosophy of Qi: A Practical Understanding* (Lanham, MD: Lexington Books, 2015), xii, 1–5.

24. Jeeloo Liu, *Neo-Confucianism: Metaphysics, Mind, the Moral Law* (Malden, MA: Wiley Blackwell, 2018), 69, 78.

25. He Bingdi, *He Bingdi sixiang zhidu shilun* [Studies of Intellectual and Institutional Histories] (Taipei: Lianjing chuban gongsi, 2013), 385–98.

26. Lin Lechang, "Qianyan" [Preface], in *Zhangzi quanshu* [Complete Works of Master Zhang Zai], ed. Lin Lechang (Xi'an: Xibei daxue chubanshe, 2015), 16–17.

27. Zhang Dainian, *Key Concepts in Chinese Philosophy*, trans. Edmund Ryden (New Haven, CT: Yale University Press, 2002), 26–27.

28. Ibid., 29.

29. Liu, *An Introduction to Chinese Philosophy*, 199.

30. For the definitions of *qi* as philosophical category, see Zhang, *Key Concepts in Chinese Philosophy*, 45–46.

31. Feng, *Zhongguo zhexue shi*, 240–41; A. C. Graham, *Two Chinese Philosophers: The Metaphysics of the Brothers Cheng* (La Salle, IL: Open Court Publishing, 1992), 14.

32. Ibid., 241.

33. Kim, *A History of Chinese Political Thought*, 127.

34. I translate *tong* as "command" because Zhu Xi explains in *Zhu zi yu lei* [Classified Conversations of Zhu Xi] that *tong* means "command" as in the term's military usage.

35. Graham, *Two Chinese Philosophers*, 65.

36. Chen, *Baihutong shuzheng*, 381. In the book, the numbers are used symbolically to match the internal organ: five *zang*s and six *fu*s as per the theory of traditional Chinese medicine.

37. Feng, *Zhongguo zhexue shi*, 240.

38. Ibid., 250–51.

39. Zhu Xi, Lü Zuqian, *Reflections on Things at Hand*, trans. Wing-Tsit Chan (New York: Columbia University Press, 1967), 8.

40. Ibid., 41.

41. Graham, *Two Chinese Philosophers*, 102.

42. Ibid., 105.

43. Joseph A. Adler, *Reconstructing the Confucian Dao: Zhu Xi's Appropriation of Zhou Dunyi* (Albany: State University of New York Press, 2014), 169.

44. Nicholas Rescher, *Rationality: A Philosophical Inquiry into the Nature and the Rationale of Reason* (Oxford: Clarendon Press, 1988), 1.

45. Ibid., 104–5.

46. Ibid., 9.

47. For an interpretation of what rationality entails, see ibid., 44.

48. Wing-Tsit Chan, *A Source Book in Chinese Philosophy* (Princeton, NJ: Princeton University Press, 1963), 635.

49. Wing-tsi Chan provides detailed explanations of the meaning of the word "*fen*"; see Chan, *Chu Hsi: New Studies*, 298–99.

50. Rescher, 153–54, 161–62.

51. Feng Youlan, in his classic study of ancient Chinese philosophy, compares *li* to "Form" in Greek philosophy. See Feng, *Zhongguo zhexue shi*, 259.

52. Chan, *Chu Hsi: New Studies*, 151.

53. Adler, *Reconstructing the Confucian Dao*, 6.

54. Qian Mu argues that Qing scholar's criticism of Zhu Xi on this twisting lost the big picture. See Qian Mu, *Zhuzi xue tigang* [Outlines of Master Zhu Xi's Scholarship] (Beijing: Sanlian shudian, 2005), 37.

55. Ibid., 87–88.

56. Ibid., 89.

57. Zhu Xi and Lü Zuqian, *Reflections on Things at Hand*, 53.

58. Ibid., 85.

59. Ibid., 143.

60. Qian, *Zhuzi xue tigang*, 49.

61. Chen Lai, "The Discussion of Mind and Nature in Zhu Xi's Philosophy," trans. Robert W. Foster, *Chinese Philosophy in an Era of Globalization*, ed. Robin R. Wang (Albany: State University of New York Press, 2004), 79.

62. Ibid., 107.

63. Chan, *Chu Hsi: New Studies*, 154, 156.

64. Ibid., 161.

65. Ibid., 541.

66. Zhu Xi, *Zhu zi yu lei.*

67. Zhang Longxi, *Allegoresis: Reading Canonical Literature East and West* (Ithaca, NY: Cornell University Press, 2005), 139–41.

68. Chan, *Chu Hsi: New Studies*, 95.

69. Daniel K. Gardner, *Chu Hsi Learning to Be a Sage: Selections from the Conversations of Master Chu* (Berkeley: University of California Press, 1990), 184.

70. Conrad M. Schirokauer, "Chu His's Political Career: A Study in Ambivalence," in *Confucian Personalities*, ed. Arthur F. Wright and Denis Twitchett (Stanford: Stanford University Press, 1962), 165–66.

71. Daniel K. Gardner, *Chu Hsi and the Ta-hsueh: Neo-Confucian Reflection on the Confucian Canon* (Cambridge, MA: Harvard University Press, 1986), 9, 17, 19.

72. Daniel K. Gardner, *Zhu Xi's Reading of the Analects: Canon, Commentary, and the Classical Tradition* (New York: Columbia University Press, 2003), 85.

73. Ibid.

74. Ibid., 89.

75. Zhu Xi, *Zhu zi yu lei.*

76. Li Minghui, *Rujia yu kangde* [Confucianism and Kant] (Taipei: Lianjing chuban shiye youxian gongsi, 1990), 131, 137. Li Minghui believes that Zhu Xi constructed a *xin-xing-qing* triad.

77. Gardner, *Zhu Xi's Reading of the Analects*, 94–95.

78. Chan, *Chu His: New Studies*, 162.

79. Gardner, *Zhu Xi's Reading of the Analects*, 100–1.

80. Zhu Xi, *Si shu zhangju ji zhu* [Collective Annotations of the Four Books] (Beijing: Zhonghua shuju, 2011), 194.

81. Hoyt Cleveland Tillman, *Confucian Discourse and Chu Hsi's Ascendency* (Honolulu: University of Hawaii Press, 1992), 75.

82. Zhu Xi, *Si shu zhangju ji zhu*, 137.

83. Zheng Zhenman, "Song yihou Fujian de jiazu xisu yu zongzu zuzhi" [Ancestral Sacrificial Customs and Lineage Organization in Fujian after the Song], in Zheng Zhenman, *Xiangzu yu guojia: Duoyuan shiye zhong de min tai chuantong shehui* [Local Lineage and the State: Fujian and Taiwan's Traditional Society from a Multifaceted Perspective] (Beijing: Sanlian shudian, 2009), 103.

84. Ibid., 104.

85. Wang Zhiyue, *Song dai lizhi yanjiu* [A Study of Song Dynasty Ritual System] (Beijing: renmin chubanshe, 2017), 126, 129.

86. I do not intend to engage in the discussion of the connotation of "lineage" in a pure and strict anthropological sense here. It can be understood as a "self-professed patrilineal descent group" or an "organized agnatic kinship," as argued in Michael Szonyi, *Practicing Kinship: Lineage and Descent in Late Imperial China* (Stanford, CA: Stanford University Press, 2002), 4–6.

87. Peter K. Bol, *Neo-Confucianism in History* (Cambridge, MA: Harvard University Press, 2008), 243.

88. Zheng Zhenman, *Family Lineage Organization and Social Change in Ming and Qing Fujian*, trans. Michael Szonyi (Honolulu: University of Hawaii Press, 2001),

271. The English word "temple" has three Chinese renditions: a Buddhist temple is *si*, a Daoist temple is *guan*, and the buildings erected in memory of great men and ancestors are called *ci* and *citang*. See Jing Jun, *The Temple of Memories: History, Power, and Morality in a Chinese Village* (Stanford, CA: Stanford University Press, 1996), 23.

89. Yang Yi, "Qing li zhi bian: Lun song dai jia li zhong de muji" [Between Emotion and Rationality: Graveyard Sacrifice in Song Dynasty's Family Rituals], *Zhongguo wenhua yanjiu* (Summer 2020).

90. Hong Mai, *Record of the Listener: Selected Stories from Hong Mai's Yijianzhi*, trans and ed. Cong Ellen Zhang (Indianapolis, IN: Hackett Publishing, 2018), 51.

91. Zhu Xi and Lü Zuqian, *Reflections on Things at Hand*, 229.

92. Randall Collins, *Interaction Ritual Chains* (Princeton, NJ: Princeton University Press, 2004), 36.

93. Ge Zhaoguang, *Qufu shi ji qita: Liu chao sui tang daojiao de sixiang shi yanjiu* [A History of Submission and Other Things: An Intellectual History Study of Daoism in the Six Dynasties, Sui, and Tang] (Beijing: Sanlian shudian, 2003), 61–62.

94. Kenneth Dean, *Taoist Ritual and Popular Cults of Southeast China* (Princeton, NJ: Princeton University Press, 1993), 12, 28.

95. Ibid., 159.

96. C. Fred Blake, *Burning Money: The Material Spirit of the Chinese Lifeworld* (Honolulu: University of Hawaii Press, 2010), 54, 65, 68.

97. The comment is seen in Zhu Xi, *Si shu zhangju ji zhu*, 66.

98. Ibid., 166.

99. Ibid., 235.

100. Ibid., 272.

101. Zhu Xi, *Zhu zi yu lei*.

102. Ibid.

103. Ibid.

104. Ibid.

105. Chan, *A Source Book in Chinese Tradition*, 645–646.

106. Zhu Xi, *Zhuzi yu lei*.

107. Ibid.

108. Li Jiansheng, *Qing dai-min'guo: Xining shehui shenghuo shi* [From the Qing to the Republic: A History of Social Life in Xining] (Beijing: renmin chubanshe, 2012), 77.

109. Patricia B. Ebrey, "Translator's Preface," in *Chu His's "Family Rituals,"* trans. Patricia B. Ebrey (Princeton, NJ: Princeton University Press, 1991), ix.

110. Zhu Xi, *Chu His's "Family Rituals,"* 6–8. *Zuting*, ancestral hall, is the term used to describe the in-home shrine, and *citang*, or *zongci*, lineage ancestral offering hall, is a separate building shared by the lineage members for worshiping the ancestors, meeting, and sometimes litigation.

111. Zhu Xi, *Chu His's "Family Rituals,"* 24.

112. Francesca Bray, *Technology and Gender: Fabrics of Power in Late Imperial China* (Berkeley: University of California Press, 1997), 155.

113. Zhu Xi, *Chu His's "Family Ritual,"* 15.

114. Ibid., 28.

115. Ibid., 32.

116. Ibid., 35.

117. Ibid., 37.

118. Ibid., 62–63.

119. Ibid., 91–92.

120. Zhu Xi, *Chu His's "Family Rituals,"* 100.

121. Ibid., 84.

122. Ibid., 144.

123. Ibid., 122.

124. Bell, *Ritual: Perspectives and Dimensions*, 82.

125. Erik Mueggler, *Songs for Dead Parents: Corpse, Text, and World in Southwest China* (Chicago: University of Chicago Press, 2017), 205.

126. Lyu Seung-kuk, *Han guo ruxue yu xiandai jingshen* [Korean Confucianism and Modern Spirit], trans. Jiang Ritian and Piao Guanhai (Beijing: dongfang chubanshe, 2008), 160.

127. Zhuang Kongshao, *Yinchi: Zhongguo de difang shehui yu wenhua bianqian* [The Silver Wings: The Local Society and Cultural Changes in China] (Beijing: Sanlian shudian, 1999), 25.

128. Chan, *Chu Hsi: New Studies*, 49–50.

129. Wang Li, *Zhongguo gudai wenhua changshi, xiuding di siban* [General Knowledge of Ancient Chinese Culture, Revised 4th Edition] (Beijing: Shijie tushu chuban gongsi, 2007), 205.

130. de Bary and Bloom, *Sources of Chinese Tradition*, 809.

131. Shu-Hsien Liu, *Essentials of Contemporary Neo-Confucianism* (Westport, CT: Praeger, 2003), 23.

132. Shu-Hsien Liu, *Understanding Confucian Philosophy: Classical and Sung-Ming* (Westport, CT: Praeger, 1998), 107.

133. Li Zehou, *Shiyong lixing yu legan wenhua* [Pragmatic Reason and a Culture of Optimism] (Beijing: Sanlian shudian, 2005), 63.

134. Wang Mingming, *Shehui renleixue yu zhongguo yanjiu* [Social Anthropology and China Studies] (Beijing: Sanlian shudian, 1997), 87.

135. Davis, *Society and the Supernatural in Song China*, 179–80.

136. There are similarities between Chinese philosophers and their European counterparts. René Descartes identifies six basic human passions—wonderment, love, hate, desire, joy, and sadness—and these passions are aroused by material objects derived from sensations. Michael Moriarty, "Introduction," in René Descartes, *The Passions of the Soul and Other Late Philosophical Writings* (Oxford: Oxford University Press, 2015), xxiv–xxv. As with Chinese philosophers, Descartes also believes that passions need to be curbed, although for him the vanquishing power should come from volition. Descartes makes more sophisticated classifications of seemingly identical emotions than Chinese philosophers. For instance, there were for him "love of benevolence" and "love of concupiscence" and the distinction of "affection, affection, and devotion." See Descartes, *The Passions of the Soul and Other Late Philosophical Writings*, 216, 227–28. Baruch Spinoza also discusses "how the

mind can have absolute control over the emotions," while "all emotions are related to desire, pleasure, and pain." Baruch Spinoza, *Ethics*: *Treatise on The Emendation of the Intellect and Selected Letters* (Indianapolis, IN: Hackett Publishing, 1992), 102, 138. Yet, for Spinoza, all emotions are contrary to reason. See Russell, *A History of Western Philosophy*, 573.

137. David Hume, *A Treatise of Human Nature* (1739; repr., Lexington, KY: Gale Ecco, 2018), 43, 126.

138. Descartes, *The Passions of the Soul and Other Late Philosophical Writings*, 277.

Chapter 4

Rediscovering *Qing* and *Li* in the Ming and Qing

During the Ming (1368–1644) and Qing (1644–1911), the last two imperial dynasties in Chinese history after the Mongol rule of China from 1279 to 1368, Zhu Xi's annotation and interpretation of the Four Books was endorsed by the imperial government as the orthodox understanding of Confucianism. Zhu Xi's School of Rational Principle was also entrenched as the pivot of Confucian cosmology, epistemology, and ethics. Yet, in Ming-Qing China philosophers questioned the too lofty and detached yet also authoritarian "Heavenly principle" and the grave and tacit personality Song Confucians promoted to maintain temperance to cultivate oneself. Starting in the Ming Dynasty, the School of Heart-Mind, founded by Wang Yangming (1472–1529) and carried on by his several generations of followers slowly switched from the objectified, all-encompassing principle to the ultimate power of the subjective and introspective heart-mind.

This critical trend precipitated the rediscovery of the value of emotion, desire, and individuality among Ming-Qing Confucian scholars, so much so that some became alienated from mainstream society. Modern scholars of late Ming thought have noticed the tendency of anti-asceticism and a call for unrestricted human nature.[1] Some late Ming followers of Wang Yangming claimed that they acquired a certain quasi-religious feeling of sudden enlightenment accompanied by bodily reactions such as sweating.[2] This intellectual group also showed an overall characteristic of anti-elitism, emphasizing daily life experience and social engagement at the grassroots level. The word *qing* pervaded the language of Ming poetry and drama as a "pure force that justified a multitude of human actions and beliefs."[3] They embraced *qing* as an outlet for both moral and aesthetic expressions and some believed "sentiment" and "propriety," rather than ritual forms alone, should "bind spouses together."[4]

In the early and mid-Qing Dynasty, while the imperial government stuck with the orthodox School of Principle of the Cheng brothers and Zhu Xi, some semi-independent Confucian scholars turned to be more scholastic and somewhat, though not completely, identified themselves with the glossing and emendation tradition of Han Dynasty Confucianism. Meanwhile, challenge of the dominant assumption of the School of Principle continued, leading to a deeper engagement with rituals and the pursuit of the legitimate expression of human emotions. Song thinkers' unrelenting search for the dormant innate natural propensity, *xing*, and the inner mental state of equilibrium, *zhong*, before emotional arousal is set "in motion," *dong*, and their emphasis on an unchangeable cosmic-ethical-political order in *li* was questioned as a restriction of dynamic, natural human emotions. Beyond the intellectual discourse contained in published books and personal letters among the scholars, Qing government disseminated Confucian values to the villages and revived the ritual system, which contributed to the protracted entrenchment of ritualized Confucianism in local society.

WANG YANGMING AND HIS FOLLOWERS' CHALLENGE OF UNIVERSAL PRINCIPLE

Wang Yangming's skepticism of Zhu Xi's rational principle and its attainment by deep inquiries into an object took place in the intellectual milieu of inward turning to assert the power of mind-heart, a trend starting from Ming Confucian philosopher Wu Yubi (1391–1469), his student Chen Xianzhang (1428–1500), to Chen's student and Wang Yangming's friend Zhan Ruoshui (1466–1560). A dramatized scenario about Wang's revelation was when he practiced quiet-sitting in a courtyard at 16, facing bamboos. The attempt to unravel the concrete principle contained in the bamboos by sitting and gazing was futile and Wang became sick. After a rumination, he realized that all things under Heaven were incomprehensible if approached from the outside, and deep inquiries could only be achieved through one's own body and mind.[5]

Here, the first premise of Wang Yangming's action was Zhu Xi's inductive assumption that even a grass leaf or a piece of wood has its own essential rational principle, and Wang, as the subject of cognition, was trying to grasp the rational principle of the bamboos as an objective of research. Again, Zhu Xi attempted to universalize the rational principle by applying it to all non-human objects, while emotion and rites do not apply to bamboo because bamboo is not a moral agent. From a modern critical point of view, we might say that Wang had a good start but what he lacked was the proper method of modern natural science which could have bridged him and the bamboos, nor did he put the bamboos under rational scrutiny by investigating their growth.

But psychologically, the quiet-sitting became a life-transforming experience for Wang, full of inner conflicts, and the frustration facilitated his decision to doubt Zhu Xi's learning and switch inward to search the spontaneous affective faculty of heart-mind and the validity of subjective experience.

Wang Yangming subverted the predominance of the rational principle by extending the introspective dimension of Zhu Xi's thought. First, he made a straightforward claim that "The sages' learning is the "learning of the Mind-and-heart.' It is learning that seeks fully to employ the mind-and-heart' by invoking an esoteric quote in the *Book of History, shangshu,* focusing on the 'human mind' and the 'mind of the Way.'[6] Wang Yangming's reasoning here cited legendary sage rulers Yao, Shun, and Yu to legitimize his emphasis on the value of mind-heart while bypassing the core conceptual pair in Zhu Xi's doctrine, Heaven and principle, and a simplified formula: Heaven is the principle. Following Wang Yangming's logic, the sages" learning was all about how to properly (re)discover and employ one's heart-mind, rather than seek the truth from the outside. Second, besides the archaeology of the concepts, Wang constructed another logic that the passing of the sages caused the obscuring of the learning of hear-mind, and this in turn causes the degeneration of human conduct to striving only for fame and profit.[7] Through this model of chain reaction, Wang Yangming showed the demoralizing consequence of losing the tradition of the learning of heart-mind, which for him had an intrinsic moral high ground.

Third, Wang Yangming did not succumb to but rather takes issues with Zhu Xi's *li*-supremacy by asserting that the old notion "the principle in each individual thing is to be sought with the mind" separates the mind and principle into two.[8] Instead, Wang argues that the principle of commiseration animated by the sight of a child about to fall into a well, as the famous Mengzi imagery tried to reveal, is already rooted in one's innate moral knowledge of heart-mind. Questioning the separation of heart-mind and rational principle, Wang attempts to establish the supremacy of heart-mind itself. Fourth, by invoking the "A means B" sentence structure, Wang introduces another concept, the primary substance, *benti,* into his exposition to link heart-mind to the intrinsically good human nature: ". . . the original substance of the mind is human nature."[9]

Regarding the essence of human nature, Wang Yangming did not differ from Zhu Xi and both believed in intrinsically good human nature and opposed Xunzi's argument about evil human nature. To battle incorrectness, Wang argues, one needs to rectify one's mind by extending one's innate moral knowledge to the utmost, *zhi liangzhi,* while this innate moral knowledge according to Wang was not external empirical knowledge but heart-mind's innate faculty of distinguishing right and wrong.[10] The basis of making the distinction, for Wang, were moral feelings such as love that serve also as the basis of one's moral actions.[11]

Wang Yangming's friend, mid-Ming philosopher Luo Qinshun (1465–1547) switched from the focus on rational principle, *li*, to *qi*, vital energy or materiel force and he did not believe *li* is prior or superior to *qi*, as Zhu Xi insisted. For Luo Qinshun, *qi*, changing from obscurity to manifestation, "is the warmth and coolness and the cold and heat of the four seasons, and the birth, growth, gathering in the preservation of all living things," and "It is the people's daily life and social relations and the success and failure, gain and loss in human affairs."[12] While acknowledging the significance of concrete daily-life experiences, Luo Qinshun disenchanted the word *li* by etymologically restoring its original meaning as "pattern."[13] Luo also engaged with the relational trio of "nature," which for him was "less a substance," "rational principle," and "emotion," but he pointed out that the basic qualities of nature encompass "human desires," together with human feelings such as "pleasure, anger, sorrow, and joy." Hence, the tension between nature and emotion, as perceived by Cheng Yi and Zhu Xi, was not a question for Luo Qinshun after he reconciled the two.[14] Both Wang Yangming and Luo Qinshun demonstrated their affirmative attitudes toward human emotions and desires, and day-to-day experiences.[15]

In the late Ming, popular Confucianism with a liberating propensity figured prominently. A poet and politician, Wang Yangming himself was not only emotional in his personal disposition but also affirmed the inevitable influence of emotion when one makes an ostensibly rational judgment.[16] Wang's stress on autonomy, spontaneity, and supremacy of hear-mind was so liberating that some of his avid followers and their disciples formed a circle of kindred minds that eschewed Song Neo-Confucianism's emphasis on reverence and quietism. They were less than bookish nor stolid but idealistic and practical-minded; they emphasized ordinary people's normal feeling, *changqing*, interests, and life experiences; and many of them were passionate about influencing others and assuming the role of the public speaker for Confucianism. Wang Ji(1498–1583), not related to Wang Yangming, "emphasized the transcendental freedom of innate knowing and its spontaneous exercise."[17] Through decades of public lectures and explicit spiritual messages, Wang Ji reached out to a large public audience and made his teaching look like an evangelical movement.[18] Wang Gen (1483–1541), another unrelated disciple of Wang Yangming had a personal background of being a salt merchant with rudimentary academic training, but he acquired a self-imposed sense of mission to "become a teacher of mankind."[19] Wang Gen talked about his love for himself, his family, and the state, and he found great spiritual ecstasy in learning with emotional intensity, and the ecstasy would render

Wang Gen bold enough to announce that "The sage and I are the same."[20] He was recorded to have had a mystic epiphany in a strange dream about Wang Yangming's world-saving power and then he woke up, sweating and totally enlightened.[21]

If rational (Heavenly) principle has been defined as *a priori* cosmological-ethical dogma which had caused the inner repression of individual emotions through the lineage institutions, then the doctrine of heart-mind allows the individual more room to use discretional power to choose what is better for himself, because heart-mind belongs to each individual and Wang Yangming never related mind-heart to Heaven. However, their passionate and sometimes unorthodox propagation of Confucianism did not preclude a respect for ritualism, which underlay the mode of interaction between them. When Wang Gen visited Wang Yangming for the first time as a disciple, he wore the *shenyi* linen robe, the ritualist artifact of atavism, as Zhu Xi did at home, to show his respect.[22]

Late Ming popular culture was characterized by two phenomena: syncretism of the three prevalent teachings in China: Confucianism, Daoism, and Buddhism, and the legitimization of human emotional arousal, especially the affection between men and women in creative writing and literary criticism.[23] Individualism, idiosyncrasy, and further recognition of human emotions and desires reached an apex in Li Zhi (1527–1602), an iconoclastic Confucian philosopher and literary scholar who turned to be a Buddhist monk at age of 61, who drew upon Wang Ji and Wang Gen's concern with mundane life, and he himself was skeptical of the authenticity or sacredness of the Six Classics. He disenchanted the sages by saying that "The sage is no different from others; it is a matter of not deceiving oneself."[24] For Li Zhi, the rational principle should not be related to the cosmological order but should be sought in secular material expressions: "To wear clothing and eat food—these are the principles of human relations. Without them, there are no human relations." [25] As a cultural radical, Li also historicized and contextualized the sacralized pre-Qin Confucian classics as an intellectual construct by putting them back into the specific time period.[26]

Although known as a maverick who was not obsequious, Li Zhi was not opposed to ritual *per se*. But for him, ritual was only worthwhile when it expressed genuine inner feelings: "What comes forth from within may be called decorum; what comes from without is not decorum."[27] Emotion became the sole criterion for defining ritual. Defying the gender hierarchy sanctioned by Song Confucian thinkers as part of the Heavenly principle, Li Zhi advocated gender equality and extolled women's talents.[28] He believes that an "ultimate man," *zhiren*, might have opposite emotions compared with philistines. When the crowd is pleased, the ultimate man alone feels sorrowful, but while everyone else is worried, the ultimate man can find joy, and that is because the ultimate man knows the constant change of good luck and bad luck into each other.[29] Because of intellectual radicalism, tensions with mainstream Confucian interpretation, and alleged wallowing in lewd lifestyle to satisfy concupiscence, which flouted social convention, Li Zhi was indicted by the inimical local government and thrown into prison, where he killed himself in 1602 with a sharp pang of desperation.

Another late Ming Confucian thinker Lü Kun (1536–1618)'s writing also demonstrated a nuanced understanding of rational principle and its relations with other key concepts. Lü asserted the moral authority of Confucian scholars by arguing that the emperor holds power, *shi*, whereas the sage holds rational principle, *li*, and he announced that rational principle was more respectable between the two.[30] In Lü's idealized good old days under the sagely and wise governance, human emotion or natural disposition, *qing*, ritual, *Li*, and government statutes, *fa*, were compatible with each other. He lamented that in a time of political decay, the emotion would prevail and take place of law, but when law figured prominently, it would overshadow ritual.[31] For Lü, although the perfect balance of *qing*, *Li*, and *fa* symbolizes a good government, *qing* as natural impulses and desires was regarded negatively: "People have five kinds of *qing* and they grow out of self-serving motives. When there is profit, people go for it; when there is a pretty woman, men love her; where there are food and drink, people become greedy; when there is an easy life, people adapt to it; when they see the weak and the uneducated people, they take advantage of them. These are all done to serve their own interests."[32] This reminds us of the negative assessment of *qing* in the Tang Confucian scholar Li Ao in chapter 3. but Lü Kun did not call for the abolition of them or coercive rectification of human nature. Even if *Qing* can be selfish, it can still be compatible with ritual and law, so long as a good ruler could coordinate and balance the three elements.

Another observation of Lü was about how people with different levels of moral self-cultivation would treat the dangerous *qing*: "A myriad of things grow out of nature, *xing*, but perish in *qing*. People with the highest level of wisdom eliminate their *qing*, the gentlemen rectify their *qing*, commoners follow their *qing*, and petty-minded men give up themselves to their *qing*."[33] Since Confucian scholars identify themselves with the image of an ideal gentleman, it is arguable that Lü Kun's own attitude toward emotion was realistic in both acknowledging its existence and stressing the necessity of controlling it. Yet he was not without sympathy at a personal level: ". . . I bent the rules, and emotions of women and children were not suppressed. As a result, virtuous and filial old women and servant girls could also live out their days. . . ."[34]

The central concern with *qing* and *Li* was tied to another major theme in late Ming discourse: human nature. When the late Ming saw the surge of a trend of thought that argued for the neutrality of human nature that transcends good and evil, implying the irrelevance of ritual propriety, the thinker and political activist Gu Xiancheng (1550–1612) felt the danger because this radicalism would lead to the abolition of *Li*. As On-Cho Ng points out, Gu Xiancheng reaffirmed that human nature was innately good and then moved on to his logical assertion that conventions, and protocols should not be subverted, because these external social norms and formal rituals realized and fulfilled the fundamental good human nature.[35] Instead of seeing emotions as the mere manifestation of human nature, Liu Zongzhou (1578–1645) argued that emotions were "integrally nature in themselves," and not a post-arousal mental state. In other words, emotions and human nature are co-immanent.[36]

During the period of Ming-Qing transition, the eminent philosopher and historian Wang Fuzhi (1619–1692) revisited the relations among natural disposition, emotion, and desire in a way similar to the elaborations on the Chu bamboo slips, which we discussed in chapter 2. Wang asserted that emotions are received from human nature, which is a repository of emotions, and emotions generate desires. "Above, emotions are received from natural disposition; below, emotions produce desires." Wang argued that "rational principle is stored in desires" and even "desire is rational principle."[37] Hence, Wang Fuzhi unified human emotions/desires and the rational principle.

RITES AND CEREMONIES WENT DOWN
TO THE COMMON PEOPLE

It is necessary to examine how Confucianism as a politicized and practical system of thoughts was implemented by the state and experienced by the people in late imperial Chinese society. The adoption of a lineage structure, which was endorsed by Song Neo-Confucian philosophers, was associated with the collective performance of rituals in the early Ming, and in the sixteenth century, the centrality of ancestor sacrifice was recognized by the late Ming state as the "linchpin connecting state authority and local communities."[38] The founder of the Ming dynasty Zhu Yuanzhang (1328–1398) legalized the restoration of the pre-Qin district libational ceremony, *xiang yinjiu Li,* usually hosted by the local county mayors to pay tribute to esteemed local elders. When one of the late Ming Confucian scholar was invited, he turned down the invitation two times because he saw the drinking ceremony as a formality and wanted the local mayor to transform some accepted ritual-customs, *Li-su* of the entire community.[39] At the grassroots level, the compound word *Li-su* hints at the complex fusion of the rituals sanctioned by the state and Confucian thinkers and local folklores, and how to adapt ritual to local custom and how to improve local custom to match ritual would become a major theme in the governing practice of Confucian scholar-officials.

Focusing on Qing governance of rural China, Xiao Gongquan (Kung-Chuan Hsiao, 1897-1981), an eminent twentieth century political scientist and historian of Chinese political thought, seems to be more cynical on the state promotion of local sacrifices. He argues that the rulers made use of sacrificial rites to honor Confucius, the god of war, the various gods of wind, clouds, land, and grain, and venerable local officials to reinforce the methods of influencing the minds of their subjects. Qing rulers schematically built temples and shrines and instituted various sacrifices in all the localities of the empire to buttress with religious sentiments the values of loyalty, self-sacrifice, and gratitude, because these values were conducive to the security of the state.[40] Xiao's emphasis on the rituals' instrumental function of political control is a pertinent observation, and it again shows the top-down character of rites as prescriptive rules imposed from above. Anthropologist Lin Yaohua, however, notes the changing function of the lineage ancestral offering hall, *zongci*, from a ritual space to a sociopolitical stage to forge linkages between clan members and to exercise the clan head's power.[41] Overall, in addition to this indisputable function of enforcing the social and moral order, the lineage group strengthened an individual member's feeling that he was not alone, but a part of an organization with its own historical pride through participating in sacrificial ceremonies.[42]

Confucian scholar-officials had long been expected to perform a leadership role in a variety of public rituals and share a religious feeling with the community. A county seat in Ming-Qing China had many sites with a certain religious character: sanctified Confucius and more folkloric ones such as the city god, *chenghuang*, the god of war, *guandi*, and the god of literature, *wenchang*, god of agriculture, *shennong*, and the gods of earth and grain, *sheji*. A local county "magistrate" had the duty of burning incense on certain days to pay homage to these gods and deified Confucius, though not all of them were "Confucian." According to Qu Tongzu (T'ung-Tsu Ch'ü, 1910-2008), "A magistrate who failed to visit the temples or offer sacrifices on schedule, or who held a banquet during a fast was subject to impeachment."[43] Although local officials' engagement in these activities was not necessarily mandated by government regulations, local people shared the expectation for their magistrate to preside over the ceremonies for supernatural aid. For them, the magistrate was the chief priest.[44] While the worship of ancestors was unconditional, the local deities might be "punished" if they were deemed to have failed to fulfill certain duties.[45] When Christian missionaries from Europe entered northern Chinese villages in the late nineteenth century, they found that temples of Buddhist origins were not only owners of land property but also sites of village theatrical performance, and agency of local power, with which they conflicted.[46]

Recent research on historical anthropology reminds us of several phenomena in Ming ritualism at central and local levels. First, there was imperial promotion of Zhu Xi's *Family Rituals*. The Ming court since the Yongle reign (1403–1424) elevated *Family Rituals* to an unprecedented high level, only next to the Four Books with Zhu Xi's annotation.[47] In fifteenth century China, the popularity of Zhu Xi's *Family Rituals* also helped expand the roster of the worshipped ancestors from the recent ones to include older ancestors.[48] The *Family Rituals* had such a deep influence among scholars that one of the earliest Chinese Christians, late Ming scholar-official Yang Tingyun ". . . both before and after his baptism, fully participated in the movement to restore Zhu Xi's *Family Rituals*."[49]

Second, a group of local part-time ritual officiants, lisheng, emerged, who administered the ritual processes. Unlike magicians or medicine men, these officiants served as secular masters of ceremony based on ritual manuals and they did not engage in supernatural activities, but also unlike more sophisticated Confucian thinkers, these ritual experts did not engage in critical reflections of Confucian ideology.[50] They were selected from local low-level officials or Confucian students with *xiucai* or *juren* degrees and thus they were educated Confucians.

Third, these Confucian liturgists played a key role in sacrificial rites although they might also appear in weddings and other rites. The Ming-Qing ritual are still performed today and Liu Yonghua in his fieldwork observed five times of performance involving sacrifice to local gods and ancestors, sacrifice to the dragon head, wedding ceremony, and funeral.[51] In the sacrifices, the officiants make sure all the steps are followed correctly to pay respect to their ancestors.

Fourth, the Master of Ceremony in the Ming court, however, was Daoist liturgists, and at the local level, Confucian sacrificial officiants collaborated with Daoist and Buddhist monks when the sacrifice was performed to pay homage to gods and deities.[52] The rise of the sacrificial officiant as a distinct social group was a consequence of the self-conscious construction of local lineage groups since the early Ming, which was accompanied by Confucian scholars' proactive introduction of the village compact, *xiangyue*, rituals into the villages.[53]

Economically, the daily maintenance of the ancestral hall, the performance of annual sacrifices, the care of communal graveyards, and the expenses for younger lineage members' education were all covered by a lineage's public property as "ritual land," also known as "charitable land" in the seventeenth century.[54] We may extrapolate that during the Ming-Qing period, Confucian ritualism had been disseminated deep down to the village level with substantial lineal support. The state, local lineages, and Confucian scholars were three pillars in this movement of spreading Confucian values and rituals to the grassroots level. For the often-illiterate villagers, Confucian rites were fused with local lore and experienced by them because it was no longer the intellectual debate among thinkers but ritual performances that they could see and participate in after being acted out.

In terms of the rituals that mixed external forms and inner sentiments, some European missionaries to Ming China in the sixteenth century found Chinese performed a sacrifice with food and wine to ancestors "in order to show the affection they displayed for the deceased and that they offered him the same things as if he were alive. . . ."[55] Here the missionary captured the gist of Chinese family sacrifice, which was understood in Confucius's time as an expression of affection with an "as if" imagination. Another way of understanding the Chinese affective worship of ancestors is a modern analysis of Chinese funeral: "(Due to) the love and respect for the dead, (we) would rather believe he/she is there."[56] The trope "would rather," *ning*, is very revealing in showing how *qing* could influence one's action.

One clan document of 1809 epitomizes local people's understanding of ritual, sacrifice, and their relationship to human emotions"

> Ritual has five constant principles, of which none is more important than sacrifice. Our family is assembled here as a lineage. The descendants hope to flourish. It is particularly important that arrangements for sacrificial matters be made in advance. . .It is only to be hoped that in every generation the descendants will prepare the objects and perform the ritual with the utmost love and respect. In [the world of] darkness this will agree with the spirits and in that of light this will encourage war feelings within the lineage.[57]

The text shows that sacrifice was considered as the most important ritual for a lineage because of its function of connecting ancestors with descendants. The ritual organizer did have his utilitarian purpose of realizing the prosperity of future generations by obtaining the blessing of the ancestors. However, the author of this document also emphasized the importance of true feelings of love and respect, so that the sacrificial ritual would not be reduced to an empty form.

While Ming Dynasty thinkers took issue with Zhu Xi's absolutization of rational principle, local elites challenged Zhu Xi's ritual regulation. With the rise of lineage's influence, one local elite questioned the Cheng brothers and Zhu Xi's regulation that the family temple should be replaced by the ancestral hall, and people who hold official positions may worship four generations of the ancestors while common scholars two generations. Ming dynasty people's doubt were two-folded: (1) The architectural requirement and spatial arrangement for an ancestral hall seemed to be too complicated and "strict." (2) The limit on the number of worshipped ancestors also too rigid. In fact, the Ming temple regulation in practice even did not allow serving officials to sacrifice to over four generations of ancestors. Local elites thus wanted the lineal ancestral hall to include the remote founding ancestors.[58] As with the state that exercised social control by building many kinds of temples, the proliferating ancestral halls served as a "means of controlling lineage members."[59] However, if we consider both the controlling function of the ancestral hall and its emotional function through collective ritual actions, then I would suggest that ritualism at the local level had both controlling and emotional aspects.

The state's role in mass moral education at the village level was more prominent in the Qing dynasty when the Kangxi Emperor compiled sixteen maxims, which were amplified by his son, the Yongzheng Emperor, to make the Sacred Edicts to be conveyed to villagers. On the first and fifteenth of every moon, the ritual officiant, *lisheng*, would call aloud to guide ritual steps; an orator, or *shijiang sheng*, would be charged with the mission of explaining the edicts.[60] This invaluable text shows the passion of the two generations of the Qing emperors in reaching out to the village level with Confucian moral teaching. Although their ultimate purpose was to achieve more effective ideological and social control, the amplified edicts themselves are indispensable source materials for understanding what was valued by the emperors, what they expected from the people, and how they thought they could reach that end.

The imperial maxims as a collective reflect several prevailing imperial concerns to steer people's choices. First and foremost, the emperors urged the people to adhere to the Confucian principle of filial piety as the foundation of humanity by incurring pangs of conscience toward their parents: "Filial piety is [founded on] the unalterable statute of heaven, the corresponding operations of earth, and the common obligations of all people. Have those who are void of filial piety never reflected on the natural affections of parents to their children?" The book heuristically admonished people to recall or to imagine the parental care they received when they were children: "Did you smile? They were happy. Did you weep? They were unhappy. Did you begin to walk? They followed at your heels. . . ."[61]

In the *Sacred Edicts*, ritual propriety was emphasized to manifest love and kindness among all family members, particularly brothers who have mutual emotional involvement as "flesh and blood."[62] To harmonize the interpersonal relations among the entire lineage group that owns the common charity field and to foster kinship solidarity, the members were expected to love each other and always yield, *rang*, to another member and extend this harmony to neighbors by forgiving and through amicable and reasonable settlement of disputes.[63] The book advised people to avoid lawsuits because neither gain nor loss was worth of the time and effort. Because people are born good, it argues, appealing to "mutual kindness, mutual affection, and constant interchanges of friendly attentions" suffices to eschew contentions and lawsuits and to establish rapport with each other.[64]

The emperors also wanted people to avoid extravagant ceremonial practices because "Economy is an excellent virtue." They instructed that "In the ceremonies of manhood, marriage, mourning, and sacrificing to the dead, keep within your proper sphere. In domestic utensils, let there be plainness and simplicity. Even in the anniversary sacrifice and feasts, let there be an accordance with propriety and the customs—all verging rather towards economy."[65] In this edict, *li*, rational principle, was deprived of the Song Neo-Confucian metaphysical meaning and only used as an equivalence to popular moral judgment: "Even if a person who knows not good from evil, should stumble against me, or rashly against me, I will abide by reason, *li*, and send him about his business."[66] Ideally, all these admonitions, if they really worked, were expected to cushion the local society from the imperial penal code and prelude interpersonal conflicts before they needed to be controlled.

The emphasis on the family bond had been entrenched in the Chinese value system by the eighteenth century. Beyond the imperial edicts aiming at building an idealized society that is free from lawsuits and based upon mutual love and understanding, Qing Code had allowed excessive controlling power to lineage groups, acquiescing to mutual "covering up" and prohibiting children's reporting of their parents and grandparents even if the latter committed non-political, common crimes.[67] The purpose was to hold clans together and thus cement and stabilize village-level society. In the mid-nineteenth century, a lineage group that shared one surname and a public ancestral offering hall could be so large that it accommodated more than 6,000 members.[68] This explains why it was so important for buttressing local political order.

A Confucian scholar-official Chen Hongmou (1669–1771), who took his office as a provincial governor in 1742, saw family as a sacred space that was "simultaneously emotional, hierarchical, and solidary." Chen attempted to retain the "affective, ritual, and ethical aspect of family" even after the family properties had been divided among siblings.[69] Chen Hongmou maintained that the entrenched lineage hall as an institution, *zongci* or *citang*, should serve as a courtroom where disputes would be mediated in public by the lineage head.[70] For Chen Hongmou, who stuck with the Song Neo-Confucian doctrines, family was a "realm where compassion reigns supreme" yet the "dictates of formal propriety" are the "supporting beams" of a family. These rituals in Chen's time included the Confucian Four (family) Rituals: capping, marriage, funerals, and ancestral sacrifice.[71] As a local administrator and social reformer, Chen focused on three aspects to change in order to foster a better community under his governance: strengthening the authority of the lineage head, promoting community granaries, and regularizing the district libational ceremony with the goal of rectifying the declining human mind-heart, for instance, morality.[72] Chen condemned the theft of communal grain as a violation of *tianli*, Heavenly principle. But here again, *tianli* was semantically understood as a secular code of behavior. In local religious life, Chen patronized the temple of the brave and loyal god of war, *guandi*, observed public rituals, and even prayed for rain on behalf of the people under his jurisdiction while convincing himself that he still stuck to the orthodox School of Principle, *lixue*, founded by the Cheng brothers and Zhu Xi.[73]

In daily usage, the term *li* could represent ethnical principle. This can be found in another local official named Wang Lüjie who observed the non-Han ethnic Miao people in southwest China in the eighteenth century and pondered the best policy to govern these "barbarians." He advocated for an appeasing and accommodating policy by saying "Though the Miao people are tough, they are also human beings. All human beings have the same heart, and all hearts have the same principle[*li*]. [The Miao] also know about respecting their fathers and elder brothers and revere their superiors. If [we] follow the policy of accommodation, how can they afford to stay outside of our culture?"[74] Wang demonstrated a Confucian paternalistic attitude toward the Miao people and in his parlance, "principle," *li*, was used in a benevolent way, stressing universal humanity regardless of ethnicity.

At the communal level, there was an innovative use of existent space for ritual and social purposes. One community school in the late eighteenth century was utilized by local elites to fulfill its potential in addition to the extolling of learning. The school was converted into an institution for solving local conflicts, substituting the litigation in a county government office, and it also became a post-sacrificial storage space for the spirit tablets of the lineage's founding ancestors, deities with national status, as well as more recent local exemplary persons who had been dead. The school therefore combined the functions of education, adjudication, and adulation.[75] As for the importance of the spirit tablet, since "soul" in Chinese was not an integral entity, some aspects of it survived independent of the part that went to the channel of reincarnation and will find their home in the ancestral tablet with the dead person's name inscribed.[76] In the Ming classical novel *Shuihu zhuan* [*Water Margin*] set against the political background of the Northern Song, the wooden spirit tablet is called *shenzhu*, "spirit lord." At the funeral of Chao Gai, the founder of the brotherhood, his *shenzhu* is erected in the center of the sacrificial hall with his surname and honorary title inscribed on it.[77]

QING SCHOLARS' APPROACH TO RITUAL,
RATIONAL PRINCIPLE, AND EMOTION

After the fall of the Ming, early Qing scholars continued to take issue with Song Confucian philosophers' reduction of all questions to their rigid, universal rational principle, *li*, but the late Ming radicals were also railed against because of their anti-intellectual stance and the hyperbolic self-confidence. Against this backdrop of reflection and rebellion, Qing scholars refocused on pre-Qin classics and the solid method of evidential research to understand them.[78] This led to a new epistemology of approaching the truth through evidence and the application of philological and phonetic knowledge.[79]

Huang Zongxi, the eminent Confucian philosopher who lived through the late Ming and early Qing years as a Ming loyalist, discussed the relationship of Heavenly principle and human emotions, acknowledging the latter's accessibility for common men and women: "Heavenly principle and human emotions are not two distinct things, but Heavenly principle is so intangible [*wuke zhuomo*] that it must be testified in human emotions."[80] Here Huang saw expression of emotions as the external manifestations of Heavenly principle that is congruent with human emotions. Early Qing Confucian philosopher Yan Yuan (1635–1704) embodied the spirit of his time in challenging Neo-Confucianism's excess of book learning and "empty talk" with revived ritualism. Doubting the value of quiet-sitting and lecturing which were prevalent during the Song and Ming periods as well as Song Confucians' verbal elaboration of issues such as human nature and moral obligation, Yan Yuan emphasized practice and observation of ritual in daily life. To Yan, who was not opposed to but followed Zhu Xi's *Family Rituals* seriously, the practice of concrete Confucian ritual acts through formalized rehearsal was a meaningful gesture to demonstrate his overall anti-Neo-Confucian attitude.[81]

The intellectual shifts since the fall of the Ming dynasty continued although the learning of Song Neo-Confucian rational principle had been upheld by the Qing court as orthodoxy and anchor of sociopolitical order by the mid-Qing. Although Yan Yuan did not associate ritual with emotional expression, eighteenth-century Confucian thinkers Dai Zhen (1724–1777), Ling Tingkan (1757–1809), and Ruan Yuan (1764–1849) believed that they needed to bring human "feelings and desires" back to the intellectual discourse because they battled the lingering "Buddhist" and "Daoist" influences relentlessly.[82] This implicitly shows that for these thinkers, the recognition of feelings and desires was quintessentially "Confucian," which had been tinged with Buddhism and Daoism since the Song dynasty. Yet rites were considered as congruent with emotions. Ling Tingkan, the mid-Qing scholar famous for his philosophical interest in *Li* and his attempt to "substitute principle with ritual," *yi Li dai li*, marked a major "shift in the intellectual center of gravity" in his time to uplift the subordinate status of *Li*.[83]

Ling Tingkan's concern with ritual studies related to the contemporaneous rise of the "cult of *qing*."[84] For Ling Tingkan, *qing* was not only a concept and abstract speculation but a concrete, private moral sentiment toward the plight of ordinary people, and he was affirmative of secular desires, believing music and drama were modes of emotional expression.[85] His interest in ritual studies was a natural consequence of his native province Anhui's deep respect for Zhu Xi's *Family Rituals*,[86] but his skepticism of the "nature-is-principle" and "heart/mind-is-principle" theories reflected a visible trend of his own time.[87] To upend the Song thinkers' assumption about the nature/emotion dichotomy, Ling proposed a legible sequence in which "nature generates emotions, and emotions generates desires," but for him, social ritual and code of conduct is needed to regulate emotion and desire so one can recover his original good nature.[88] This linear, emanating sequence from nature to emotion challenged Zhu Xi's dualism of the tranquil nature and the volatile emotion, a dialectical *yin-yang* structure.[89]

If there was an assumed connection between ritual and emotion, and nature was considered not a part of the Song "nature-principle" structure but part of the nature-emotion assemblage, then Ling Tingkan proposed the ritual-nature-emotion triad because for him, ritual and inherent human emotion were commensurate with each other and enhanced each other. Yet, for Ling, the supreme "Heavenly principle" which overrules rituals as their ontological foundation, could be incompatible with both rituals and emotions. By inflicting a blow on the Cheng-Zhu theory and reviving, or imagining, the Western Zhou polity and ritual system, Confucian scholars like Ling Tingkan and his friend Dai Zhen undermined the sanctity of *li* and shared an atavistic concern with "a serious reconstruction of the classical world in eighteenth-century China."[90] The pre-Qin ritual and emotional theory of Xunzi lent support to the pro-ritual argument of the late Qing. For Xunzi, rituals were created by the ancient sages to guide the people, and the Qing theory emphasizes the sages' human and sometimes flexible aspects. Therefore, Ling Tingkan commended Xunzi by saying "How great Xunzi was!" in his book.[91] It is arguable that they were unhappy with the *li*-centered absolutized dominant ideology of their time, hoping for a restoration to the more humane world of ritual-emotion during the pre-Qin period.

Qing Confucians might need to face a challenge: why were those complicated ritual actions or the many codes of conduct, as *Li* entails in different contexts, not as rigid, restrictive, and undesirable as "Heavenly principle"? One scholar Zhang Chengsun provided a cogent theory that reconciles ritual and emotion, which suggested that rituals were not only created to express human feelings but were, in the first place, based upon human feeling.[92] Zheng Zhen (1806–1864), a late Qing poet and specialist in ritual studies and a student of Ling Tingkan's student Cheng Enze, believed the ancient sages were very thoughtful and rational so when they created ritual propriety they sized up complex circumstances: they "created rituals based on normal human situation-emotion" [*shengrun yuan qing zhi Li*], thus a woman should not be considered a widow and observe the ritual code, if the husband had died before all the ritual steps of the wedding were completed.[93] When Zheng Zhen's baby son died in 1830, he enacted the ancient rite recorded in the Tan'gong chapter of the *Record of Rites* by exposing his left arm, howling for three times at the tomb to express his emotional pain, which a father who lost a child was supposed to do according to the rites.[94] Nevertheless, one flip side of ritualism in the lifeworld was that Confucian scholars' common practice of ritual by following ritual manuals in the early Qing might lead to the instrumentalization and manipulation of it.[95]

Dai Zhen dealt with the relationship between Heavenly principle and human feelings. Dai argued that "Heavenly principle is nothing but natural distinction; natural distinction means using my feeling to match others' feeling and the result will naturally be balance and fairness, *ping*," and that "When emotion reaches balance and fairness, it reaches the state of the regulated judgment of liking and disliking. This is in accordance with Heavenly principle."[96] Dai Zhen reinterpreted "Heavenly principle" as the secular, proper relationship between one's liking and disliking, i.e., benevolence, *ren*, and justice, *yi*, and he excoriated the Song Neo-Confucian proposition "Heaven is tantamount to rational principle" as "particularly erroneous."[97] For Dai Zhen, overemphasis on the impassive "rational principle" had three negative consequences: (1) It set a too high moral standard to be imposed on worthy people; (2) Scholars had become too pompous themselves and too harsh on judging others. (3) The promotion of principle and rejection of desire had created many hypocrites.[98] Dai Zhen assumes that human nature is composed of three parts: desire, *yu*, emotion, *qing*, and intellect, *zhi* and see the acquisition of human intellect as the prerequisite to fulfilling emotions and desires.[99]

Through his seminal book *A Philological Study of the Mengzi* [*Mengzi zi yi shu zheng*], Dai Zhen attempt to establish his own philosophy despite its modest title, by which Dai Zhen wanted to show his detractors that his study was not only ambitious but also solid.[100] The book aims at mounting rebuttal against the Cheng-Zhu learning of rational principle. As Dai wrote to a friend, "The Way of the sages was letting All-Under-Heaven free from emotions that are not expressed and free from unfulfilled desires. All-under-Heaven will be thus governed properly."[101] In *A Philological Study of the Mengzi*, Dai Zhen reiterated that "When the sages ruled All-under-Heaven, they emphasized with the people's emotion and satisfy people's desires, and thus the kingly Way was complete."[102] After examining the book through a modern, comparative lenses, late Qing reformer and scholar Liang Qichao (1873–1927) made a brisk comment, "To sum up, the content of the book was nothing but replacing the 'philosophy of rationality,' *lixing zhexue*, with the 'philosophy of emotion,' *qinggan zhexue*. In terms of this feature, it was very similar to the trend of thought during the Enlightenment movement in Europe."[103] Other scholars paid attention to Dai Zhen's political stance: he condemned the absolutized rationality without elasticity and he sympathized with the people who were ruled by the imperial government.[104] Dai Zhen bashed Song philosophers by exposing how they distorted and abused the original meaning of the word "*li*." In actual life, the term *li* had been cited repeatedly by people in superior positions to blame inferior people and *li* was nothing but their personal prejudices and habits. Modern thinker Hu Shi (1891–1962) was impressed by Dai Zhen's advocacy of emotion/desire-centered political philosophy and he compared it to Jeremy Bentham's utilitarianism.[105]

Dai Zhen's more polemical *Inquiry into Goodness* [*Yuan shan*] justified human senses and feelings in a lengthy passage as the centerpiece of his polemics,

> The five colors, the five sounds, the five smells, and the five tastes are the norms of Heaven and Earth relative to the senses; joy, anger, sorrow and happiness, love, resentment, cares and misgivings, irascibility and indignation, fear and melancholy, the desires for food and for sex, enduring moodiness and rampant feelings of misfortune, grief and exaltation, like and dislikes—these are all due to nature at the very beginning of its formation and are therefore called the Way.[106]

His view of gender relations in marriage was also revolutionary:
> The perfect or ideal relationship between husband and wife is comparable to that between father and son regarding the feelings of love and gratitude that should obtain between them; it is comparable to that between elder and younger brothers regarding the feelings of harmony between them."[107]

Dai was never advocating carefree self-indulgence. For him, natural human desires and ritual propriety were the two things that one should attend to simultaneously: "If men pay attention only to their own desires and are not benevolent and hence are devoid of the feelings of propriety and righteousness, then trouble, disaster, danger, and destruction will ensue."[108] In Dai's view, balancing the satisfaction of emotions and desires and the observance of propriety was a prudent and mindful way of life.

Qing classical studies and hermeneutics continued to approach the ritual-emotion interplay by interpreting the Han dynasty studies of

Confucianism. For instance, Eastern Han classist Zheng Xuan believed filial sons were expected to perform sacrifice to parents who died recently on a daily basis because they "cannot bear to abandon their rite of serving parents on a single day, so they perform daily sacrifices as if the parents are still alive" in his annotation of the *Classic of Filial Piety* [109] Late Qing classicist Pi Xirui continued to explicate Zheng Xuan's annotation by emphasizing that in the pre-Qin time only after certain days did the filial sons treat their parents no longer as living people but as true ancestral ghosts and spirits, and they stopped daily serving thereafter.[110]

By the end of the nineteenth century, Confucianism had been institutionalized as a pervasive non-Western belief, value, and ritual system entrenched in Chinese society. The Board of Rites of the Ming and Qing central governments devised ritual details in their handbooks and monitor the implementation. The Board classified the state ceremonies into two groups: quasi-religious sacrifices to deities and the imperial ancestors, and another group observed the more secular political, military, and diplomatic rituals. When the Manchu Qing forces entered Beijing in 1644, the emperor performed a sacrifice at the altar to Heaven built by the Ming.[111] The hierarchical yet paternalistic and reciprocal state guest ritual that distinguishes supreme and lesser lords caused tensions in China's diplomatic engagement with Britain in the late eighteenth century.[112]

CONCLUSION

Among scholars engaged in independent and reflective thinking and writing during the Ming-Qing period, there emerged a shared trend of reasserting human emotions and desires. At the same time, the rituals were rediscovered as a source of inspiration to check the power of the detached, indifferent Heavenly principle that was deemed not as humane, emotionally charged, and resilient as the rituals. Whereas Song Dynasty thinkers gave a more prominent place to the overarching cosmological-rational principle in this triad, their Qing critics established a stronger bond between ritual and emotion after doubting the absolutism of rational principle as the ultimate value that buttressed the hierarchical and oppressive moral order and questioning if Song philosophers distorted the original meaning of the word *li*. Ming-Qing thinkers also found the "Heavenly (rational) principle" had been abused by the superiors and elders in the lineage power structure in real life only to reinforce the status and power of the monarch, the father, and the husband. Instead, they took the mundane world of daily life and human normal sentiments more seriously. The pleasure they sought was connected with the fulfillment of desire, or it might be called "practical pleasure."[113]

At the same time, lineage groups prevalent in the Ming-Qing period sustained ritualism and financially supported their young members to prepare for the imperial Civil Service Examination.[114] Despite their controlling, authoritarian, and oppressive aspects that might smother individuality, lineage groups also provided social spaces to facilitate the emotional cohesiveness and reciprocity among the members, and the institution was encouraged by the early Qing rulers to play the stabilizing role. The emperors, governors, and patriarchs believed that through the lineage-based ritual actions at the grass-roots level, mutual feelings could be cultivated, reinforced, and communicated, and hence society could achieve solidarity with the rectified human heart-mind and collective moral transformation.

The Confucian attempt to balance emotion, rationality, and ritual propriety can be reconsidered from a global, comparative perspective.[115] Adam Smith admitted that for private misfortunes, "our feelings are apt to go beyond the bounds of propriety."[116] Confucian philosophers' cautious legitimization of emotions and their taming in a relational entanglement was certainly not as bold as Fredrich Nietzsche who sees feelings not as a consequence or outgrowth of something else but a driving force, a cause that arouses human actions.[117] However, we should keep in mind that Confucian thinkers' self-imposed ultimate goal was to attain sagehood, which required the appropriateness of conduct through balancing and integrating one's emotion, rationality, and ritual propriety, and through both internal self-cultivation and external sociopolitical engagements.[118]

NOTES

1. Wang Fansen, *Wan Ming Qing chu sixiang shilun* [Ten Studies of the Thoughts in Late Ming and Early Qing] (Shanghai: Fudan daxue chubanshe, 2004), 93.

2. Many of this kind of anecdote are recorded in late Ming-early Qing Confucian scholar Huang Zongxi's Ming ru xue an [Intellectual Biographies of Ming Confucian Scholars].

3. Jonathan D. Spence, *Return to Dragon Mountain: Memories of Late Ming Man* (New York: Penguin Group, 2007), 38. For the expression of affections in Chinese theatricality in the late Ming, also see Lam, *The Spatiality of Emotion in Early Modern China*.

4. Hinsch, *Women in Imperial China*, 160–61.

5. Dong Ping, *Wang Yangming de shenghuo shijie* [The Lifeworld of Wang Yangming] (Beijing: zhongguo renmin daxue chubanshe, 2009), 8–9.

6. WM. Theodore de Bary and Irene Bloom, *Sources of Chinese Tradition*, 843. I translate *xin* as "mind-heart," rather than "mind-and-heart" because for me it is just one character containing two modern meanings, and it does not have any hint of "A and B" in Chinese.

7. Ibid., 844.

8. Ibid., 849.

9. Ibid., 846.

10. Ibid., 846. I modified de Bary and Irene Bloom's translation of *liangzhi* as "innate knowledge" to "innate moral knowledge," because Wang Yangming makes it clear that this is knowledge about external things but the ability of knowing good and evil, and thus I think *liangzhi* is a moral concept.

11. For the importance of *qing* in Wang Yangming's doctrine, see Yinghua Lu, "Wang Yangming's Theory of the Unity of Knowledge and Action Revisited: An Investigation from the Perspective of Moral Emotion," *Philosophy East and West* 69, no. 1 (2019): 197–14.

12. Irene Bloom, "Philosophy of Lo Ch'in-shun," in *Principle and Practicality*, eds. WM. Theodore de Bary and Irene Bloom (New York: Columbia University Press, 1979), 83.

13. Ibid., 84.

14. Ibid., 96.

15. Ibid., 97–98.

16. Yang Guorong, *Zinxue zhi si: Wang Yangming zhexue de chanshi* [The Contemplation of the Learning of the Heart-Mind: Interpreting the Philosophy of Wang Yangming] (Beijing: Sanlian shudian,1997), 36, 122.

17. WM. Theodore de Bary and Irene Bloom, *Sources of Chinese Tradition*, 857.

18. Ibid., 858.

19. Ibid., 859.

20. Ibid., 862.

21. Huang Zongxi, *Ming ru xue an.*

22. Huang Zongxi, *Ming ru xue an.*

23. Chih-P'ing Chou, *Yüan Hung-tao and the Kung-an School* (Cambridge, UK: Cambridge University Press, 1988), 2–3.

24. WM. Theodore de Bary and Irene Bloom, *Sources of Chinese Tradition*, 871.

25. Ibid., 873.

26. Qiong Zhang, *Making the New World Their Own: Chinese Encounters with Jesuit Science in the Age of Discovery* (Leiden: Brill, 2015), 220.

27. WM. Theodore de Bary, "Individualism and Humanitarianism in Late Ming Thought," in *Self and Society in Ming Thought*, eds. WM. Theodore de Bary and the conference on Ming thought (New York: Columbia University Press, 1970), 197.

28. This tendency was commended by twentieth century Chinese Marxist intellectual historians as "progressive" and "anti-feudal." See Hou Wailu, *Zhongguo sixiang shi gang* [An Outline of Chinese Intellectual History] (Shanghai: shiji chuban jituan, 2008), 335.

29. Li Zhi, *Fen shu* [Book to be Burned] (Beijing: Jiuzhou chubanshe, 2001), 116.

30. Lü Kun, *Shenyin yu/xiaochuang youji* [Murmuring Speeches/Anecdotal Records under the Small Window] (Beijing: Zongjiao wenhua chubanshe, 2002), 45.

31. Ibid., 165.

32. Ibid., 166.

33. Ibid., 49.

34. WM. Theodore de Bary and Irene Bloom, *Sources of Chinese Tradition*, 896.

35. On-Cho Ng, *Cheng-Zhu Confucianism in the Early Qing* (Albany: State University of New York Press, 2001), 31–32.

36. Ibid., 45–46.

37. Meng Peiyuan, *Lixue de yanbian: cong Zhu Xi dao Wang fuzhi Dai Zhen* [Evolution of Neo-Confucianism: from Zhu Xi and Wang Fuzhi and Dai Zhen] (Beijing: Fangzhi chubanshe, 2007), 318–19.

38. David Faure, *Emperor and Ancestor: State and Lineage in South China* (Stanford, CA: Stanford University Press, 2007), 10, 75.

39. Jia Qianchu, *Zhudong de chenmin: Mingdai Taizhou xuepai pingmin ruxue zhi zhengzhi wenhua yanjiu* [Imperial Subjects Who Take the Initiative: A Study of the Political Culture of the Popular Confucianism of Ming Dynasty's Taizhou School] (Beijing: zhishi chanquan chubanshe, 2018), 84–85.

40. Kung-Chuan Hsiao, *Rural China: Imperial Control in the Nineteenth Century* (Seattle: University of Washington Press, 1960), 220–21.

41. Lin, *Yixu de zongzu yanjiu*, 28. Lin renders the Chinese word *zongzu* as "clan," while Maurice Freedman uses the word "lineage" to describe a single-surname village.

42. C.K. Yang, *A Chinese Village in Early Chinese Transition* (Cambridge, MA: The MIT Press, 1959), 97.

43. T'ung-Tsu Ch'ü, *Local government in China under the Ch'ing* (Cambridge, MA: Harvard University Press, 1962), 164.

44. Ibid., 165.

45. Arthur P. Wolf, "Gods, Ghosts, and Ancestors," in *Religion and Ritual in Chinese Society*, ed. Arthur P. Wolf (Stanford, CA: Stanford University Press, 1974), 144.

46. Charles A. Litzinger, "Rural Religion and Village Organization," in *Christianity in China: From the Eighteenth Century to the Present*, ed. Daniel Bays (Stanford, CA: Stanford University Press, 1996), 41–42.

47. Liu Yonghua, *Liyi xiaxiang: Ming dai yijiang min xi sipu de liyi biange yu shehui zhuanxing* [Ritual and Etiquettes Go to Villages: Ritual Reform in the Sipu Region of Western Fujian and Social Transformation] (Beijing: sanlian shudian, 2019), 13.

48. Ibid., 139.

49. Nicolas Standaert, *The Interweaving of Rituals: Funerals in the Cultural Exchange Between China and Europe* (Seattle: University of Washington Press, 2008), 93.

50. T'ung-Tsu Ch'ü, *Local government in China under the Ch'ing*, 19.

51. Liu, *Liyi xiaxiang*, 51, 73.

52. Ibid., 56, 237.

53. Ibid., 198, 234.

54. Hilary J. Beattie, *Land and Lineage in China: A Study of T'ung-Ch'eng County, Anhwei, in the Ming and Qing Dynasties* (Cambridge, UK: Cambridge University Press, 1979), 117–19.

55. Standaert, *The Interweaving of Rituals*, 171–72.

56. Li, *Yili yu liji de shehuixue yanjiu*, 15.

57. Zheng Zhenman, *Family Lineage Organization and Social Change in Ming and Qing Fujian*, trans. Michael Szonyi with the Assistance of Kenneth Dean and Dave, 72.

58. Ibid., 197.

59. Ibid., 201.

60. Rev. William Miline, "Translator's Preface," *in The Sacred Edicts, containing sixteen maxims of the Emperor Kang-he, Amplified by His Son, the Emperor Yoong-ching; together with a Paraphrases on the Whole by a Mandarin* (London: Black, Kingsbury, Parbury, and Allen, 1817), x.

61. Ibid., 30, 36.

62. Ibid., 59.

63. Ibid., 66.

64. Ibid., 76.

65. Ibid., 98.

66. Ibid., 73–74.

67. Shen Daming, *"Da Qing Lüli"* yu Qing dai de shehui kongzhi [Qing Code and the Social Control of the Qing Dynasty] (Shanghai: Shanghai renmin chubanshe, 2007), 125.

68. This is based on the eminent modern Chinese scholar Hu Shi's (1891–1962) knowledge of his own clan in Jixi, Anhui province. See Hu Shi, "Zhi Hu Jinren, Hu Enyu" [Letter to Hu Jinren and Hu Enyu], in *Hu Shi shuxin ji*, eds. Geng Yunzhi, Ouyang Zhesheng [Collected Letters of Hu Shi] (Beijing: Beijing daxue chubanshe,1996), 513.

69. William Rowe, "Ancestral Rites and Political Authority in Late Imperial China: Chen Hongmou in Jiangxi," in *Modern China* 24, no. 4 (1998): 379–80.

70. Gan Chunsong, *Zhidu hua rujia jiqi jieti* [Institutionalized Confucianism and Its Disintegration] (Beijing: Zhongguo renmin daxue chubanshe, 2003), 89.

71. Rowe, "Ancestral Rites and Political Authority in Late Imperial China: Chen Hongmou in Jiangxi," 380.

72. Ibid., 395.

73. William Rowe, *Saving the World: Chen Hongmou and Elite Consciousness in Eighteenth Century China* (Stanford, CA: Stanford University Press, 2001), 96–97.

74. Guo Wu, "Accommodation and Conflict: The Incorporation of Miao Territory and Construction of Cultural Difference during the High Qing Era," *Frontiers of History in China* 7, no. 2 (2012): 251.

75. Luo Yixing, "Territorial Community at Lubao," in David Faure and Helen Siu eds., *Down to Earth: The Territorial Bond in South China* (Stanford, CA: Stanford University Press, 1995), 59–61.

76. For discussions on Chinese death ritual, see *Death Ritual in Late Imperial and Modern China*, eds. James L. Watson and Evelyn S. Rawski (Berkeley: University of California Press, 1988).

77. Shi Naian, Luo Guanzhong, *Shuihu quan zhuan* [Water Margin] (Wuhan: Chongwen shuju, 2006), 379.

78. Chen Zuwu, Zhu Tongchuang, *QianJia xuepai yanjiu* [A Study of the Confucian Scholarship during the Qianlong-Jiaqing Reign] (Shijiazhuang: Hebei renmin chubanshe, 2007), 81–82.

79. Benjamin Elman, *From Philosophy to Philology: Intellectual and Social Aspects of Change in Late Imperial China* (Cambridge, MA: Council on East Asian Studies, Harvard University, 1984), 43–44.

80. Huang Zongxi, *Ming ru xue an.*

81. Shang Wei, *Rulin waishi and Cultural Transformation in Late Imperial China* (Cambridge, MA: Harvard University Asia Center, 2003), 36–41.

82. Kai-wing Chow, *The Rise of Confucian Ritualism in Late Imperial China: Ethics, Classics, and Lineage Discourse* (Stanford, CA: Stanford University Press, 1994), 201.

83. Ori Sela, *China's Philological Turn: Scholars, Textualism, and the Dao in the Eighteenth Century* (New York: Columbia University Press, 2018), 172–73.

84. Ibid.

85. Zhang Shouan, *Ling Tingkan yu Qing dai zhongye ruxue sixiang zhi zhuanhuan* [Ling Tingkan and the Transition of Mid-Qing Confucianism] (Shijiazhuang: Hebei jiaoyu chubanshe, 2001), 14–15.

86. Ibid., 23.

87. Ibid., 32.

88. Ibid., 45.

89. He Bingsong correctly points out the Daoist component in Zhu Xi's philosophy, see He Bingson, *Zhe dong xuepai suyuan* [Tracing the Origins of the Eastern Zhejiang Academic School] (Guilin: Guangxi shifan daxue chubanshe, 2004), 45.

90. Minghui Hu, *China's Transition to Modernity: The New Classical Vision of Daizhen* (Seattle: University of Washington Press, 2015), 108.

91. Qian Mu, *Zhongguo jin sanbai nian xueshu shi* [An Intellectual History of China in the Last Three Hundred Years] (Beijing: Shangwu yinshu guan, 1997), 544–45.

92. Zhang, *Ling Tingkan yu Qing dai zhongye ruxue sixiang zhi zhuanhuan*, 134.

93. Guo Wu, "Zheng Zhen and the Rise of Evidential Research in Late Qing Northern Guizhou," *Journal of Chinese History* 2, no. 1 (2018): 158.

94. Dai Mingxian, *Ziwu shan hai Zheng Zhen: ren yu shi* [The Child of the Meridian Hill: Zheng Zhen, The Man and His Poetry] (Beijing: renming wenxue chubanshe, 2013), 31. The ritualist and emotional treatment of a dead infant here contradicts with modern anthropological observations about how callously Chinese treat young children who die untimely deaths, see Wolf, "Gods, Ghosts, and Ancestors," in *Religion and Ritual in Chinese Society*, 148. My interpretation is that Zheng Zhen demonstrated an attitude of a sophisticated cultural elite who could cite Confucian classics to justify his emotional expression.

95. Shang, *Rulin waishi and Cultural Transformation in Late Imperial China*, 14–15.

96. Chen Zuwu, Zhu Tongchuang, *QianJia xuepai yanjiu*, 281.

97. Qian, *Zhongguo jin sanbai nian xueshu shi*, 373.

98. Chai Degeng, *Qing dai xueshu shi jiangyi* [Lecture Notes of History of Qing Scholarship] (Beijing: Shangwu yinshuguan, 2013), 107.

99. Wang Xuequn, *Qing dai xuewen de minjin* [Approaches to Qing Scholarship] (Beijing: Zhonghua shuju, 2009), 241.

100. For this motivation, see Yu Yingshi, *Lun Dai Zhen yu Zhang Xuecheng* [On Dai Zhen and Zhang Xuecheng] (Beijing: Sanlian shudian, 2005), 124.

101. Liang Qichao, *Qing dai xueshu gailun* [An Outline Discussion on Qing Scholarship] (Guilin: Guangxi shifa daxue chubanshe, 2010), 44.

102. Ibid., 45.

103. Ibid., 47.

104. Tan Pimo, *Qing dai sixiang shi gang* [An Outline History of Qing Dynasty Ideas] (Shanghai: Shanghai guji chubanshe, 2013), 59.

105. Hu Shi, *Dai Dongyuan de zhexue* [The Philosophy of Dai Zhen (Dongyuan)] (Shanghai: Shanghai guji chubanshe, 2013), 39. 41.

106. Chung-ying Cheng, *Tai Chen's Inquiry into Goodness* (Honolulu: University of Hawaii Press, 1971), 84.

107. Ibid., 112.

108. Ibid., 111.

109. Pi Xirui, *Xiao jing Zheng zhu shu* [Explanation of Zheng Xuan's Annotation of the Classic of Filial Piety] (Beijing: Zhonghua shuju, 2016), 43.

110. Ibid.

111. Evelyn S. Rawski, *The Last Emperors: A Social History of Qing Imperial Institutions* (Berkeley: University of California Press, 1998), 201–3.

112. For a discussion of the ritual actions on their own terms, see James Hevia, *Cherishing Men from Afar: Qing Guest Ritual and the Macartney Mission of 1793* (Durham. NC: Duke University Press, 1995).

113. Kant, *The Metaphysics of Morals*, trans. Mary Gregor, 40.

114. See Ping-ti Ho, *The Ladder of Success in Imperial China: Aspects of Social Mobility, 1368–1911* (New York: Columbia University Press, 1962).

115. Immanuel Kant held the opinion that people fundamentally cannot control their emotions, but in public people are morally responsible for treating each other with respect, not because of the genuine feeling but because the person you dislike is a human being. See Bryan W. Van Norden, *Introduction to Classical Chinese Philosophy* (Indianapolis, IN: Hackett Publishing, 2011), 28. In contrast to the Kantian emphasis on the absolute purity of motive in a moral action, as Justin Tiwald argues, Dai Zhen was realistic and fair enough to recognize "self-interest as an important source of morality" in his pursuit of "good shared-end relationships" of "mutual fulfillment." See Justin Tiwald, "Shared Ends: Kant and Dai Zhen on the Ethical Value of Mutuality Fulfilling Relationships," *Journal of Confucian Philosophy and Culture* 33 (2020): 107.

116. Adam Smith, *The Theory of Moral Sentiments* (Los Angeles: Logos Books, 2018), 123.

117. Friedrich Nietzsche, *Twilight of the Idols*, trans. Richard Polt (Indianapolis, IN: Hackett Publishing, 1997), 34–35.

118. For Wang Yangming's self-imposed sense of mission to become a sage, see Yang, *Xinxue zhi si*, 36.

Conclusion

Reinventing Confucian Ritualism and the Modern Fate of the Triad

The three key intellectual strands in the pre-Qin, Tang-Song, and Ming-Qing periods, which I delineated in chapters 2, 3, 4, met the criteria of "Science/ Intellectual Movements (SIM)" in that the first one responded to political chaos and moral disorientation during the pre-Qin period, focusing on rites/ etiquettes/social protocols and their relations with human emotions; the second one responded to the challenge of Buddhism, which entails "void" for Confucianism, and Confucian scholars of the Tang-Song period added a metaphysical and ontological dimension, the "Heavenly principle," to the Confucian discourse while also elaborating on rites on both polemical and practical levels; and the Ming-Qing Confucian scholars refocused on the power and legitimacy of human emotions and tried to supplant the dominant rational principle concept with the more tangible and resilient rites. Each generation of Confucianists had their specific challenges to respond to and their own complaints and doubts to address, and each had its own intellectual leaders and followers who formed a collective of proponents.[1] Does the twenty-first century revival of Confucianism qualify as a SIM? I think it is already very close to it. At least, it is a response to modern Western culture and globalization, with its own discontents, leaders, resources, and venues. According to Guy Alitto, there are two types of modern Confucianism: high-level, self-conscious, text-based Confucianism as an academic discourse and Confucianism as a social or spiritual practice.[2]

REVIVAL OF CONFUCIAN RITUALISM
IN CHINESE SOCIETY

The early twenty-first century has witnessed the triumphant "revival of traditional culture," *chuantong wenhua fuxing,* in mainland China, centering on Confucianism-related institutions, spaces, and cultural activities. At the state level, official ceremonies to commemorate the birth of Confucius have been held in many Confucian temples around the country, attended by important CCP and government leaders, scholars, students, and tourists. In Qufu, Shandong province, which is proud of being the birthplace of Confucius and the home of the Kong clan since the pre-Qin time, the commemorative ceremony celebrating the birthday of Confucius was revived in 1984. The institutionalized annual birthday celebration on September 28 in the Confucian Temple in Qufu has become official and it means no admittance of tourists for one day because important state and provincial leaders make speeches, and carefully chosen honored guests and organized school students attend. The entire process of speeches and atavistic worshiping, sacrifice, dancing, and musical instrument playing is televised live to the world, introduced by local TV anchors and commented on by specially invited scholars of Confucianism.

The nationwide celebration of Confucius's birthday has been highly politicized and the image of Confucius appropriated by the state to showcase its respect for China's "traditional culture." This is not based upon real, direct "social memory" but a "social reconstruction."[3] This reconstruction and appropriation is perhaps not different from how past dynasties treated the Kong clan, the Confucian Temple, although the "birthday" of Confucius based on the Gregorian calendar seems to be the modern invention of the twentieth century. At least, the birthday celebration for Confucius is a modern ritual, even if the date is accurate. The ceremonial use of the archaic four-character sentences sounds a little strange to modern ears when read out by a government official.

Why is there such a fever? Inspired by the patriotic yet iconoclastic cultural climate of the May Fourth movement of 1919, the first generation CCP leaders were hardly friendly to Confucianism. The best treatment of Confucianism before the insulting "Criticize Confucius" campaign of the 1970s was perhaps studying it as part of "traditional culture," but all the studies after 1949 had to be ideologically streamlined to comply with the methodology of Marxist historical materialism, in which Confucius was "feudal" and Zhu Xi's doctrine of Principle idealistic and reactionary. The Cultural Revolution was a time of passion and the invention of new political rituals.[4] However, associated with personality cult and the public good, Maoist political rituals failed to fulfill people's "expectations of reciprocity and human feeling."[5]

For over a century, the modern Chinese state and the intelligentsia have been deeply involved in defining modern China as a unified nation with multiple ethnic minorities.[6] Yet Confucius and Confucianism in China do not appeal to non-Han peoples who have their own cultural heritage and belief systems. The changed official attitude and the state's enthusiastic patronage of Confucian resurgence symbolizes the state's turn to (Han) cultural nationalism: In an age of global capitalism and hegemonic Western technology and popular culture, the image of Confucius and the performed Confucianism serve as an asset make "us" feel our "non-Western" (Han) Chinese identity and proud cultural heritage. To be sure, "cultural heritage" and its reinvention are always entangled with government ideology and political agenda in contemporary China.[7]

China's rising urban middle class joined the cultural enterprise of reviving Confucianism and became infatuated with the rites. Invested in by a group of Guizhou businessmen and located on a hilltop, Guiyang's large-scale Confucian Academy was open to the public in 2012. It works like an NGO devoted to hosting free "public interest" lectures to local citizens and cultural events related to traditional festivities rather than merely worshipping Confucius and other sages, who have their beautiful statues there, though. As a theme-park-like site of cultural heritage, the academy also patronizes academic research and a journal on Confucianism and collectively hosts the "Four Rites of the Confucian School," *Kong men si li*— "opening the pen," for instance, matriculation for the young first graders; "initiation," targeting young adults who just turned eighteen; "revering the elders"; and "Chinese traditional wedding ceremony." These public "ceremonials" and their variations in other regions are all secular and interpersonal, aiming to launch socialization processes by forging and reinforcing the affective ties between children and their parents, pupils and their teachers, the young and the old, and husband and wife, as well as the moral duty of young men and women who just entered adulthood. A modified private Confucian-style wedding ceremony based upon Zhu Xi's *Family Rituals* was performed by a descendent of Zhu Xi in 2009 and two similar Confucian wedding ceremonies took place in 2010 and 2011.[8] As mentioned in chapter 4, as late as the Qing dynasty, the state-sanctioned "Four Confucian Rituals" were capping, marriage, funeral, and ancestral sacrifice, but the modern "Four Rituals" are apparently an invention and combination. Through new ritual steps such as pupils' collective writing of the Chinese character *ren*, or "person," the young participants are expected to learn respect, mutual love, and responsibility and thus acquire a virtuous disposition.

Rituals are changing. Even during the Ming-Qing period, not all localities adhered to Zhu Xi's *Family Rituals*, although the manual held an orthodox status in theory. In real life, local activists created new rituals by incorporating indigenous worship or by adding new rituals.[9] Since the late 1970s, the ancestral shrine and ancestral rites, which had been suspended in the early 1950s because of the Communist confiscation of the ancestral trust land, have been revived, but the destroyed ancestral tablet was replaced by a photograph, if available.[10]

One significant modern reform is that while in Confucius's time, the initiation rite was differentiated by gender, today's Four Rites have no gender
distinction. In contrast with the traditional, more rural "communal libational
rite," which had been abandoned, these four new rites are very urban in terms
of their location and participants. They were also no longer lineage-based but
public spectacles for visitors and journalists. Acting out some pellucid core
Confucian values through ritual performance, the organizers nationwide have
provided an alternative, public and performative pedagogical venue outside
of the school system that focuses on academic learning and exam preparation. One thing that remains unchanged in some non-commercialized local
rituals is the distribution and consumption of cooked sacrificial meat among
the participants, just as Confucius himself was treated as a Lu state official,
based upon one's status in the hierocracy, gender, and seniority.[11]

Reinvented Confucian ceremonies as a mode of conveying emotions and
forging comity largely appeal to the spiritual sensibilities of the rising urban
middle class, who want their children to "experience the traditional culture"
through the atavistic recreation of rituals, and to strengthen the parent-child
relationship in a ritualized way. According to my remote, online interview
with the contact person in Qufu's Confucian Temple, while the Confucian
Temple has its own research institute where scholars publish books and host
international symposiums, the organization of the popular ceremonies is con-
tracted to a ceremony company. Is an urban middle class of China trying to
fulfill a religious sentiment while Buddhism and Daoism are less "civic" and
Communism too lofty? Filial piety, respect for education and marriage, and
a sense of ethical duty—affective relationality might be the essence that has
been submerged and needs to be fostered today. At least, the prevalence of
neo-traditionalist rituals in China testifies that there is a stability of Chinese
values and worldview, and perhaps it is true that "[p]rogressive Confucianism
needs to find more room for ritual to play a constructive role. . . ."[12]

Questioning "authenticity" always appears; people have asked whether
those were "real ancient rites," but most of the time, it was irrelevant. Even
if the organizer of the event explains that they consulted the Ming Dynasty
ritual handbook beforehand, it can hardly be "authentic" because the Ming
rituals were already reconstructed or reinvented *in toto* compared with the
genuine "ancient rites" of Confucius' time. The *shidian* ritual to commemorate the purported birthday of Confucius on September 28 also shows great
regional variations in terms of ritual details, from the sacrificial objects that
are used to the number of dancers who perform. Apparently, the politicized
reinvention of the *shidian* rite to commemorate the birthday of Confucius and
the social invention of the "Four Rites (of passage)" were not unconscious
evolution of custom but artificial "invention of tradition" through which "[s]
tate, nation, and society converged."[13] The new "Four Rites," local variations

notwithstanding, all require the young attendees to be dressed in Han dynasty style clothing, and all involve bodily movements such as bowing.

But these phenomena in the contemporary Chinese lifeworld are all new to me. There was a revival of Confucianism in the Chinese academic world beginning in the 1980s, and Arif Dirlik very aptly grasps its "ideological meaning" regarding "the place of non-Euro/American intellectual traditions in the contemporary discourse on culture."[14] However, diffusion and ritualization did not occur until the early twenty-first century. When I grew up as a schoolchild in the 1980s, we only had the ceremony of joining Young Pioneers for first graders and national flag-raising ceremony and singing the national anthem on a daily basis. Before I left China in 2000, I had never heard of these public "Confucian" rites or celebration of Confucius's birthday, nor did I dare to imagine the reinvention of "Han dynasty style clothing" among college students to accompany the rites of passage, based upon a romanticized image of the great Han dynasty.[15]

The purpose of reinventing these collective rituals is to assert the codified idioms in which the state and society select signals and invent new cultural forms that are regarded as compatible with a (Han) Chinese identity. Through this performative reinvention of affective actions, the organizers aroused human feelings toward the shared heritage and each other. As David Couch argues, "Repetition and ritual, or performance, can bring affects that, in the way of performativity, can effect."[16] Together, these can also be understood as new folklore, *xin minsu*, to use the current Chinese term or even more derogatory "fakelore," or *wei minsu* in Chinese. Cultural productions like these modern rituals in the PRC exemplify the "late socialist cultural condition" and the "cultural logic of late socialism," to use Ka-ming Wu's terminologies.[17] The "rediscovery and piecing together" of tradition and the use of performative "visual representations of the sacred communities,"[18] is part of the modern Chinese nationalist project. According to political scientist Zheng Yongnian, the popularity of Confucian activities marks a significant ideological transition in the early twenty-first century PRC, in which the ruling Communist Party's own modern, radical revolutionary ideology accommodated and returned to a tradition-based nation-state ideology; between these two ideologies, the ritualized nation-state ideology, which is derived from Confucianism, is easier than the Party ideology for people from different social walks to accept.[19] The only remaining problem is one that has been approached by anthropologists: the tension between the public "performative nature" of ritual and the genuine inner "sincerity of feeling."[20] But as we have also shown in chapter 2, Confucius has encountered this conflict and he chose to prioritize emotional honesty.

Confucian influence on private rites seems to be more natural. Martin C. Yang's observation of the Chinese funeral based on his fieldwork in the 1940s is still valid for understanding the relationship between ritual, emotion, and Confucianism: (1) Providing a proper funeral is the filial duty of the surviving children of the deceased, and failure to do so is socially despicable; (2) the ceremonies and feasts were devised by ancient sages to preclude the descendants' forgetting of ancestors, while the descendants already tended to "pretend" that parents were still alive; (3) deceased parents and ancestors were remembered and missed but not "worshipped" in the Western sense.[21] All these are the features that should be considered when Confucianism is now entering inevitable cross-cultural dialogues with other cultural traditions. In fact, the most detailed studies of Chinese funeral rites in modern Western languages are done by anthropologists in south and central China, according to Susan Naquin, a historian with deep anthropological interest, and based on her study on Chinese funeral practice from the late nineteenth century to the mid-twentieth century, Naquin concludes that "Funerals were intended to give formal expression not only to the feelings of grief and loss that a death generated but also to the ensuing rearrangement of relationships."[22] For Naquin, funeral rituals, which can find the most authoritative reference in Confucian classics, are the quintessential expression of the Confucian value of *xiao*, or filial piety.[23] This observation reaffirms the conclusion of Martin C. Yang and also my own funeral experience.

While anthropological studies on Chinese rituals toward a plethora of gods and deities emphasize the resemblance between the image and role of high gods and government officials and the ritual performances were used to exercise social control and political authority, I tweak this politicized perspective in my current research.[24] Whether in the Confucian thought reflected in the remarks of Confucius, Cheng Yi, and Zhu Xi or in real-life, true human, affective emotions, their expressions are not only desired but also practiced through participatory, interpersonal ritual procedures taking place in ritual spaces. As I have shown in this book, Confucian philosophers not only presented their thoughts in a detached and abstract way; they lived Confucian lives, and they were immersed in rituals, clan and community construction, and all sorts of social relations. Confucianism, despite its distinctive external ritualism, is about how to "carry out one's civil duties as a good citizen" and how to attain "the highest good," and John Rawls's description of ancient Greek moral philosophy applies to Confucianism.[25] Confucian thinkers such as Zhu Xi and Wang Yangming took the attainment of sagehood as the "endpoint" of their "ultimate transformation," and as Rodney L. Taylor argues, the goal of moral intellectual perfection is "the Absolute" for Zhu Xi and Wang Yangming and some of their followers.[26]

ACADEMIC INQUIRIES INTO
CONFUCIAN EMOTIONALISM

Yet, the genuine academic interest in Confucianism should not be neglected. In the academic field of researching Confucianism as a philosophy, there have been two new foci: an interest in emotion and a reassessment of Xunzi. Contemporary philosopher Li Zehou notices the emphasis on *qing* in the Guodian bamboo slip texts, and he correctly points out the dual meaning of *qing* as both situation and emotion. An ideal Chinese mind is aesthetic, Li argues, and it is both within the nexus of emotions and can also transcend it. Fundamentally, Li believes that for Confucianism, all external rational regulations, imperatives, and ritual systems must hinge on internal emotional needs.[27] There is no real tranquility, Li debunks the Neo-Confucians, because even the no-joy, no-sorrow condition is also a kind of mood and mental state, and the dynamic *qing* is primarily a changing process of "becoming" (Li used the English word here), yet this dynamism and change is by itself "being" (Li used the English word here, too).[28] Li advances this theory of "emotion-as-primary-substance," *qingbenti*, to reinterpret the essence of Confucianism. For Li Zehou, "Classical Confucianism . . . regards emotion as the basis, substance, and origin of human nature and human life."[29] In his 1994 preface to his newly annotated *Analects*, Li confirmed that the recognition of "emotion-as-substance" means the restoration of the "truly lively and concrete delight in the lifeworld" reflected in the *Analects*.[30] For him, this affirmation of emotion as the essence was the reason Confucianism is more this-worldly than otherworldly, simply because this world is good and beautiful.[31] Li Zehou acknowledges that A.C. Graham is correct in understanding *qing* as fact and situation, which I discussed in the introduction, but Li argues that the word's semantic transition to feeling and emotion was more significant.[32] In the Chinese cultural tradition, the often perturbed *qing* stems from the presumably stable nature, *xing*. *Qing* is unrelated to the Chinese "soul," *hun*, which is never a thinking entity that forms a dichotomy with the body, as in the Western cultural tradition. But in the West, "[p]assions . . . are generally understood to be thoughts and states of the soul. . . ."[33] Another factor is that in the Western Christian cultural tradition, "God has equipped us with passions."[34] Without the concepts of the soul, God, and being, the Chinese *qing* as a substance by itself must be approached in its own cultural and customary context of secular ritualism.

In an interview with Taiwanese Confucian philosopher Liu Youming, Li Zehou identified his own thought with the philosophy of Xunzi, who had long been marginalized by Song Neo-Confucianists, who promoted Mencius and particularly affirmed Mencius's theory on intrinsically good human nature.[35]

Liu Youming formally advocated for "Contemporary New Xunzi Learning," *dangdai xin Xun xue*, in 2006.[36] Liu argues that the past detractors of Xunzi exaggerated Xunzi's stress on evil human nature. For Liu, Xunzi's stance was nothing but an alternative form of the good human nature theory, a "weak" one though, which merely demands artificial or self-reflective cultivation. Liu argues that ritual and righteousness stressed by Xunzi are hidden inside human emotions and desires, but these emotions and desires must be controlled by the rules of ritual and righteousness, which are made by the ancient sages. However, because ritual and righteousness are realistic affairs, as long as people adjust them under the change of the emotion-situation, *qingjing*, it will not be stagnant and thus oppressive to human nature.[37] Western scholars have also paid attention to Xunzi's doctrines' emphasis on the conscious construction of *Li* and Xunzi's dual identity as both a "believer" and a scholar who treated Li "by taking a more removed stance."[38]

It is beyond the scope of this study to overhaul the broad spectrum of "contemporary new Confucians" who try to promote Confucianism with various motivations and from various intellectual and political backgrounds. I believe some of them are more academic and some others harbor a feeling of missionary vocation and entertain a high ambition of influencing politics and society.[39] The historian Yu Yingshi (Ying-shih Yu) provides a fair and balanced assessment of the modern fate of Confucianism. For Yu, Confucianism's key contribution to traditional China was its offering of stable sociopolitical order, but to maintain its modern relevance it must abandon its old ambition of comprehensively arranging the order of human life. As a "rootless, wandering soul" [*youhun*] with the absence of imperial institutions that buttressed it prior to the fall of the Qing empire, modern Confucianism might still gain a new life in the climate of intellectual freedom and globalization as part of Chinese collective memory and China's "national culture."[40] Even with the demolition of the old social structure, its essential values "remain inherent in Chinese psychology and underl East Asian attitudes and behavior."[41]

The missionary-style passion for making Confucianism more visible and more relevant in modern times is not new. As Confucians with moral commitment, improving humanity and saving the world still concern them. The "last Confucian" Liang Shu-ming believed that he "held the key to the salvation of not only China, but all humankind, and was under the awful imperative to impart it to others."[42] I want to share two observations about what the self-conscious "Confucian" scholars can do in today's China, no matter which camp they come from. First, Professor Guo Qiyong cited the Confucian allusion of father and son covering up each other in the *Analects*, to legitimize his advocacy that the current Chinese legal system should tolerate the concealing of kin, or at least the criminal justice practice should avoid implicating spouses as each other's witnesses, because this would challenge basic human moral feelings.[43] The second case is that Professor Zhang Xinmin, whom I met in 2013, co-signed an open letter in 2019, along with nine other professors, one being a leading advocate of Confucianism as China's cultural mark, Chen Ming. The letter protested against some Chinese colleges' encouragement of students to report on professors' "incorrect speeches" in and outside of the classroom. For Zhang et al., who played out the role of critical public intellectual, this policy undermines the traditional trustful and emotional relationship between the teacher and the students, a "key ethical relationship" highly valued in "Chinese traditional culture."[44]

The two cases show that contemporary Confucian scholars are still critical of the status quo, and they consider how to invoke the Confucian emphasis on ritual propriety, human feeling, and the spirit of rationality to mitigate the power abuse of the state and its delegates on college campuses and in legal practices. Contemporary Confucians are still after the Confucian high ideal of perfect personality: With a self-imposed sense of mission, one shows "love" and "empathy" for others and his own submissiveness to "the mores and the norms," *Li*, but also uses "prudence" and "caution" in daily life.[45] In 2013 I visited a "Chinese Culture Academy" located in Guizhou University in Guiyang, the flagship institution of higher education in Guizhou Province, with Zhang Xinmin as the then director. The academy is not part of the established schools or departments but an added complementary institution modeled on Song Neo-Confucian scholars' *shuyuan*, with its original purpose of encouraging serious and independent intellectual inquiry and dialogue, not for test preparation. This type of modern Neo-Confucian style *shuyuan*, like the New Asia Academy founded by the Confucianist historian Qian Mu in Hong Kong, epitomizes an effort to "rescue Chinese culture through academic learning," assuming the culture has been corrupted by "the fragmentation of academic disciplines, the instrumental purpose of degree programs," and "the alienation of learning from living as well as teachers from students. . . ."[46] In the "Chinese Culture Academy," I could feel the founders' aspiration for injecting human feelings and ritual propriety into a modern university.

THE TRIAD AND ITS FUTURE

Twentieth-century thinkers look at emotion and ritual through different lenses and not always positively. The eccentric writer and cultural critic Gu Hongming defined the Chinese people as having "the power of sympathy" because "they live wholly a life of the heart—a life of emotion or human affection." He also referred to *Li* as the "pre-Confucian" "law of propriety, good taste or good manners," and *Li* for him was more the "fine feeling and good taste of a gentleman" than mere ceremony and propriety.[47] John Dewey was optimistic about the value of the non-coercive customs and rituals, and he emphasized the balance of reason and feeling.[48] Indeed, even today in China, the ideal solution of a dispute or an explanation of a puzzling situation is still *he qing he li*—it fits both individual human feelings and the more external, objective rational principle. But the preeminent Chinese anthropologist Fei Xiaotong (1916-2005) found in the 1940s that Chinese village life was largely dominated by interpersonal ties, *guanxi*, and each tie "consists of an explicit category of social relationship that requires specific, prescribed 'ritual'(*li* in Fei's usage or *Li* in my usage) behavior."[49] Fei Xiaotong also found that different from law, rituals are sustained by personal habits, and they "work through the feelings of respect and of obedience that people themselves have cultivated."[50] Fei emphasized that "the force to maintain rituals comes not from the outside but from the inside, from one's conscience."[51] Modern Confucian philosopher Liang Shu-ming (1893-1988) also believes that rationality, *lixing* in modern Chinese, is embodied in Confucian rites and etiquette and it "consists of extending family emotions to all social relationships. . . ."[52] For me, the contemplation of Liang was implicitly entangled in the triad we discussed in this book, demonstrating the deep Confucian concern with human mental state and interpersonal relations.

My understanding of Fei Xiaotong's key concern in his influential book *From the Soil* was how rural China finally could be modernized and democratized. Fei's comparative perspective led him to think that impersonal "calm thinking" and "reason" dominated modern contractual activities, i.e., rational reflection, negotiation, and compromise in everyday social life, and this is what rural society "lacks."[53] Confucianism never lacks appreciation of aesthetic experiences, and its "aesthetic dimension" deserves to be stressed more.[54] But Confucianism might fall short of cultivating modern, rational economic men for its emotional particularism. Following Fei's modernization logic, the surviving *Li* and *qing* in the trio are rural, traditional, and particularistic, but *li* in the sense of contractual, rational-legal institutions (no longer the unchangeable yet cognitively meaningless cardinal concept "Heavenly principle" in its metaphysical sense) is urban and modern.

Modern Confucian thinkers concerned with China's reform and progress are still obsessed by the balance of the three titular ideas—*Li, qing*, and *li*—while Fei Xiaotong provides a salient perspective to reconsider the meaning of embedding modern rationalism based upon impersonal relations into the Chinese mode of thinking to balance the entrenched *Li-qing* dual structure, which fundamentally hinges on the pre-modern rural lineage system. Rationality, critical thinking, and democracy, i.e., the modern *li*, and a renovated assemblage of *Li, qing*, and *li* is perhaps what China needs to achieve political and educational modernization and its balanced combination with tradition. Recent anthropological research shows that modern rationality has been increasingly reflected in the law enforcement in Chinese villages since the 1980s, but "overemphasizing the authority of law might bring forth the loss of the reciprocal relations in a rural, intimate community."[55] This statement suggests the latent conflict between modern legal rationality and human emotions in Chinese villages.

Whether Confucianism has a "religious or spiritual *dimension*" (italicization original) is still a moot question.[56] For orthodox Confucians in the Qing dynasty, ancestor worship was a "secular rite" to express human feelings of love and respect for the dead.[57] In mainland China today, Confucianism is not recognized as one of the five world religions, for instance, Buddhism, Daoism, Islam, Protestantism, and Catholicism, and in Taiwan, the "Museum of World Religions" also excludes Confucianism in its list of eight.[58] I agree with the sociologist C. K. Yang that Confucianism never altered "its basic this-worldly orientation," and "Confucianism did address itself to the ultimate meaning of life and death, but only in terms of moral responsibility to man, not to any supernatural power."[59] As C. K. Yang points out, Confucianism can be regarded as a "faith" that combines "an emotional attitude" with "a body of rational teaching" while not without some adopted "religious elements."[60] Yet if I add the dimension of ritual actions, then these factors again form the *Li-qing-li* triad that characterizes the faith.

The sociologist of religion Fenggang Yang defines quasi-religion as having supernatural beliefs, practices, and "diffused" organization and argues it cannot develop into a full religion in modern times.[61] In this sense, Confucianism can be seen as a quasi-religion between magic and atheism, and the Confucian obsession with the *shenyi* robe from the pre-Qin period to the Ming dynasty is not "philosophical" in any modern sense. It is fair to abandon the "religion vs. philosophy" mode of thinking today and to accept the judgment that Confucianism is a complex cultural assemblage that combines spiritual, philosophical, social, and ritualist dimensions.[62]

The debate around the religious-spiritual dimension of Confucianism notwithstanding, the modern value of Confucian ritualism and sentimentalism and the position of rationalism has global relevance. Alfred North Whitehead points out that "[t]he primitive form of physical experience is emotional—blind emotion," and "*sympathy* (italicization original)" is a "primitive element."[63] The Western-centric imagination, as Bryan W. Van Norden sums up, that "'we' are rational, self-controlled, just, and civilized, whereas 'they' are illogical, impassioned, unfair, and barbaric"[64] is also problematic. Anthropological studies have revealed that modern American minds are fraught with tense emotions of fear and insecurity,[65] although in the world of pure polemics, "the heirs of the rationalist rather than sentimentalist Enlightenment now dominate both philosophy and social science."[66] There is also a gendered "Western" notion that suggests women are by nature more emotional than men.[67] In real-life political practice in contemporary America, however, "affective (i.e., emotional) experience affects political reasoning and facilitates low-information rationality."[68]

That ritualization entails socialization, and civilization is a cross-cultural experience. In late-nineteenth-century America, there were etiquette manuals instructing social etiquette and rituals to the rising middle class, and like what had happened to the Chinese *Li*, there were also reflections on whether the etiquette was formal, false, or insincere, and how these external manners might reflect inner qualities and dispositions.[69] In the field where philosophical studies and China studies converge, a group of "Boston Confucians" resonated with the revival of Confucian ritualism: "Confucianism's most unique contribution to contemporary world philosophy is its deployment of ritual to interpret conjoint action and practice reason," and decided that "Contemporary Confucians should develop rituals that allow all persons to take part with regard to political power and be rewarded with placement and wealth according to their merit and that allow persons to interact respectfully and concretely with people very different from themselves."[70] Here the new expectation for contemporary Confucianism is how to make rituals equal, inclusive, and open to diversity while a recognition of the value of ritualism still points the way.

While American society needs to think about how it can continue to be truly inclusive and open to diversity, Confucianism has the potential to become a "rooted global philosophy" that inspires other cultures. But for me, the traditional pursuit of morally perfect sagehood might be too high an aim for average people these days.[71] Chas W. Freeman Jr., an American diplomat and the Chinese interpreter for Richard Nixon, finds that *Li* should be placed at the center of Western understanding of China: "the social disciplines of propriety (*Li*; Chas W. Freeman Jr. uses Chinese character礼)" are "the primary regulators of economic behavior in China, much as law is in the West." And he believes that the Chinese rank "emotional bonds" (*qing*; he provides the Chinese character 情) above the "calculus of selfishness" which is his rendition of *li* (理).[72] Given the contradiction between the presupposed hyper-rationalism and rationality's limit in the lifeworld, in my view, the Confucian emphasis on a sense of proportion and balance among ritual propriety, true human sentiments, and the rational self-control of emotional excess is an indispensable intellectual asset for the rest of the world to construct a moderate and mindful lifestyle.

NOTES

1. For a study of SIM from the point of view of sociology of knowledge, see Scott Frickel and Neil Gross, "A General Theory of Scientific/Intellectual Movements," *American Sociological Review* 70 (2005): 204–32.

2. Guy Alitto, "Reconstituting Confucianism for the Contemporary World," in *Contemporary Confucianism in Thought and Action,* ed. Guy Alitto (Heidelberg: Springer, 2015), 2–9.

3. See Paul Connerton, *How Societies Remember* (Cambridge, UK: Cambridge University Press, 1989), 13–14.

4. Guo Wu, "Ritual, Reading, and Resistance in the Prison and Cowshed during the Cultural Revolution," *Journal of Contemporary China* 29, no.124 (2020): 632–46.

5. Stephan Feuchtwang, *Popular Religion in China: The Imperial Metaphor* (Richmond, Surrey: Curzon Press, 2001), 217.

6. Susan D. Blum, *Portraits of "Primitives": Ordering Human Kinds in the Chinese Nation* (Lanham, MD: Roman & Littlefield, 2001), 7. Also see Wu, *Narrating Southern Chinese Minority Nationalities*, 13–35.

7. Zhengfu Chen et al., "Cultural Heritage as Rural Development: Batik Production Amongst China's Miao Population," *Journal of Rural Studies*, no. 81 (2021): 184.

8. Margaret Mih Tillman and Hoyt Cleveland Tillman, "Modernizing Tradition or Restoring Antiquity as Confucian Alternatives: A View from Reading Rituals in Contemporary China," in *Contemporary Confucianism in Thought and Action*, ed. Alitto, 80–81.

9. Szonyi, *Practicing Kinship*, 143–45.

10. Huang Shu-min, *The Spiral Road: Change in a Chinese Village Through the Eyes of a Communist Party Leader* (Boulder, CO: Westview Press, 1998), 28, 161.

11. Jing, *The Temple of Memories*, 67.

12. Stephen C. Angle, *Contemporary Confucian Political Philosophy* (Cambridge, UK: Polity Press, 2012), 91.

13. Eric Hobsbawm, "Mass-Producing Traditions: Europe, 1870–1914," in *The Invention of Tradition*, ed. Eric Hobsbawm and Terence Ranger (Cambridge, UK: Cambridge University Press, 1983), 263–64.

14. Arif Dirlik, *Culture and History in Post-Revolutionary China: The Perspective of Global Modernity* (Hong Kong: The Chinese University Press, 2011), 98–99.

15. For the combination of cultural nationalism and ritualism in China today, see Kevin Carrico, *The Great Han: Race, Nationalism, and Tradition in China Today* (Berkeley: University of California Press, 2017).

16. David Crouch, "Affect, Heritage, Feeling," in *The Palgrave Handbook of Heritage Research* eds. Emma Waterton and Steve Watson (London: Palgrave McMillan, 2015), 181.

17. Ka-Ming Wu, *Reinventing Chinese Tradition: The Cultural Politics of Late Socialism* (Urbana: University of Illinoi Press, 2015), 20, 147.

18. Benedict Anderson, *Imagined Communities* (London: Verso, 1991), 22, 74.

19. Zheng Yongnian, *Zai su yishi yingtai* [Rebuild Ideology] (Beijing: Dongfang chubanshe, 2015), 7–12, 51, 133.

20. Adam B. Seligaman et al., *Ritual and Its Consequences: An Essay on the Limits of Sincerity* (Oxford, UK: Oxford University, 2008), 103–5.

21. Martin C. Yang, *A Chinese Village: Taitou, Shantung Province* (New York: Columbia University Press, 1945), 89–90.

22. Susan Naquin, "Funerals in North China," in *Death Ritual in Late Imperial and Modern China*, eds. James Watson and Evelyn S. Rawski (Berkeley: University of California Press, 1988), 62–63.

23. Ibid., 63.

24. For this approach, see Emily Martin Ahern, *Chinese Ritual and Politics* (Cambridge, UK: Cambridge University Press, 1981).

25. John Rawls, *Political Liberalism* (New York: Columbia University Press, 1996), xxi–xxii.

26. Taylor, "The Religious Character of the Confucian Tradition," 90–91.

27. Li Zehou, *Lishi benti lun/Jimao wu shuo* [Historical Ontology/Five Essays from 1999] (Beijing: Sanlian shudian, 2003), 105–6, 305.

28. Ibid., 106–7.

29. Jinhua Lu, "Li Zehou's Preconception of the Confucian Ethics of Emotion," *Philosophy East and West* 66, no. 3 (2016): 763.

30. Li Zehou, *Lunyun jindu* [A Contemporary Reading of the Analects] (Beijing: Zhongshu shuju, 2015), 7.

31. Ibid., 68.

32. Ibid., 243. Also see Graham, *Studies in Chinese Philosophy and Philosophical Literature*. In late imperial China, if an official and particularly a military general had to have his mourning period waived or shortened per the state's need, the practice was called *duoqing*, literally, "(expediently) deprive someone of personal emotions." For the discussion of *duoqing*, see Norman Kutcher, *Mourning in Late Imperial China* (Cambridge, UK: Cambridge University Press, 2006), 25. My literal translation of *duoqing* above is different from Kutcher's "cut short the emotions" because the word *duo* means deprive and take away.

33. Susan James, *Passion and Action: The Emotions in Seventeenth-Century Philosophy* (Oxford, UK: Oxford University Press, 1997), 4.

34. Ibid., 7.

35. Liu Youming, *Yige dangdai de, dazhong de ruxue: dangdai xin Xun xue lungang* [A Contemporary, Popular Confucianism: An Outline Thesis of Contemporary New Xunzi Learning] (Beijing: Zhongguo renmin daxue chubanshe, 2019), 68.

36. Ibid., 69.

37. Ibid., 71.

38. Kurtis Hagen, *The Philosophy of Xunzi: A Reconstruction* (Chicago: Open Court, 2007), 39, 114.

39. For instance, one Confucian promoter, Zhou Beicheng, hopes that Confucianism can one day become China's state religion; see Billioud and Thoraval, *The Sage and the People*, 156.

40. Yu's argument here is a little complex and my summary tries to capture the gist of his somewhat ambivalent attitude. See Yu Yingshi, *Xiandai ruxue de huigu*

yu zhanwang [The Past and Prospect of Modern Confucianism] (Beijing: Sanlian shudian, 2004), 177–83.

41. Xinzhong Yao, *An Introduction to Confucianism* (Cambridge, UK: Cambridge University Press, 2000), 275.

42. Guy S. Alitto, *The Last Confucian: Liang Shu-ming and the Chinese Dilemma of Modernity* (Berkeley: University of California Press, 1986), 59.

43. Guo Qiyong, *Zhongguo ruxue zhi jingshen* [The Spirit of Chinese Confucianism] (Shanghai: Fudan daxue chubanshe, 2009).

44. Rujia shi jiao shou [Ten Confucian Professors], "Dui dangqian gaoxiao dongyuan guli xuesheng gaomi wenti de kanfa" [Our Views on Institutions of Higher Education's Mobilization of the Students to Report on Professors], Rujia wang [The Confucian Net] www.rujiazg.com accessed April 10, 2019.

45. For the enumeration of the "persisting" characteristics of Confucian personalities, see Arthur F. Wright, "Preface," in *Confucian Personalities*, 6–8.

46. Chueng Chan Fai, "Tang Junyi and the Philosophy of General Education," in Wm. Theodore de Bary with Contributions by Cheung Chan Fai and Kwan Tze-wan, *Confucian Tradition and Global Education* (Hong Kong: The Chinese University of Hong Kong, 2007), 61.

47. Gu Hongming, *The Spirit of the Chinese People* (Beijing: Foreign Language Teaching and Research Press, 1998), 13, 36, 49.

48. Sor-hoon Tan, "The Dao of Politics (Ritual/Rites) and Laws as Pragmatic Tools of Government," *Philosophy East and West* 61, no. 3 (2011): 478–82.

49. Fei Xiaotong, *From the Soil: The Foundations of Chinese Society*, trans. Gary G. Hamilton and Wang Zheng (Berkeley: University of California Press, 1992), 22.

50. Fei, *From the Soil*, 99.

51. Ibid., 103.

52. Allito, *The Last Confucian*, 184–85.

53. Ibid., 127.

54. David L. Hall and Roger T. Ames, *Thinking Through Confucius* (Albany: State University of New York, 1987), 105, 248.

55. Zhao Xudong, *Quanli yu gongzheng: xiangtu shehui de jiufen jiejue yu quanwei duoyuan* [Power and Justice: Dispute Settlement and Authority Diversity in Rural Society] (Tianjin: Tianjin guji chubanshe, 2003), 134.

56. For a detailed examination of this issue, see Rodney L. Taylor, "The Religious Character of the Confucian Tradition," *Philosophy East and West* 48, no. 1 (1998): 80–107.

57. Richard J. Smith, *China's Cultural Heritage: The Ch'ing Dynasty, 1644–1912* (Boulder, CO: Westview Press, 1983), 152.

58. Michael J. Walsh, *Stating the Sacred: Religion, China, and the Formation of the Nation-State* (New York: Columbia University Press, 2020), 67, 83.

59. C.K. Yang, *Religion in Chinese Society: A Study of Contemporary Social Functions of Religion and Some of Their Historical Factors* (Berkeley: University of California Press, 1961), 26.

60. Ibid, 244–45.

61. For the criterion, see Fenggang Yang, *Religion in China: Survival and Revival under Communist China* (Oxford, UK: Oxford University Press, 2012), 36–38.

62. John Bethrong and Evelyn Nagai Bethrong, *Confucianism: A Short Introduction* (Oxford, UK: Oneworld Publications, 2000), 2, 28.

63. Alfred North Whitehead, "Process and Reality: An Essay in Cosmology," in *Gifford Lectures Delivered in the University of Edinburgh During the Session 1927–28*, eds. David Ray Griffin and Donald W. Sherburne (New York: The Free Press, 1978), 162–63.

64. Bryan W. Van Norden, *Taking Back Philosophy: A Multicultural Manifesto* (New York: Columbia University Press, 2017), 86.

65. Francis L.K. Hsu, *Americans and Chinese: Reflections on Two Cultures and Their People* (Garden City, NY: Doubleday Natural History Press, 1970), 347–48.

66. Michael L. Frazer, *The Enlightenment of Sympathy: Justice and the Moral Sentiments in the Eighteenth Century and Today* (Oxford, UK: Oxford University Press, 2012), 4.

67. Reddy, *The Navigation of Feeling*, 41, 43.

68. See Wendy R. Rahn, "Affect as Information: The Role of Public Mood in Political Reasoning," in *Elements of Reason: Cognition, Choice, and the Bounds of Rationality*, eds. Arthur Lupia (Cambridge, UK: Cambridge Press, 2000), 130–52.

69. Shirley Yeung, "Natural Manners: Etiquette, Ethics, and Sincerity in American Conduct Manuals," in *Ordinary Ethics*: *Anthropology, Language, and Action*, ed. Michael Lambek (New York: Fordham University Press, 2010), 235–48.

70. Robert Cummings Neville, *Boston Confucianism: Portable Tradition in the Late-Modern World* (Albany: State University of New York Press, 2000), 78, 80.

71. For sagehood in Confucianism and its global relevance, see Stephen C. Angle, *Sagehood: The Contemporary Significance of Neo-Confucianism* (Oxford, UK: Oxford University Press, 2010). Yet I doubt sagehood is a desirable and attainable goal for modern people.

72. Chas W. Freeman Jr., *Interesting Enemies: China, America, and the Shifting Balance of Prestige* (Charlottesville, VA: Just World Books, 2012), 31.

Bibliography

Adler, Joseph A.. 2014. *Reconstructing the Confucian Dao: Zhu Xi's Appropriation of Zhou Dunyi*. Albany: State University of New York Press.

_____. 2002. *Chinese Religious Traditions*. Upper Saddle River, NJ: Prentice Hall Inc.

Ahern, Emily Martin. 1981. *Chinese Ritual and Politics*. Cambridge, UK: Cambridge University Press.

Alitto, Guy S. 2015. Reconstituting Confucianism for the Contemporary World." In *Contemporary Confucianism in Thought and Action*, ed. Guy Alitto, 2–9. Heidelberg: Springer.

_____. 1986. *The Last Confucian: Liang Shu-ming and the Chinese Dilemma of Modernity*. Berkeley: University of California Press.

Anderson, Benedict.1991. *Imagined Communities*. London: Verso.

Angle, Stephen C. 2012. *Contemporary Confucian Political Philosophy*. Cambridge, UK: Polity Press.

_____. 2010. *Sagehood: The Contemporary Significance of Neo-Confucianism*. Oxford, UK: Oxford University Press.

Aristotle. 2011. *The Philosophy of Aristotle: A Selection with an Introduction and Commentary by Renford Bambrough*. Trans. J.L. Creed and A.E. Wardman. New York: Penguin Group.

Ayer, A.J. 1946. *Language, Truth and Logic*. London: Penguin Books.

Beattie, Hilary J. 1979. *Land and Lineage in China: A Study of T'ung-Ch'eng County, Anhwei, in the Ming and Qing Dynasties*. Cambridge, UK: Cambridge University Press.

Beatty, Andrew. 2019. *Emotional Worlds: Beyond an Anthropology of Emotion*. Cambridge, UK: Cambridge University Press.

Bell, Catherine. 1997. *Ritual: Perspectives and Dimensions*. Oxford, UK: Oxford University.

Bell, Daniel A. and Hahm Chaibom. 2003. "The Contemporary Relevance of Confucianism." In *Confucianism for the Modern World*, eds. Daniel A. Bell and Hahm Chaibom,1–30. New York: Cambridge University Press.

Bella, Robert N. 1991. *Beyond Belief: Essays on Religion in a Post-Traditionalist World*. Berkeley: University of California Press.

Benedict, Ruth. 1989. *The Chrysanthemum and the Sword: Patterns of Japanese Culture*. Boston: Houghton Mifflin Company.

Bethrong, John and Evelyn Bethrong. 2000. *Confucianism: A Short Introduction* (Oxford, UK: Oneworld Publications.

Biehl, João. 2014. "Ethnography in the Way of Theory." In *The Ground Between: Anthropologists Engage Philosophy*, eds., Veena Das et al. 94–118. Durham, NC: Duke University Press.

Billioud, Sébastien, and Joël Thoraval. 2014. *The Sage and the People: The Confucian Revival in China*. Oxford, UK: Oxford University Press.

Blake, C. Fred. 2010. *Burning Money: The Material Spirit of the Chinese Lifeworld*. Honolulu: University of Hawaii Press.

Blum, Susan D. 2001. *Portraits of "Primitives": Ordering Human Kinds in the Chinese Nation*. Lanham, MD: Roman & Littlefield.

Bloom, Irene. 1979. "Philosophy of Lo Ch'in-shun." In *Principle and Practicality*, eds., WM. Theodore de Bary and Irene Bloom, 69–123. New York: Columbia University Press.

Bol, Peter K. 2008. *Neo-Confucianism in History*. Cambridge, MA: Harvard University Press.

Book of Documents. 2016. Trans. James Legge. Middletown, DE: Dragon Books.

Bourdieu, Pierre. 1984. *Distinction: A Social Critique of the Judgement of Taste*. Trans. Richard Nice. Cambridge, MA: Harvard University Press.

Bray, Francesca. 1997. *Technology and Gender: Fabrics of Power in Late Imperial China*. Berkeley: University of California Press.

Broadie, Sarah. 2001. "Soul and Body in Plato and Descartes." *Proceedings of the Aristotelian Society*, 101: 295–308.

Cai, Liang. 2014. *Witchcraft and the Rise of the First Confucian Empire*. Albany: State University of New York Press, 2014.

Carrico, Kevin. 2017. *The Great Han: Race, Nationalism, and Tradition in China Today*. Berkeley: University of California Press.

Chai Degeng. 2013. *Qing dai xueshu shi jiangyi* [Lecture Notes of History of Qing Scholarship]. Beijing: Shangwu yinshuguan.

Chan, Wing-Tsi. 1989. *Chu Hsi: New Studies*. Honolulu: University of Hawaii Press, 1989.

——————. 1963. *A Source Book in Chinese Philosophy*. Princeton, NJ: Princeton University Press.

Chang, Kuang-Chih. 1983. *Art, Myth, and Ritual: The Path to Political Authority in Ancient China*. Cambridge, MA: Harvard University Press, 1983.

——————.1 983. "Sandai Archaeology and the Formation of States in Ancient China: Processual Aspects of the Origins of Chinese Civilization." In *The Origins of Chinese Civilization*, ed. David N. Keightley, 495–521. Berkeley: University of California Press.

——————. 1980. *Shang Civilization*. New Haven, CT: Yale University Press.

Chen, Huaiyu. 2020. *Dongwu yu zhongguo zhengzhi zongjiao zhixu* [Animals and the Politicoreligious Order in Medieval China]. Shanghai: Shanghai guji chubanshe.

Chen Lai. 2004. "The Discussion of Mind and Nature in Zhu Xi's Philosophy." Trans. Robert W. Foster. In *Chinese Philosophy in an Era of Globalization*, 75–98, ed. Robin R. Wang. Albany: State University of New York Press.

Chen Li. 1994. *Baihutong shu zheng* [The Annotated Treatise of the White Tiger Hall]. Beijing: Zhonghua shuju.

Chen Zhengfu et al. 2021. "Cultural Heritage as Rural Development: Batik Production Amongst China's Miao Population." In *Journal of Rural Studies*, 81: 1820–93.

Chen Zuwu, Zhu Tongchuang. 2007. *QianJia xuepai yanjiu* [A Study of the Confucian Scholarship during the Qianlong-Jiaqing Reign]. Shijiazhuang: Hebei renmin chubanshe.

Cheng, Chung-ying. 1971. Tai *Chen's Inquiry into Goodness*. Honolulu: University of Hawaii Press.

Chou, Chih-P'ing. 1988. *Yüan Hung-tao and the Kung-an School*. Cambridge, UK: Cambridge University Press.

Chow, Kai-wing. 1994. *The Rise of Confucian Ritualism in Late Imperial China: Ethics, Classics, and Lineage Discourse*. Stanford, CA: Stanford University Press.

Ch'ü, T'ung-Tsu. 1962. *Local government in China under the Ch'ing*. Cambridge, MA: Harvard University Press.

Chun, Allen. 1996. "The Lineage-Village Complex in Southeastern China: A Long Footnote in the Anthropology of Kinship," in *Current Anthropology*, 37, 3: 429–50.

Clifford, James, and George E. Marcus eds. 1986. *Writing Culture: The Poetics and Politics of Ethnography*. Berkeley: University of California Press.

Collins, Randall. 2004. *Interaction Ritual Chains*. Princeton, NJ: Princeton University Press.

Confucius et al. 2013. *The Book of Rites*. Ed. Dai Sheng. Trans. James Legge. Beijing: Intercultural Press.

Connerton, Paul. 1989. *How Societies Remember*. Cambridge, UK: Cambridge University Press.

Cook, Scott. 2013. *The Bamboo Texts of Guodian: A Study and Complete Translation*. Ithaca, NY: Cornell University East Asia Program.

Critchley, Simon. 2001. *Continental Philosophy: A Very Short Introduction*. Oxford, UK: Oxford University Press.

Crouch, David. 2015. "Affect, Heritage, Feeling." In *The Palgrave Handbook of Heritage Research*, Emma Waterton and Steve Watson eds., 177–87. London: Palgrave McMillan.

Dai Mingxian. 2013. *Ziwu shan hai Zheng Zhen: ren yu shi* [The Child of the Meridian Hill: Zheng Zhen, The Man and His Poetry]. Beijing: renming wenxue chubanshe.

Damasio, Antonio. 1994. *Descartes' Error: Emotion, Reason, and the Human Body*. New York: The Penguin Group.

Davis, Edward L. 2001. *Society and the Supernatural in Song China*. Honolulu: University of Hawaii Press.

Davis, James, and Dimitrina Spencer, eds. 2010. *Emotions in the Field: The Psychology and Anthropology of Fieldwork Experience*. Stanford, CA: Stanford University Press.

de Bary, Wm. Theodore, and Irene Bloom. 1999. *Sources of Chinese Tradition, second edition vol.1* From Earliest Times to 1600. New York: Columbia University Press.

_____. 1970. "Individualism and Humanitarianism in Late Ming Thought." In *Self and Society in Ming Thought*, eds. WM. Theodore de Bary and the conference on Ming thought, 145–247. New York: Columbia University Press.

Dean, Kenneth. 1993. *Taoist Ritual and Popular Cults of Southeast China*. Princeton, NJ: Princeton University Press.

Deleuze, Gilles, and Félix Guattari. 1994. *What is Philosophy?* Trans. Hugh Tomlinson and Gram Burchell. New York: Columbia University Press.

Descartes, René. 2015. *The Passions of the Soul and Other Late Philosophical Writings*. Oxford, UK: Oxford University Press.

Desmond, Mathew. 2014. "Relational Ethnography." In *Theory and Society*, 43:547–79.

Dirlik, Arif. 2011. *Culture and History in Post-Revolutionary China: The Perspective of Global Modernity*. Hong Kong: The Chinese University Press.

Dong Ping. 2009. *Wang Yangming de shenghuo shijie*. The Lifeworld of Wang Yangming. Beijing: zhongguo renmin daxue chubanshe.

Douglas, Mary. 1999. *Implicit Meanings: Selected Essays in Anthropology*, 2nd edition. London: Routledge.

Du Zexun. 2001. *Wenxian xue gaiyao* [A General Outline of the Studies of Ancient Chinese Texts]. Beijing: Zhonghua shuju.

Durkheim, Émile. 2001. *The Elementary Forms of Religious Life*. Trans. Carol Cosman. Oxford, UK: Oxford University Press.

Elman, Benjamin. 1984. *From Philosophy to Philology: Intellectual and Social Aspects of Change in Late Imperial China*. Cambridge, MA: Council on East Asian Studies, Harvard University.

Elvin, Mark. 2004. *The Retreat of the Elephants: An Environmental History of China*. New Haven, CT: Yale University Press.

Emirbayer, Mustafa. 1997. "Manifesto for a Relational Sociology." *American Journal of Sociology* 103, 2: 281–317.

Eno, Robert. 1990. *The Confucian Creation of Heaven: Philosophy and the Defense of Ritual Mastery*. Albany: State University of New York Press.

Evans-Pritchard, E. E., 1965. *Theories of Primitive Religion*. Oxford:, UK Oxford University Press.

Fai, Chueng Chan. 2007. "Tang Junyi and the Philosophy of General Education." In *Confucian Tradition and Global Education*, ed. Wm. Theodore de Bary with Contributions by Cheung Chan Fai and Kwan Tze-wan, 59–73. Hong Kong: The Chinese University of Hong Kong.

Falkensausen, Lothar Von. 2006. *Chinese Society in the Age of Confucius (1000-250 BC)*. Los Angeles: Costen Institute of Archaeology.

Faure, David. 2007. *Emperor and Ancestor: State and Lineage in South China*. Stanford, CA: Stanford University Press.

Feleppa, Robert. 2009. "Zen, Emotions, and Social Engagement." *Philosophy East and West* 59, 3: 263–93.

Feng Youlan. 1964. *Zhongguo zhexueshi xinbian* [A Revised History of Chinese Philosophy]. Beijing: renmin chubanshe.

Feuchtwang, Stephan. 2001. *Popular Religion in China: The Imperial Metaphor.* Richmond, Surrey: Curzon Press.

Frazer, James George. 1994. *The Golden Bough, A New Abridgement.* Oxford, UK: Oxford University Press.

Frazer, Michael L. 2012. *The Enlightenment of Sympathy: Justice and the Moral Sentiments in the Eighteenth Century and Today.* Oxford, UK: Oxford University Press.

Freeman Jr., Chas W. 2012. *Interesting Enemies: China, America, and the Shifting Balance of Prestige.* Charlottesville, VA: Just World Books.

Frickel, Scott and Neil Gross. 2005."A General Theory of Scientific/Intellectual Movements." *American Sociological Review*, 70: 204–32.

Fung You-lan. 1976. *A Short History of Chinese Philosophy: A Systematic Account of Chinese Thought from Its Origins to the Present Day.* Derk Bodde, ed. New York: The Fee Press.

Gardner, Daniel K. 2003. *Zhu Xi's Reading of the Analects: Canon, Commentary, and the Classical Tradition.* New York: Columbia University Press.

_____. 1990. *Chu Hsi Learning to Be a Sage: Selections from the Conversations of Master Chu.* Berkeley: University of California Press.

_____. 1986. *Chu Hsi and the Ta-hsueh: Neo-Confucian Reflection on the Confucian Canon.* Cambridge, MA: Harvard University Press.

Gan Chunsong. 2003. *Zhidu hua rujia jiqi jieti* [Institutionalized Confucianism and Its Disintegration]. Beijing: Zhongguo renmin daxue chubanshe.

Ge Zhaoguang. 2003. *Qufu shi ji qita: Liu chao sui tang daojiao de sixiang shi yan-jiu* [A History of Submission and Other Things: An Intellectual History Study of Daoism in the Six Dynasties, Sui, and Tang]. Beijing: Sanlian shudian.

Geertz, Clifford. 1983. *Local Knowledge: Further Essays in Interpretive Anthropology.* New York: Basic Book.

_____. 1976. "Art as a Cultural System." In *Comparative Literature* 91, 6: 1473–99.

_____. 1973. *The Interpretation of Cultures.* New York: Basic Books.

Goldin, Paul Rikita. 1999. *Rituals of the Way: The Philosophy of Xunzi.* Chicago: Open Court.

Goossaert, Vincent. 2005. "The Concepts of Religion in China and the West." *Diogenes* 52, 1: 13–20.

Gordon, Ronald D. 2007. "Beyond the Failures of Western Communication Theory." *Journal of Multicultural Discourses* 2, 2: 89–107.

Graham, A.C. 1992. *Two Chinese Philosophers: The Metaphysics of the Brothers Cheng.* La Salle, IL: Open Court Publishing Company.

_____. 1989. *Disputers of the Tao: Philosophical Argument in Ancient China.* La Salle, Il: Open Court Publishing Company.

_____. 1986. *Studies in Chinese Philosophy and Philosophical Literature.* Singapore: The Institute of East Asian Philosophies.

Granet, Marcel. 1932. "Introduction." In Marcel Granet and E.D. Edwards. *Festivals and Songs of Ancient China*. New York: E. P. Dutton.

Gu Hongming. 1998. *The Spirit of the Chinese People*. Beijing: Foreign Language Teaching and Research Press.

Guan Xianzhu et al. eds. 1997. *Lü shi Chunqiu Quanyi* [Complete Modern Translation of the Spring and Autumn Annals of Lü Buwei]. Guiyang: Guizhou renmin chubanshe.

Guo Qiyong. 2009. *Zhongguo ruxue zhi jingshen* [The Spirit of Chinese Confucianism]. Shanghai: Fudan daxue chubanshe.

Hagen, Kurtis. 2007. *The Philosophy of Xunzi: A Reconstruction*. La Salle, Il: Open Court.

Hansen, Chad. 2020. *Language and Logic in Ancient China*. Socoro, MN: Advanced Reasoning Forum. Reproduction of the text originally published in 1983.

He Bingdi. 2013. *He Bingdi sixiang zhidu shilun* [Studies of Intellectual and Institutional Histories]. Taipei: Lianjing chuban gongsi.

_____. 2004. *Zhe dong xuepai suyuan* [Tracing the Origins of the Eastern Zhejiang Academic School]. Guilin: Guangxi shifan daxue chubanshe.

He Yixin. 2020. "The Rise of the School of Heart/Mind-Nature of Confucianism: The Intellectual Innovation of Ziyou and His Orthodoxy Status" [Rujia xinxing zhixue de zhuanchu—lun ziyou de sixiang chuangzao ji qi daotong diwei]. *Fudan xuebao shehuikexue ban* [Journal of Fudan University: Social Sciences] 4: 105–17.

Herzfeld, Michael. 1985. *The Poetics of Manhood: Contest and Identity in a Cretan Mountain Village*. Princeton, NJ: Princeton University Press.

Hevia, James. 1995. *Cherishing Men from Afar: Qing Guest Ritual and the Macartney Mission of 1793*. Durham, NC: Duke University Press.

Hinsch, Bret. 2006. *Women in Early Imperial China*. Lanham, MD: Roman & Littlefield.

Ho, Ping-ti. 1975. *The Cradle of The East: An Inquiry into the Indigenous Origins of Techniques and Ideas of Neolithic and Early Historic China 5000-1000 B.C.* Hong Kong: The Chinese University of Hong Kong Press.

_____. 1962. *The Ladder of Success in Imperial China: Aspects of Social Mobility, 1368-1911*. New York: Columbia University Press.

Hobsbawm, Eric. 1983. "Mass-Producing Traditions: Europe, 1870-1914." In *The Invention of Tradition*, eds. Eric Hobsbawm and Terence Ranger, 263–307.Cambridge, UK: Cambridge University Press.

Hong Mai. 2018. *Record of the Listener: Selected Stories from Hong Mai's Yijianzhi*. Trans and ed. Cong Ellen Zhang. Indianapolis, IN: Hackett Publishing.

Hou Wailu. 2008. *Zhongguo sixiang shi gang* [An Outline of Chinese Intellectual History]. Shanghai: shiji chuban jituan.

_____. 2003. *Zhongguo gudai shehui shilu* [Essays on Ancient Chinese Society]. Shijiazhuang, Hebei jiaoyu chubanshe.

Hsu, L.K.. 1970. *Americans and Chinese: Reflections on Two Cultures and Their People*. Garden City, NY: Doubleday Natural History Press.

_____. XXXX. *Under Ancestor's Shadow: Kinship, Personality and Social Mobility in China*. Stanford, CA: Stanford University Press.

Hsun Tzu Basic Writings. 1963. Trans. Burton Watson. New York: Columbia University Press.

Hu, Minghui. 2015. *China's Transition to Modernity: The New Classical Vision of Daizhen.* Seattle: University of Washington Press.

Hu Pingsheng, Chen Meilan eds. 2007. *Liji/Xiaojing* [Book of Rite/Classics of Filial Piety]. Beijing: Zhonghua shuju.

Hu Shi. 2013. *Dai Dongyuan de zhexue* [The Philosophy of Dai Zhen (Dongyuan)]. Shanghai: Shanghai guji chubanshe,

_____. 1996. "Zhi Hu Jinren, Hu Enyu" [Letter to Hu Jinren and Hu Enyu] In *Hu Shi shuxin ji* [Collected Letters of Hu Shi] eds. Geng Yunzhi, Ouyang Zhesheng, 513. Beijing: Beijing daxue chubanshe.

Huang, Shu-min. 1998. *The Spiral Road: Change in a Chinese Village Through the Eyes of a Communist Party Leader.* Boulder, CO: Westview Press.

Huang Zongxi. 2018. *Ming ru xue an* [Intellectual Biographies of Ming Confucian Scholars] e-book. Yiya chubanshe.

Hume, David. 2018. *A Treatise of Human Nature.* Lexington, KY. reprint.

I-Ching The Classic of Changes. 1996. Trans. Edward L. Shaughnessy. New York: Ballantine Books.

Ing, Michael David Kaulana. 2012. *The Dysfunction of Ritual in Early Confucianism.* Oxford, UK: Oxford University Press.

Ingold, Tim. 2000. *The Perception of the Environment: Essays on Livelihood, Dwelling, and Skill.* London: Routledge.

James, Susan. 1997. *Passion and Action: The Emotions in Seventeenth-Century Philosophy.* Oxford, UK: Oxford University Press.

James, William. 1982. *The Varieties of Religious Experience: A Study in Human Nature.* New York: Penguin Books.

Jia Qianchu. 2018. *Zhudong de chenmin: Mingdai Taizhou xuepai pingmin ruxue zhi zhengzhi wenhua yanjiu* (Imperial Subjects Who Take the Initiative: A Study of the Political Culture of the Popular Confucianism of Ming Dynasty's Taizhou School. Beijing: zhishi chanquan chubanshe.

Jing, Jun. 1996. *The Temple of Memories: History, Power, and Morality in a Chinese Village.* Stanford, CA: Stanford University Press.

Jung, Carl Gustav. 1966. *Psychology and Religion.* New Haven, CT: Yale University Press.

Kagan, Shelley. 2012. *Death.* New Haven, CT: Yale University Press.

Kalmanson, Leah. 2017. "The Ritual Methods of Comparative Philosophy." *Philosophy East and West* 67, 2: 399–418.

Kant, Immanuel. *Groundwork for the Metaphysics of Morals.* Accessed June 29, 2020. https://www.earlymoderntexts.com/assets/pdfs/kant1785.pdf

_____. 2019. *The Critique of Pure Reason.* Trans. J.M.D. Meiklejohn. Middletown, DE, reprint.

_____. 1991. *The Metaphysics of Morals.* Trans. Mary Gregor. Cambridge, UK: Cambridge University Press.

Keightley, David N. 2000. *The Ancestral Landscape: Time, Space, and Community in the Late Shang* China, ca.1200-1045 B.C. Berkeley: University of California Press.

_____. 1985. *Sources of Shang History: The Oracle-Bone Inscriptions of Bronze Age China*. Berkeley: University of California Press.

_____. "The Late Shang State: When, Where, and What?" 1983. In *The Origins of Chinese Civilization*, ed. David N. Keightley, 553–64. Berkley: University of California Press.

Kenny, Anthony.2 004. *Ancient Philosophy*. Oxford, UK: Clarendon Press.

Kim, Jung-Yeup. 2015. *Zhang Zai's Philosophy of Qi: A Practical Understanding*. Lanham, MD: Lexington Books.

Kim, Youngmin. 2018. *A History of Chinese Political Thought*. Medford, MA: Polity Press.

Kleinman, Arthur. 2014. "The Search for Wisdom." In *The Ground Between: Anthropologists Engage Philosophy*, eds, Veena Das et al. 119–27. Durham, NC: Duke University Press.

Kósa, Gábor. 2003. "The Shaman and the Spirits: The Meaning of the Word 'Ling' in the Jiuge," *Acta Orientalia Academicae Scientiarrum Hungaricae*, 56, 2: 145–86.

Koselleck, Reinhart. 2002. *The Practice of Conceptual History: Timing History, Spacing Concepts*. Trans. Todd Samuel Presner et al. Stanford, CA: Stanford University Press.

Kuhn, Philip. 1990. *Soul Stealers: The Chinese Sorcery Scare of 1768*. Cambridge, MA: Harvard University Press.

Kutcher, Norman. 2006. *Mourning in Late Imperial China*. Cambridge, UK: Cambridge University Press.

Kung-Chuan Hsiao. 1960. *Rural China: Imperial Control in the Nineteenth Century*. Seattle: University of Washington Press.

Lam, Ling Hon. 2018. *The Spatiality of Emotion in Early Modern China*. New York: Columbia University Press.

Lambek, Michael. 2010. "Introduction" In *Ordinary Ethics: Anthropology, Language, and Action*, ed. Michael Lambek, 3–6. New York: Fordham University Press.

Laozi. 2001. *Dao De Jing The Book of the Way*. Trans. Moss Roberts. Berkeley: University of California Press.

Laufer, Berthold. 1974. *Jade: A Study of Chinese Archaeology and Religion*. New York: Dover Publications.

Lévi-Strauss, Claude. 1963. *Structural Anthropology*. New York: Basic Books.

Lewis, Mark Edward. 2007. *Early China*. Cambridge, MA: Harvard University Press.

_____. 1990. *Sanctioned Violence in Early China*. Albany: State University of New York Press.

Li Anzhai. 2005. *Yi-li yu Liji de shehuixue yanjiu* [A Sociological Study of *Ceremonials and Rites* and *Records of Rites*]. Shanghai: Shanghai shiji chuban jituan.

Li Ao. *Fu xing shu* [A Treatise on Recovering Nature]. Accessed July 11, 2020. https://zh.wikisource.org/wiki/%E5%BE%A9%E6%80%A7%E6%9B%B8%E4%B8%8A.

Li, Feng. 2013. *Early China: A Social and Cultural History*. Cambridge, UK: Cambridge University Press.

Li Jiansheng. 2012. *Qing dai-min'guo: Xining shehui shenghuo shi* [From the Qing to the Republic: A History of Social Life in Xining]. Beijing: renmin chubanshe.

Li Ling. 2001.*Zhongguo fangshu kao* [An Examination of the Early Chinese Craft of Medicine, Astrology and Divination]. Beijing: Dongfang chubanshe.

Li Minghui. 1990. *Rujia yu kangde* [Confucianism and Kant]. Taipei: Lianjing chuban shiye youxian gongsi.

Li Xueqin. 2009. *Zhongguo dudai wenming yanjiu* [Studies in Ancient Chinese Civilization]. Shanghai: Huadong shifan daxue chubanshe.

_____. 2007. *Zhonggguo gudai wenming qiyuan*. Origins of Ancient Chinese Civilization]. Shanghai: Shanghai kexue jishu wenxian chubanshe.

_____. 2005. *Zhongguo gudai wenming shijiang*. Ten Essays on Ancient Chinese Civilization]. Shanghai: Fudan University Press.

_____. ed. 1999. *Zhou Li zhu shu* [Annotations and sub-annotations of *Rites of Zhou*]. Beijing: Beijing daxue chubanshe.

Li Zehou. 2012. *Shuo wushi chuantong* [On the Tradition of Shamans and Historians]. Shanghai: Shanghai yiwen chubanshe.

_____. 2005. *Shiyong lixing yu legan wenhua* [Pragmatic Reason and a Culture of Optimism]. Beijing: Sanlian shudian.

_____. 2015. *Lunyun jindu* [A Contemporary Reading of the Analects]. Beijing: Zhonghua shuju.

_____. 2004. *Zhongguo gudai sixiangshi lu* [Studies in Ancient Chinese Intellectual History]. Tianjin: Tianjin renmin chubanshe.

_____. 2003. *Pipan zhexue de pipan: Kangde shuping* [A Critique of the Philosophy of Critique: A Study of Kant]. Tianjin: Tianjin shehui kexue chubanshe.

_____. 2003. *Lishi benti lun/Jimao wu shuo* [Historical Ontology/Five Essays from 1999]. Beijing: Sanlian shudian.

Li Zhi. 2001. *Fen shu* [Book to be Burned]. Beijing: Jiuzhou chubanshe.

Liang Qichao. 2010. *Qing dai xueshu gailun* [An Outline Discussion on Qing Scholarship]. Guilin: Guangxi shifa daxue chubanshe.

Lin Lechang. 2015. "Qianyan" [Preface]. In *Zhangzi quanshu* [Complete Works of Master Zhang Zai], ed. Lin Lechang. Xi'an: Xibei daxue chubanshe.

Lin Yaohua. 2000. *Yixu de zongzu yanjiu* [A Study of the Lineage at Yixu]. Beijing: Sanlian shudian.

Litzinger, Charles A. 1996. "Rural Religion and Village Organization." In *Christianity in China: From the Eighteenth Century to the Present*, ed. Daniel Bays, 41–52. Stanford, CA: Stanford University Press.

Liu, Jeeloo. 2018. *Neo-Confucianism: Metaphysics, Mind, the Moral Law*. Malden, MA: Wiley Blackwell.

_____. 2006. *An Introduction to Chinese Philosophy*. Malden, MA: Blackwell Publishing.

Liu, Shu-Hsien. 2003. *Essentials of Contemporary Neo-Confucianism*. Westport, CT: Praeger.

_____. 1998. *Understanding Confucian Philosophy: Classical and Sung-Ming*, Westport, CT: Praeger.

Liu Xiaoxin. 2001. "The Yi Health Care System in Liangshan Chuxiong." In *Perspectives on the Yi of Southwest China* ed. Stevan Harrell, 267–82. Berkeley: University of California Press.

Liu Yonghua. 2019. *Liyi xiaxiang: Ming dai yijiang min xi sipu de liyi biange yu shehui zhuanxing* [Ritual and Etiquettes Go to Villages: Ritual Reform in the Sipu Region of Western Fujian and Social Transformation]. Beijing: sanlian shudian.

Liu Youming. 2019. *Yige dangdai de, dazhong de ruxue: dangdai xin Xun xue lungang* [A Contemporary, Popular Confucianism: An Outline Thesis of Contemporary New Xunzi Learning]. Beijing: Zhongguo renmin daxue chubanshe.

Liu Zehua. 2004. *Xianqin shiren yu shehui* [Pre-Qin Scholars and Society]. Tianjin: Tianjin renmin chubanshe.

Lloyd, G.E.R. 2002. *The Ambitions of Curiosity: Understanding the World in Ancient Greece and China*. Cambridge, UK: Cambridge University Press.

Lovejoy, Arthur O. 2001. *The Great Chain of Being*: A Study of the History of an Idea. Cambridge, MA: Harvard University Press.

Lu Huiliang and Yu Li eds. 2011. *Xi Zhou jinwen ying yi* [English Translation of Western Zhou Bronze Inscriptions]. Beijing: Yuwen chubanshe.

Lu Xun. 1998. *Lu Xun xueshu lunzhu* [Academic Writings of Lu Xun]. Hangzhou: Zhejiang renmin chubanshe.

Lutz, Catherine A. 1988. *Unnatural Emotions: Everyday Sentiments on a Micronesian Atoll and Their Challenge to Western Theory*. Chicago: University of Chicago Press.

Luo. Yixing. 1995. "Territorial Community at Lubao." In *Down to Earth: The Territorial Bond in South China*, eds. David Faure and Helen Siu, 44–64. Stanford: Stanford University Press.

Lü Kun. 2002. *Shenyin yu/xiaochuang youji* [Murmuring Speeches/Anecdotal Records under the Small Window]. Beijing: Zongjiao wenhua chubanshe.

Lyu Seung-kuk. 2008. *Han guo ruxue yu xiandai jingshen* [Korean Confucianism and Modern Spirit]. Trans. Jiang Ritian, Piao Guanhai. Beijing: dongfang chubanshe.

Machle, Edward J. 2014. "Xunzi as a Religious Philosopher." In *Ritual and Religion in the Xunzi*, eds. T.C. Cline and Justin Tiwald, 21-42. Albany: State University of New York Press.

Macintyre, Alasdair. 2007. *After Virtue: A Study in Moral Philosophy*, third edition. Notre Dame, IN: University of Notre Dame Press.

Malinowski, Bronislaw. 1944. *A Scientific Theory of Culture and Other Essays*. Chapel Hill: The University of North Carolina Press.

Marcus, George E. and Michael M.J. Fischer. 1999. *Anthropology as Cultural Critique: An Experimental Moment in the Human Sciences*. Chicago: University of Chicago Press.

Mauss, Marcel. 1990. *The Gift: The Form and Reason for Exchange in Archaic Societies*. New York: W. W. Norton.

McDaniel, June. 1995. "Emotion in Bengli Religious Thought: Substance and Metaphor." In *Emotions in Asian Thought: A Dialogue in Comparative Philosophy*, eds. Joel Marks and Roger T. Ames, 39–63. Albany: State University of New York Press.

Meng Peiyuan. 2007. *Lixue de yanbian: Cong Zhu Xi dao Wang fuzhi Dai Zhen* [Evolution of Neo-Confucianism: from Zhu Xi and Wang Fuzhi and Dai Zhen]. Beijing: Fangzhi chubanshe.

Meng Wentong. 2006. *Jingxue jueyuan* [Tracing the Origins of the Classical Studies]. Shanghai: shiji chuban jituan.

Mengzi with Selections from Traditional Commentaries. 2008. Trans. Bryan W. Van Norden. Indianapolis, IN: Hackett.

Miline, Rev. William. 1817. *The Sacred Edicts, containing sixteen maxims of the Emperor Kang-he, Amplified by His Son, the Emperor Yoong-ching; together with a Paraphrases on the Whole by a Mandarin*. London: Black, Kingsbury, Parbury, and Allen.

Mote, Frederic. 1971. W. *Intellectual Foundations of China*. New York: Alfred A. Knopf.

Mueggler, Erik. 2017. *Songs for Dead Parents: Corpse, Text, and World in Southwest China*. Chicago: University of Chicago Press.

Naquin, Susan. 1988. "Funerals in North China." In *Death Ritual in Late Imperial and Modern China*, eds. James Watson and Evelyn S. Rawski, 37–68. Berkeley: University of California Press.

Neville, Robert Cummings. 2008. *Ritual and Deference: Extending Chinese Philosophy in a Comparative Context*. Albany: State University of New York Press.
_____. 2000. Boston Confucianism: Portable Tradition in the Late-Modern World. Albany: State University of New York Press.

Ng, On-Cho. 2001. *Cheng-Zhu Confucianism in the Early Qing*. Albany: State University of New York Press.

Nichols, Ryan. 2011. "A Genealogy of Early Confucian Moral Psychology." *Philosophy East and West*, 61, 4: 609–29.

Nietzsche, Friedrich. 1997. *Twilight of the Idols*. Trans. Richard Polt. Indianapolis, IN: Hackett Publishing Company.

Nylan, Michael. 2015. "Lots of Pleasure but Little Happiness." *Philosophy East and West*, 65, 1: 196–226.
_____. 2001. *The Five Confucian Classics*. New Haven, CT: Yale University Press.

Owen, Stephen. "Foreword." 1996. In *The Book of Songs: The Ancient Chinese Classic of Poetry*. Trans. Arthur Waley. Edited and Additional Translations by Joseph R. Allen. New York: Grove Press.

Palecek, Martin and Mark Risjord. 2012 "Relativism and the Ontological Turn within Anthropology." In *Philosophy of the Social Sciences*, 43, 1: 3–23.

Panner, Hans H. 1989. "Rationality, Ritual, and Science." In *Religion, Science, and Magic: In Concert and in Conflict*, eds. Jacob Neusner et al. New York: Oxford University Press.

Peng Lin ed. 2011. *Yi-Li* [Etiquette and Rites]. Zhengzhou: Zhongzhou guji chubanshe.

Peterman, James F. 2015. *Whose Tradition? Which Dao? Confucius and Wittgenstein on Moral Learning and Reflection*. Albany: State University of New York Press.

Petroppoulou, Maria-Zoe. 2008. *Animal Sacrifice in Ancient Greek Religion, Judaism, and Christianity, 100 BC—AD 200*. Oxford, UK: Oxford University Press.

Pi Xirui. 2017.*Jing xue tong lun* [A General Survey of Confucian Classics]. Beijing: Zhonghua shuju.

_____. 2016. *Xiao jing Zheng zhu shu* [Explanation of Zheng Xuan's Annotation of the Classic of Filial Piety]. Beijing: Zhonghua shuju.

_____. 2016. *Xiao Jing Zheng zhu shu* [Classic of Filial Piety, annotated by Zheng Xuan and explicated by Pi Xirui]. Beijing: Zhonghua shuju.

Pines, Yuri. 2016. "Social Enginnering in Early China: The Ideology of the Shangjunshu Revisited." In *Oriens Extremus*, 55: 1–37.

Plato. 2007. *The Republic*. London: Penguin Books.

Pu Maozuo ed. 2014. *Shanghai bowuguan cang Chu zhu shu Kongzi shilun, zigao, Lubang dahan* [Collection of the Shanghai Museum: Chu State Bamboo Books: Confucius on Poetry, Zigao, Great Draught in the Lu State]. Shanghai: Zhongxi shuju.

Puett, Michael J. 2014. "Ritual Disjunctions." In *The Ground Between: Anthropologists Engage Philosophy*, eds. Veena Das et al. 218–33. Durham, NC: Duke University Press.

_____. 2004. "The Ethics of Responding Properly: The Notion of Qing in Early Chinese Thought." In *Love and Emotions in Traditional Chinese Literature*, ed. Halvor Eifring, 37–68. Leiden: Brill.

_____. 2002. *To Become a God: Cosmology, Sacrifice, and Self-Divinization in Early China*. Cambridge, UK: Harvard University Asia Center.

Qian Mu. 2005. *Zhuzi xue tigang* [Outlines of Master Zhu Xi's Scholarship]. Beijing: Sanlian shudian.

_____. 2002. *Song dai lixue san shu sui zha* [Random Notes on the Three Books of the Song Learning of Principle]. Beijing: Sanlian shudian.

_____. 1997. *Zhongguo jin sanbai nian xueshu shi* [An Intellectual History of China in the Last Three Hundred Years]. Beijing: Shangwu yinshu guan.

Qiu Xigui. 2013. *Wenzi xue gaiyao* [A General Outline for Chinese Philology]. Beijing: Shangwu yinshu guan.

Radcliffe-Brown, A.R. 1958. *Method in Social Anthropology*, ed., M. N. Srinivas. Chicago: University of Chicago Press.

Radin, Paul. 1957. *Primitive Religion: Its Nature and Origin*. New York: Dover Publications, Inc.

Rahn, Wendy R. 2000. "Affect as Information: The Role of Public Mood in Political Reasoning." In *Elements of Reason: Cognition, Choice, and the Bounds of Rationality*, eds. Arthur Lupia et al., 130–52. Cambridge, UK: Cambridge Press.

Reddy, William M. 2004. *The Navigation of Feeling: A Framework for the History of Emotions*. Cambridge, UK: Cambridge University Press.

Redfield, Robert. 1941. *The Folk Culture of Yucatan*. Chicago: University of Chicago Press.

Reinhart, Katrinka. 2015. "Ritual Feasting and Empowerment at Yanshi Shangcheng," in *Journal of Anthropological Archaeology*, 39: 76–109.

Rescher, Nicholas. 1988. *Rationality: A Philosophical Inquiry into the Nature and the Rationale of Reason*. Oxford, UK: Clarendon Press.

Rawls, John. 1996. *Political Liberalism*. New York: Columbia University Press.

Rawski, Evelyn S. 1998. *The Last Emperors: A Social History of Qing Imperial Institutions*. Berkeley: University of California Press.

Rowe, William. 2001. *Saving the World: Chen Hongmou and Elite Consciousness in Eighteenth Century China*. Stanford, CA: Stanford University Press.

_____. 1998. "Ancestral Rites and Political Authority in Late Imperial China: Chen Hongmou in Jiangxi." *Modern China*, 24, 4:379–80.

Russell, Bertrand. 1972. *A History of Western Philosophy*. New York: Simon & Schuster.

Rujia shi jiao shou [Ten Confucian Professors]. "Dui dangqian gaoxiao dongyuan guli xuesheng gaomi wenti de kanfa" [Our Views on Institutions of Higher Education's Mobilization of the Students to Report on Professors]. Accessed April 10, 2019. www.rujiazg.com

Ryle, Gilbert. 2000. *The Concept of Mind*. Chicago: University of Chicago Press.

Sahlins, Marshall. 1996. *How "Natives" Think: About Captain Cook, For Example*. Chicago: University of Chicago Press

_____. 1976. *Culture and Practical Reason*. Chicago: University of Chicago Press.

_____. 1972. *Stone Age Economics*. London: Routledge.

Charles Sanft. 2014. "Paleographic Evidence of Qin Religious Practice from Liye and Zhoujiatai." In *Early China*, 37: 327–58.

Schirokauer, Conrad M. 1962. "Chu His's Political Career: A Study in Ambivalence." In *Confucian Personalities*, eds. Arthur F. Wright and Denis Twitchett, 162–88. Stanford, CA: Stanford University Press.

Schwartz, Adam C. 2019. "Shang Sacrificial Animals: Material Documents and Images." in Roel Stercks ed., *Animals Through Chinese History: Earliest Times to 1911*. Cambridge, UK: Cambridge University Press.

Sela, Ori. 2018. *China's Philological Turn: Scholars, Textualism, and the Dao in the Eighteenth Century*. New York: Columbia University Press.

Seligaman, Adam B. et al. 2008. *Ritual and Its Consequences: An Essay on the Limits of Sincerity*. Oxford, UK: Oxford University.

Shang, Wei. 2003. *Rulin waishi and Cultural Transformation in Late Imperial China*. Cambridge, MA: Harvard University Asia Center.

Shaughnessy, Edward L. 1997. *Before Confucius: Studies in the Creation of the Chinese Classics*. Albany: State University of New York Press.

Shen Daming. 2007. *"Da Qing Lüli"* yu Qing dai de shehui kongzhi [Qing Code and the Social Control of the Qing Dynasty]. Shanghai: Shanghai renmin chubanshe.

Shi Naian, Luo Guanzhong. 2006. *Shuihu quan zhuan* [Water Margin]. Wuhan: Chongwen shuju.

SigurÐsson, Geir. 2015. *Confucian Propriety and Ritual Learning: A Philosophical Interpretation*. Albany: State University of New York Press.

Slater, Michael R. 2018. "Xunzi on Heaven, Ritual, and the Way." *Philosophy East and West*, 68, 3: 887–908.

Smith, Adam. 2018. *The Theory of Moral Sentiments*. Los Angeles: Logos Books.

Smith, Richard J. 1993. *Fortune-tellers and Philosophers: Divination in Traditional Chinese Society*. Boulder, CO: Westview Press.

_____. 1983. *China's Cultural Heritage: The Ch'ing Dynasty, 1644-1912*. Boulder, CO: Westview Press.

Soames, Scott. 2015. *Rethinking Language, Mind, and Meaning*. Princeton, NJ: Princeton University Press.

Soloman, Robert C. 2001. "'What Is Philosophy?' The Status of World Philosophy in the Profession." *Philosophy East and West* 51, 4: 100–4.

Spence, Jonathan D. 2007. *Return to Dragon Mountain: Memories of Late Ming Man*. New York: Penguin Group.

Spinoza, Baruch. 1992. *Ethics: Treatise on The Emendation of the Intellect and Selected Letters*. Indianapolis, IN: Hackett Publishing Company.

Stalnaker, Aaron. 2007. *Overcoming Our Evil: Human Nature and Spiritual Exercises in Xunzi and Augustine*. Washington DC: Georgetown University Press.

Standaert, Nicolas. 2008. *The Interweaving of Rituals: Funerals in the Cultural Exchange Between China and Europe*. Seattle: University of Washington Press.

Sterckx, Roel. 2011. *Food, Sacrifice, and Sagehood in Early China*. Cambridge, UK: Cambridge University Press.

Stock, Brian. 1996. *Listening for the Text: On the Uses of the Past*. Philadelphia: University of Pennsylvania Press.

Su Bingqi. 2010. *Su Bingqi wenji* [Collected Essays of Su Bingqi]. Beijing: Wenwu chubanshe.

Sun, Ana. 2013. *Confucianism as a World Religion: Contested Histories and Contemporaries Realities*. Princeton, NJ: Princeton University Press.

Sun Yongdu, Meng Zhaoxing. 2006. *Zhongguo lidai zhiguan zhishi shouce* [A Manual of Chinese Official Titles in the Past Dynasties]. Tianjin: Baihua wenyi chubanshe.

Szonyi, Michael. 2002. *Practicing Kinship: Lineage and Descent in Late Imperial China*. Stanford, CA: Stanford University Press.

Tan Shaojiang. 2017. *Li Ao* [Li Ao]. Xi'an: Shaanxi shifan daxue chubanshe.

Tan Pimo. 2013. *Qing dai sixiang shi gang* [An Outline History of Qing Dynasty Ideas]. Shanghai: Shanghai guji chubanshe.

Tang Lan. 2005. *Zhongguo wenzi xue* [The Science of Chinese Characters]. Shanghai: Shanghai shiji chuban jituan.

Tang Yongtong. 2010. *Sui Tang fojiao shigao* [A Draft History of Sui-Tang Buddhism]. Beijing: Bejing daxue chubanshe.

_____. 2006. *Han Wei liang Jin nanbei chao fojiao shi*. [A History of Buddhism in Han, Wei, the Two Jins and the Southern-Northern Dynasties]. Beijing: Kunlun chubanshe.

Taylor, Rodney L. 1998. "The Religious Character of the Confucian Tradition." *Philosophy East and West*, 48, 1: 80–107.

Tillman, Hoyt Cleveland. 1992. *Confucian Discourse and Chu Hsi's Ascendency*. Honolulu: University of Hawaii Press.

Tillman, Margaret Mih and Hoyt Cleveland Tillman. 1992. "Modernizing Tradition or Restoring Antiquity as Confucian Alternatives: A View from Reading Rituals in

Contemporary China" In *Contemporary Confucianism in Thought and Action*, ed. Guy Alitto, 79–100. Heidelberg: Springer.

Tiwald, Justin. 2020. "Shared Ends: Kant and Dai Zhen on the Ethical Value of Mutuality Fulfilling Relationships." In *Journal of Confucian Philosophy and Culture*, 33: 105–37.

Turner, Victor. 1966. *The Ritual Process: Structure and Anti-Structure*. Ithaca, NY: Cornell University Press.

Tylor, Edward Burnett. 2016. *Primitive Culture*. Mineola, NY: Dover Publications, Inc.

Van Norden, Bryan W. 2017. *Taking Back Philosophy: A Multicultural Manifesto*. New York: Columbia University Press.

_____. 2011. *Introduction to Classical Chinese Philosophy*. Indianapolis, IN: Hackett Publishing.

Vandermeersch, Léon. 2017. *Zhongguo sixiang de liangzhong lixing: biaoyi yu zhanbu* [The Two Rationalities in Chinese Thought: Divination and Ideograph] Trans. Jin Siyan from *Les Deux Raisons de la Pensée Chinoise Divination et Idéographie*. Beijing: Beijing daxue chubanshe.

Vernant, Jean-Pierre. 1982. *The Origins of Greek Thought*. Ithaca, NY: Cornell University Press.

Virag, Curie. 2017. *The Emotions in Early Chinese Philosophy*. Oxford, UK: Oxford University.

Waley, Arthur. 1973. *The Nine Songs: A Study of Shamanism in Ancient China*. San Francisco: City Lights Books.

Walker, James R. 1999. *Lakota Belief and Ritual*. Lincoln: University of Nebraska Press.

Walsh, Michael J. 2020. *Stating the Sacred: Religion, China, and the Formation of the Nation-State*. New York: Columbia University Press.

Wandering on the Way, Earliest Tales and Parables of Chuang Tzu. 1994. Trans. Victor H. Mair. Honolulu: University of Hawaii Press.

Wang Fansen. 2004. *Wan Ming Qing chu sixiang shilun*. [Ten Studies of the Thoughts in Late Ming and Early Qing]. Shanghai: Fudan daxue chubanshe.

Wang Guoxuan, Wang Xiumei eds. 2016. *Kongzi jiayu* [Family Talk of Confucius]. Beijing: Zhonghua shuju.

Wang, Huaiyu. 2007. "From the Principle of Rational Autonomy of the Virtuosity of Empathetic of Embodiment: Reclaiming the Modern Significance of Confucian Civilization." *Philosophy East and West* 67, 4: 1222–47.

Wang Jiafan. 2012. *Zhongguo lishi tonglun* [A Comprehensive Study of Chinese History]. Beijing: sanlian shudian.

Wang Li. 2007. *Zhongguo gudai wenhua changshi, xiuding di siban* [General Knowledge of Ancient Chinese Culture, Revised 4th edition]. Beijing: Shijie tushu chuban gongsi.

Wang Mingming. 1997. *Cunluo shiye zhong de wenhua yu quanli: Min Tai sancun wu lun*. Culture and Power from the Perspective of Villages: Five Theses on the Three Villages of Fujian and Taiwan]. Beijing: sanlian shudian.

_____. 1997. *Shehui renleixue yu zhongguo yanjiu* [Social Anthropology and China Studies]. Beijing: sanlian shudian.

Wang Xuequn. 2009. *Qing dai xuewen de minjin* [Approaches to Qing Scholarship]. Beijing: Zhonghua shuju,.

Wang Zhiyue. 2017. *Song dai lizhi yanjiu* [A Study of Song Dynasty Ritual System]. Beijing: renmin chubanshe.

Watson, James L. and Evelyn S. Rawski eds. 1988. *Death Ritual in Late Imperial and Modern China*. Berkeley: University of California Press.

Weber, Max. 1964. *The Religion of China*. Trans. Hans H. Gerth. New York: The Free Press.

Whitehead, Alfred North. 1978. *Process and Reality: An Essay in Cosmology Gifford Lectures Delivered in the University of Edinburgh During the Session 1927-28*, eds. David Ray Griffin and Donald W. Sherburne. New York: The Free Press.

Wilhelm, Richard. 1967. *The I Ching or the Book of Changes*. Trans. Cary F. Barnes. New York: Bollingen Foundation Inc.

Willerslev, Rane. 2007. *Soul Hunters: Hunting, Animism, and Personhood Among Siberian Yukaghirs*. Berkeley: University of California Press.

Wittgenstein, Ludwig. 2019. *Major Works: Selected Philosophical Writings*. New York: Harper Collins Publishes.

_____. 2018. *The Mythology in Our Language: Remarks on Frazer's Golden Bough*. Translated by Stephan Palmié. Chicago: HAU Books.

Wolf, Arthur P. 1974. "Gods, Ghosts, and Ancestors" In *Religion and Ritual in Chinese Society*, ed. Arthur P. Wolf, 131–82. Stanford, CA: Stanford University Press.

Wu Fei. "Zheng Xuan 'Li zhe ti ye' shiyi" [An Explication of Zheng Xuan's Proposition "Ritual is Tantamount to Human Body]. Accessed September 16, 2020. https://www.rujiazg.com/article/19217.

Wu, Guo. 2020. Ritual, Reading, and Resistance in the Prison and Cowshed during the Cultural Revolution." *Journal of Contemporary China*, 29, 124: 632–46

_____. 2019. *Narrating Southern Chinese Minority Nationalities: Politics, Disciplines, and Public History*. Singapore: Palgrave MacMillan.

_____. 2018. "Zheng Zhen and the Rise of Evidential Research in Late Qing Northern Guizhou." *Journal of Chinese History*, 2,1: 145–67.

_____. 2012. "Accommodation and Conflict: The Incorporation of Miao Territory and Construction of Cultural Difference during the High Qing Era." *Frontiers of History in China*, 7, 2: 240–60.

Wu, Ka-Ming. 2015. *Reinventing Chinese Tradition: The Cultural Politics of Late Socialism*. Urbana: University of Illinoi Press.

Xiao Gongquan (Kung-Chuan Hsiao). 1998. *Zhongguo zhengzhi sixiang shi* [A History of Chinese Political Thought]. Shenyang, Liaoning jiaoyu chubanshe.

Xu Hong. 2016. *Heyi zhongguo: gongyuan qian 2000 nian de zhongyuan tujing* [How China Came in Being: The Landscape of the Central Plains around 2000 BCE]. Beijing: Sanlian shudian.

Xu Shen. 2013. *Shuo wen jie zi* [*Explication of Words and Characters*]. Beijing: Zhonghua shuju.

Xu Zhongshu. 2008. *Xu Zhongshu qian Qin shi jiangji* [Xu Zhongshu's Lectures on Pre-Qin History]. Tianjin: Tianjin guji chubanshe.

Yan, Yunxiang. 1996. *The Flow of Gift: Reciprocity and Social Networks in a Chinese Village*. Stanford, CA: Stanford University Press.

Yang Bojun, D.C. Lau. 2008. *Chinese-English Edition, Confucius, The Analects.* Beijing: Zhonghua shuju.

Yang, C.K. 1961. *Religion in Chinese Society: A Study of Contemporary Social Functions of Religion and Some of Their Historical Factors*. Berkeley: University of California Press, 1961

_____. XXXX. *A Chinese Village in Early Chinese Transition*. Cambridge, MA: The MIT Press.

Yang, Fenggang. 2012. *Religion in China: Survival and Revival under Communist China*. Oxford, UK: Oxford University Press.

Yang Guorong. 1997. *Zinxue zhi si: Wang Yangming zhexue de chanshi* [The Contemplation of the Learning of the Heart-Mind: Interpreting the Philosophy of Wang Yangming]. Beijing: Sanlian shudian.

Yang Kuan. 2008. *Xian Qin shi shi jiang* [Ten Essays on Pre-Qin History]. Shanghai: Fudan daxue chubanshe.

Yang, Martin C. 1945. *A Chinese Village: Taitou, Shantung Province*. New York: Columbia University Press.

Yang, Mayfair Mei-hui. 1994. *Gifts, Banquets, and Favors: The Art of Social Relationship in China*. Ithaca, NY: Cornell University Press.

Yang Yi. 2020. "Qing li zhi bian: Lun song dai jia li zhong de muji" [Between Emotion and Rationality: Graveyard Sacrifice in Song Dynasty's Family Rituals]. *Zhongguo wenhua yanjiu*.

Yao, Xinzhong. 2000. *An Introduction to Confucianism.* Cambridge, UK: Cambridge University Press.

Yates, Robin D. S. 2002. "Slavery in Early China: A Socio-Cultural Approach," *Journal of East Asian Archaeology*, 3, 1: 283–331.

Yearly, Lee H. 1990. *Mencius and Aquinas: Theories of Virtue and Conceptions of Courage*. Albany: State University of New York Press.

Yeung, Shirley. 2010. "Natural Manners: Etiquette, Ethics, and Sincerity in American Conduct Manuals." in *Ordinary Ethics, Anthropology, Language, and Action*, ed. Michael Lambek, 235–48. New York: Fordham University Press.

Yu Yingshi. 2005. *Lun Dai Zhen yu Zhang Xuecheng* [On Dai Zhen and Zhang Xuecheng]. Beijing: Sanlian shudian.

_____. 2004. *Zhongguo zhishi ren zhi shi de kaocha* [An Examination of the History of Chinese Intellectuals]. Gulin: Guangxi shifan daxue chubanshe.

_____. 2004. *Xiandai ruxue de huigu yu zhanwang* [The Past and Prospect of Modern Confucianism]. Beijing: Sanlian shudian.

Zhang Dainian. 2002. *Key Concepts in Chinese Philosophy*. Trans. Edmund Ryden. New Haven, CT: Yale University Press.

Zhang, Longxi. 2005. *Allegoresis: Reading Canonical Literature East and West*. Ithaca, NY: Cornell University Press.

_____. 1992. *The Tao and the Logos: Literary Hermeneutics, East and West.* Durham, NC: Duke University Press.

Zhang, Qiong. 2015. *Making the New World Their Own: Chinese Encounters with Jesuit Science in the Age of Discovery.* Leiden: Brill.

Zhang Shouan. 2001. *Ling Tingkan yu Qing dai zhongye ruxue sixiang zhi zhuanhuan* [Ling Tingkan and the Transition of Mid-Qing Confucianism]. Shijiazhuang: Hebei jiaoyu chubanshe.

Zhangsun Wuji et al. 2019. *Tang lü shu yi* [Annotated Tang Code] e-book. Yiya chubanshe. Zhang Taiyan. 2015. *Guoxue jiangyi* [Lectures on National Learning]. Shenyang: Wanjuan chuban gongsi.

Zhang Xuecheng. 2008. *Wenshi tongyi* [A General Discussion on Literature and History]. Shanghai: shanghai shiji chuban jituan.

Zhao Xudong. 2003. *Quanli yu gongzheng: xiangtu shehui de jiufen jiejue yu quanwei duoyuan* [Power and Justice: Dispute Settlement and Authority Diversity in Rural Society]. Tianjin: Tianjin guji chubanshe.

Zheng Zhenman. 2009. "Song yihou Fujian de jiazu xisu yu zongzu zuzhi" [Ancestral Sacrificial Customs and Lineage Organization in Fujian after the Song]. In *Xiangzu yu guojia: Duoyuan shiye zhong de min tai* chuantong shehui [Local Lineage and the State: Fujian and Taiwan's Traditional Society from a Multifaceted Perspective], ed. Zheng Zhenman, 103–16. Beijing: Sanlian shudian.

Zheng Zhenman. 2001. *Family Lineage Organization and Social Change in Ming and Qing Fujian.* Trans. Michael Szonyi with the Assistance of Kenneth Dean and David Wakefield. Honolulu: University of Hawaii Press.

_____. 2001. *Family Lineage Organization and Social Change in Ming and Qing Fujian.* Trans. Michael Szonyi. 2015. Honolulu: University of Hawaii Press.

Zhouyi. [Book of Changes from the Zhou]. Beijing: Zhonghua shuju.

Zheng Yongnian. 2015. *Zai su yishi yingtai* [Rebuild Ideology]. Beijing: Dongfang chubanshe.

Zhu Xi. 2011. *Si shu zhangju ji zhu* [Collective Annotations of the Four Books]. Beijing: Zhonghua shuju.

_____. 1991. *Chu His's "Family Ritual."* Trans. Patricia B. Ebrey. Princeton, NJ: Princeton University Press.

_____, Lü Zuqian. 1967. *Reflections on Things at Hand.* Trans. Wing-Tsit Chan. New York: Columbia University Press.

Zhuang Kongshao. 1999. *Yinchi: Zhongguo de difang shehui yu wenhua bianqian* [The Silver Wings: The Local Society and Cultural Changes in China]. Beijing: Sanlian shudian.

Zhuangzi. 2009. *Zhuangzi: The Essential Writings with Selections from Traditional Commentaries.* Trans. Brook Ziporyan. Indianapolis, IN: Hackett Publishing.

Zhuo, Xinping. 2015. "Western and Chinese Philosophical and Religious Thought in the Twentieth Century," *Studies in Chinese Religions* 1, 1: 93.

Ziprin, Brook. 2012. *Ironies of Oneness and Difference: Coherence in Early Chinese Thought; Prolegomena to the Study of Li.* Albany: State University of New York Press.

Zito, Angela. 1997. *Of Body and Brush: Grand Sacrifice as Text/Performance in Eighteenth-Century China.* Chicago: University of Chicago Press.

Index

About the Author

Guo Wu is an associate professor of history at Allegheny College, and he received his PhD in Chinese history from State University of New York at Albany in 2006. He is also the author of *Narrating Southern Chinese Minority Nationalities: Politics, Disciplines, and Public History* (2019), *Zheng Guanying, Merchant Reformer in Late Qing China and His Influence on Economics, Politics, and Society* (2010), and a dozen peer-reviewed journal articles on late imperial and twentieth-century Chinese cultural history.

www.ingramcontent.com/pod-product-compliance
Lightning Source LLC
Chambersburg PA
CBHW022321280326
41932CB00010B/1187